8-11-07

To Bob,

Get that Big One —

Jaws for Sport

Frank Mundus

FIFTY YEARS
A HOOKER

FIFTY YEARS
A HOOKER

FRANK AND JEANETTE MUNDUS

Library of Congress Number: 2005900390
ISBN :   Hardcover   1-4134-8429-8
                Softcover   1-4134-8428-X

This book was printed in the United States of America.

To order additional copies of this book, contact:
Xlibris Corporation
1-888-795-4274
www.Xlibris.com
Orders@Xlibris.com
27353

CONTENTS

Part III: The Middle Years

DEDICATION

I would like to thank all the people who fished with me, and most of all, my wife Jenny, who helped put this book together.

To all the mates who worked for me. Without them, the big fish we caught would be just fish stories:

Mates

Davie Bowse
Dick Bracht
John DiLeonardo
Ted Feurer Jr.
Tommy Hoffman
Johnny Lyche
Stanley Lennox
Stevie Lennox
Rob Osinski
Mike Scarimbas

Thanks also to:

Friends

Paul DiAngelo
Capt. Joe DiBella
Jon Dodd
Paul Makuakane
Harry Hoffman
Jay Hoffman
Bill Masin
Bill Peebles
Bob Rando
Debbie Tuma

Family

Barbara (Mundus) Crowley
Tammy (Mundus) Greene
Janet Mundus
Pat Mundus
Christine Mundus Zenchak

PREFACE

This book is about my past adventures on land and sea. It's not just about fishing. If something in it offends you, for instance the way I used to kill lots of sharks before I educated myself about conservation, remember that this does not start to compare with the way that thousands of catch-and-release gut-hooked sharks die every day. I learned from the past and hope that this book will encourage sport fishermen to carry conservation-friendly circle hooks in their tackle box. I think it's a good thing that many species of sharks are protected these days, and that most importantly, commercial shark finning has been banned. I popularized sport fishing for sharks, and now I'm hoping to popularize their conservation.

For fifty years, I was indeed a hooker: I sold my services, took good care of my customers, and saw to it that they had a good time, hoping that they went away satisfied and would return next season. They had to come back the second time to try and figure out what really happened the first time!

INTRODUCTION

WHITE SHARK, WHITE PINEAPPLE

The art of growing pineapples is, in some ways, like going fishing—both take time, and lots of it. Now that I am retired from fishing, I discovered that farming and fishing are somewhat alike: you have to have plenty of time and patience to get good results.

It takes over a year to grow a pineapple, but all I do is plant it and move on to something else. With a white shark, I did something similar: I was busy catching other fish; and when he came along, I was ready for him.

Waiting for a good writer to come along is a lot like growing pineapples or chumming for a white shark. Time goes by and nothing happens.

In the late 1960s, I spread the word around that I was looking for a writer and along came the sportswriter, Bill Wisner. Bill and I coauthored my first book *Sport Fishing for Sharks*. It was the hardest book of all to write because this was before the days of word processors. Bill used a typewriter, and each time I read and corrected a page that he mailed me, Bill had to retype the whole page again. Consequently, the book took four years to complete. That's the equivalent, time wise, of growing four pineapples.

Once I had written about how to catch sharks, I then wanted to tell everyone about many of the funny, yet true, stories that happened aboard the *Cricket II* and how much fun fishing can be. This time, I didn't find a writer, the writer found me.

One day in 1976, when I returned from a day's fishing, a clean-shaven, spectacled young man stepped forward on the dock and introduced himself to me as "Bob Boggs." This was about a year after the movie *Jaws*, and the young man looked and acted a lot like the character "Hooper." He was soft-spoken, and seemed to know what he was talking about. By sheer coincidence, Bob mentioned he wanted to write a humorous book about all the funny things that happened to me in past years. I was surprised, because I hadn't mentioned to anybody about how I had always wanted to tell all those crazy but true stories to the public. I told Bob Boggs, or "Boggsy" as I called him, that he could write about how the sky was pink or the grass was blue, but the stories were to be kept a hundred percent true—no bullshit, no fiction.

Because I was newly divorced and lived alone, Boggsy said he would stay for a couple of weeks to begin the book. Those two weeks turned into two years as we continued working on the book. This was at the same time that I had my other boat, the *Cricket III*, in the Caribbean. Boggsy even came down to St. Maarten with me, working on the book, and found himself caught up in some of my wacky adventures there. Once the book was written, Boggsy and I shopped around for a publisher but had no luck, so we published it ourselves. Boggsy had ten thousand copies printed in Massachusetts and we sold most of those on Long Island and at the Sports Shows.

Eventually, it was picked up by Lorenz Press in Dayton, Ohio. They renamed it *Sharkman* and printed seven thousand or so copies. To help publicize the book, Boggsy and I were sent on a book tour from Boston to Miami, with numerous stops along the way. Unfortunately for us, there was some kind of mix-up, because wherever we stopped, Boggsy and I had no books to sign.

Because we spent a lot of time together, Boggsy and I became good friends, living like the two bachelors in TV's *The Odd Couple*. People in Montauk told me I reminded them of "Felix Unger," while Boggsy was more like "Oscar Madison," the sportswriter in that TV comedy.

I wanted Boggsy to write my autobiography, but he was tangled up in too many projects in California. Ten years and five writers went by, then another Frank Mundus biography came out, written by a man who claimed to know all the facts on me. But that book is full of inaccuracies and distortions, even though this person used anecdotes and information that he got from me during numerous taped interviews. This was the final straw that made Jenny and me pick up our pens (or word processor) and write my autobiography. One of my favorite anonymous quotes tells the whole story:

> *We, the unwilling, led by the unqualified, have been doing the unbelievable for so long with so little, we now attempt the impossible with nothing . . . .*

Everything in this book is 100 percent true—I wouldn't have it any other way.

*　　*　　*

By around 6:00 p.m., we were on our way home, towing the monster that I had waited a lifetime to catch. We had thirty miles to go. I figured our running time, and the way it looked to me, we would reach the dock in about four and a half hours.

I hate pushing the button on my marine radio, but I had to call Montauk Marine Basin ahead of time so they could get ready to handle a potential rod-and-reel world record. My estimate was 3,000 to 3,500 pounds, and Montauk Marine Basin was the only place in Montauk that could handle a fish of this size. I also knew that in order to weigh the shark, they had to send a runner halfway down Long Island to bring back a very large scale. So I had to give them my estimated time of arrival, guessing it to be around 11:00 p.m. As I sat alone on the flying bridge that night, I had plenty of time to think about how it had all begun almost five decades ago, when an eight-year-old boy sat on a rock in Prospect Park Lake, New York, catching freshwater minnows with nothing but a cane pole, a string, and a piece of bread on a bent pin.

PART I

MY EARLY YEARS

CHAPTER 1

AN UNUSUAL CHILDHOOD

On October 21, 1925, a huge black cloud appeared over the top of Long Branch Hospital, New Jersey. Perhaps the doctor should have picked up my mother by the ankles and spanked her for bringing the likes of me into the world. Instead, he whacked *me* on the ass to make me cry, and then things got worse.

My mother and father were living in Point Pleasant, New Jersey, at the time, raising my six-year-old brother, Tony (Anthony), and my sister, "Chickie" (Christine), who was three. After I was born, my parents decided to move to the big city of Brooklyn so that Pop could get a good-paying job. As far back as I can remember, my father worked as a steam fitter in New York City power houses and nobody would dare call him a plumber to his face.

"A plumber is someone who cleans out toilets. I'm not a plumber, I'm a steam-fitter," Pop told everybody, adding proudly, "*We* make the steam that keeps New York moving." At that time, he was making $2.00 an hour, a lot of money in those days, but whenever we had visitors and they asked me what Pop did for a living, just for a joke I told them he was a plumber!

And so the first ten years of my horrible life were spent in the concrete jungles of Brooklyn. We lived in the second house at Number 4 McDonough Street, just past Troop Avenue. On the corner was a five-storey building belonging to the telephone company. Our back yard was right up against this brick building. I once tried climbing up the side of it by putting my fingers and toes in the cracks of the bricks. After getting up there about ten feet, gravity took over and I wound up falling head first into an iron grate—yet another visit to the emergency room.

Apart from my mischief, the Bedford-Stuyvesant area was a peaceful neighborhood in those days. A place where everybody knew each other and people took pride in caring for their property, even to the point of sweeping and scrubbing the front stone stoops and steps with soap and water each week. Most of the families in that area were German-American and proud of their German heritage. My mother and father were both of German descent. Mom and Dad often spoke German to my grandmother, but when they talked to me, they spoke English. My brother and sister knew a little bit of German, but I knew less, and it got me into trouble one day when a German peddler came to our house, selling flowers. He was a small guy with grey hair and some teeth. The peddler began speaking to my mother in German and they soon struck up a lengthy conversation, which must have been about the flowers he was selling. I was playing nearby when my mother hollered out to me in English that she had just bought some geraniums from the man and I should go out back with him where he would show me how to plant them.

I followed him into the backyard as he carried the two flower pots in his hands, and the peddler started telling me in German how to plant the flowers. But I just looked at him and laughed because I didn't know what he was talking about. This only made matters worse, and by then, I think he was mad at me. He threw the flower pots on the ground and stormed back to his truck while hollering something to my mother in German. I was still laughing and wanted to find out what was going on, so I asked my mother. She translated, "How come a nice boy like him can't speak German? You should be ashamed of yourself for not teaching him our language!"

Since I was the youngest child in our family, my brother and sister considered me the runt of the litter; both of them pushed me around like older siblings sometimes do. Even worse, Anthony got his kicks out of scaring me half to death every chance he could. That meant that I had to go off alone to find my own mischief, something I have done ever since!

One of the earliest turning points in my life happened one spring, when I was around four years old. Following a heavy rainstorm, our backyard lay submerged beneath a foot and a half of water. After a couple of weeks, this water became stagnant and you-know-who was still playing boats in it. I wound up getting double diphtheria and was confined to the house for a couple of weeks. The confinement left its mark on me as I lay in bed, listening to the kids playing kick-the-can outside. Although I felt jealous of them, for some reason isolation and I got along well and I learned to enjoy being alone, doing everything by myself.

As they had house calls in those days, our family doctor came over to investigate. After examining me, he laid me on the kitchen table and ran a heavy wire with a bent hook that looked like a clothes hanger down my throat. When the doctor yanked the wire out, it had hooked onto a ball of phlegm the size of a small golf ball. Now I could breathe again with ease, but still spent another couple of weeks lying in bed, watching the other kids playing games outside.

My first time back on the streets after three weeks of house confinement due to a bout of double diphtheria.

This first major illness had another lasting effect on me: I became restless and overactive and a regular at the hospital emergency room; the doctors soon knew me by my first name because of all the deep cuts and bruises I accumulated. Each time I got busted up one way or another, Mom put a bunch of Band-Aid blow out patches on me, but when she started to run out of Band-Aids, she would say, "Why don't you kids go to the movies?" Then she gave each of us a dime and a large dog biscuit to eat while we were there. The dog biscuits were large enough to last through the entire movie. Even our German shepherd, Teddy, liked them! In those days, the pet food manufacturers put good ingredients in dog biscuits! I think this tradition of Mom's Depression-era ersatz movie snacks began after I tossed Teddy a dog biscuit and started chewing on one myself.

But movie-going didn't deter me for long from injuring myself. In fact, it inspired me to imitate my celluloid heroes, and I really gave the doctors something to work on when I broke my right arm in 1932, on the way home from the movies after seeing Johnny Weissmuller's *Tarzan of the Apes*. Naturally, I tried to ape Tarzan's aerial vine-swinging by jumping from stoop to stoop. The last thing I remember hearing—before I tripped and fell five feet into someone's entrance way and broke my right arm—was my mother's warning: "Stop that before you get hurt!" Because I had broken my writing arm, it was put in a cast and I missed about two months of school and was kept back a grade. School always was a lot of nothing as far as I was concerned. The great outdoors, particularly the ocean, had always beckoned me. In fact, as soon as I was old enough, my mother had taken Anthony, Chickie, and me on the underground train to Coney Island or Brighton Beach each Saturday. This is where I learned to swim. These outings involved one hour of pushing, shoving, and fighting for survival—and that was just to get a seat on the train!

The only time I came out of the ocean was to eat and go home; I can still hear my mother hollerin', "Frankie, come on. We're going home!" Then, on Sundays, it was church, cake-eating clothes and visits from cheek-pinching relatives.

During the summer, the temperature in our neighborhood became hellish hot: Brooklyn style. All day long, the sun beat down on the cement streets and brownstone houses. The sidewalks and buildings retained this heat until daylight when the cycle was repeated. We kids eagerly awaited that one day when the fire department sent a man around to turn on the fire hydrant. On our block, all the kids came out and swam in two inches of gutter water. The ones who couldn't swim splashed around in the spray! Maybe this is why, as a child, I appreciated the ocean so much. To escape some of this heat, I often slid down a construction site passageway where the Eighth Avenue Subway was being excavated and watched the men at work.

When I was eight years old, I got my first and only taste of summer camp. If the truth were to be told, my parents signed me up for camp to get rid of me for a couple of weeks. It was the first and last time that they would send me away.

My mother took me to register for the summer camp at its business office somewhere in Brooklyn. I was excited about their swimming pool, especially after looking at pictures of it in the fancy color brochure. The rest of the pictures didn't get me excited at all. I had not been too happy with the idea of going away to camp, but the pool pictures soon clinched it. I visualized myself splashing in that pool from daylight until dark.

All the arrangements were made and the date was set. My mother threw together a care package of clothes that she thought I would need. The scary part was getting on the bus and waving goodbye to her. As I remember it, the bus ride from our home in Brooklyn to the camp in New Jersey was only two or three hours long.

Me at the beach with my brother Tony (left) and sister Christine "Chickie."

As soon as I got there, I jumped off the bus with my suitcase in hand and ran directly to the swimming pool. Oh, man, was I horrified! There was only six inches of water in the deep end and a lot of dead leaves and branches. I immediately asked somebody, "How come there's no water in the pool?" The answer was, "It didn't rain enough yet. We have to wait for the rain to fill it up!"

It soon became obvious I would never see any water in the two weeks I was supposed to be there. The other kids didn't seem to care about the pool. They were just happy to sit around a campfire, telling stories. I was so angry about the pool because it was the only reason I had gone to camp.

I wanted my mother to take me home right away, and just like the kid did in that Alan Sherman song, "Hello Mudda, Hello Fadda," I made a mayday phone call from the camp. But apparently, Mom had already given them one week's down payment so I was stuck there for that first week at "Camp Drywell" where I spent most of my time moping around homesick, crying in my bunk. For once, I longed to be back home where at least the firemen came around each week to turn on the hydrants so I could swim in the gutter.

After returning from summer camp, my stuttering became more pronounced as my words didn't! I think the stuttering coincided with my brother's frequent attempts to scare me to death when I was somewhere between six and eight years old. Tony often terrorized me in the evenings by leaping out in the long dark hallway that led from the front of our house all the way back to the kitchen. I always used this lower entrance when I returned home for supper. When it got dark, I ran for the last thirty or forty yards until I reached the front gate and slammed the big entrance door behind me. Scared and shaking, I knew the devil himself or the Headless Horseman was chasing after me.

Now I had the ordeal of walking through the long dark hallway. I knew that I wasn't safely in the kitchen yet and that my brother would get me before I could reach it. Tony always hid behind the stairway that led to the cellar. Although I knew he was going to be there every chance he got, I was still terrified each time my brother jumped out and roared like a big black bear. One time, I half-fainted and fell to the floor with fright. Tony just laughed, stepped over me, and headed for the kitchen as I lay gasping and stammering for help.

The stuttering didn't do my "book learning" any good, either. Every time I tried to say something, it came out all jumbled up just like the way Porky Pig talks. The more I stuttered, the more the kids at Our Lady of Victory Catholic Elementary School made fun of me, and the more my stutter got worse.

"My name is Fuf-Fuf-Fuf-Fuf-Fuf-Frank, not F-F-Francis."

"Your name *cannot* be 'Frank.' You *must* have been baptized Francis," Sister Fingerwhacker[1] hissed, turning her head to keep from laughing at my stammer.

"I *said* my name is Fuf-Fuf-Fuf-Fuf-Fuf-Frank," and figured I'd better stop there. You don't contradict a ruler-rapping nun too many times.

Third grade was the toughest two years of my life, especially the time Sister Fingerwhacker grabbed me by the hair and slammed my head half a dozen times into the blackboard. "I'll drive something into your empty head one way or another, Francis," she rasped as I convulsed in a cloud of chalk dust and my classmates giggled.

"How come you're all roughed up, Frankie?" Mom asked later that day, noticing my hair full of chalk dust and two lumps on the side of my forehead. "Did you get into a fight at school today?" Reluctantly, I told her about Sister Fingerwhacker's grand slam and Mom decided it was time she gave the nuns a talking to. The next day, she went to school with my baptismal certificate in her hand, hoping to end the grudge match between Little Frankie and Raging Nun.

"Don't ever slam my Frankie's head into the blackboard

again!" Mom yelled. "And by the way, my son was baptized 'Frank,' not 'Francis,'" she said, thrusting my certificate into Sister Fingerwhacker's face. Nothing was said by the nun. She turned on her heels and left the room. But Mom's little fireside chat did no good. As far as I can remember, Sister Fingerwhacker's bad habit of calling me Francis continued until the end of third grade when our family eventually moved to Point Pleasant, New Jersey.

In the meantime, my stutter lasted for about a year and a half before my parents found a doctor who could cure me. This doctor literally filled my mouth with marbles and instructed me to say one word then spit out one marble. I had to repeat this process with each word I pronounced until I finished a sentence. As a result, for the rest of my life I have had to talk slowly or the stutter will come back. Even today, every once in a while, when I catch myself trying to speak fast, I have to come to a complete stop and start over.

And then there was my German-American uncle who was tough on kids. Until I got cured of my stammer, he didn't exactly help matters. We knew him as "Unc," but I nicknamed him "Uncle Leatherjacket" because he always wore the same old dark three-quarter-length leather jacket. When he was around sixteen years old, Unc had come to America with his sister (my grandmother). He never did talk about his past or what he had done for a living in the old country. Unc was short and stocky, a direct contrast to his six-foot tall sister! He had a round face, a full crop of hair, and flat teeth from constantly smoking a pipe. I often heard Mom, Dad, Unc, and Grandma playing pinochle in the evenings and I could always tell they were playing cards. Everybody would be hollering and screaming, but Unc was always the loudest, especially when he was losing, because Unc was a sore loser. You could tell when Unc was winning because he would always be laughing.

The only story we heard about him from my grandmother attests to Unc's stubbornness and eccentricity.

Unc once worked in a furniture factory, operating a wood lathe. One day when he was turning a piece of wood down on the lathe, it flew out. He picked it up off the floor and jammed it back in. The wood flew out again, and as Unc picked it up again to jam the wood back in, he screamed, "It's got to *vork*!" This happened three times, until it flew out for the last time and hit him square between the eyes! Even after they picked him up off the floor, he never did figure out why the piece of wood wouldn't stay in the lathe.

Another of Unc's unusual traits was that he always waited for a full moon to do anything important. For example, Uncle Leatherjacket did not get his hair cut or buy a pair of shoes unless the moon was full. He even died during a full moon! This was when the family finally confirmed that Unc had been a "mooner!"

I have two memories of fishing trips with Unc. The first one was of the time that he took my twin cousins and me flounder fishing on the Manasquan River in a flat-bottomed row boat. Unc wanted us three boys to be like him: a serious, sour-faced fisherman. If we dared laugh or giggle, he hollered at us in broken English, screaming, "*Ach vat*, either you fish or you fool!" raising his hand like he was going to hit us. In addition to being a cantankerous old man, Uncle Leatherjacket was also a very bad sport. As Unc went to flip a flounder into the boat, the hook pulled and the fish swam home. Unc's poor sportsmanship reared its head in a torrent of curse words, all in German—some words we knew, as kids do.

After this, the fish stopped biting, but the fish hawks (ospreys) were circling and diving close to us, then surfacing and flying away with flounders. For some reason, this made Unc mad and that was when he made his fatal mistake of standing up in the rowboat, looking up at the birds in the sky while shaking his fist and cursing them. Suddenly, he lost his balance and fell backward, overboard. The twins and I spent the next fifteen minutes getting Unc back into the boat. At a time like this, we didn't dare laugh. To this day, I don't know how we got him back in as his heavy leather jacket and hip boots were filled with salt water. That was the end of our fishing trip. But on the way home, things got worse. Unc had to row the boat and one of the oars kept slipping out of the oar lock. Every time it did, Unc got mad and slammed it back in. "It's got to *vork*!" This happened a bunch of times until the oar lock was on its last legs. We held our breath, scared to death that we might not make it home, but by an act of God, we did. Like the old saying goes, "Fisherman's luck: a wet ass and a hungry gut!"

My other Unc memory is a much happier one, of the time he took me on my first ocean fishing trip for sea bass and porgies on an open boat (or head boat). After the third or fourth wave on the way out, I got seasick and remember lying on the cabin top for most of that trip. I can still hear Unc trying to get me up to catch a fish. When we returned to the dock, a lot of people were milling around and Unc was talking to somebody about the big fish that got away. When we were almost home, I realized I had left behind the fishing pole that Unc had loaned me. I thought at first he was going to kill me when I told him, but to my surprise (and relief) he didn't. I guess the pole wasn't any good! After we got home, Unc emptied his burlap bag of fish into our kitchen sink and my mother asked, "Which one did Frankie catch?"

Uncle Leatherjacket leaned over the sink, and after searching through the pile of fish, he picked up a large sea bass and replied, "This one." As I hadn't caught anything that day, I wondered why Unc had softened up at a time like this, crediting me with a fish I didn't catch.

Uncle Leatherjacket was definitely a man of contradictions, but at the same time, he was also a great wine maker. Unc also made rock and rye whisky from whatever was left over from wine making. I remember the whole family going into the countryside to pick wild cherries and elderberries for Unc's wine making. It was supposed to be a picnic but there was no relaxing with Unc around, and when we got home, my mother, brother, sister, and I had to pick and pull most of the stems off the berries. This was no job for a fidgety kid like myself, but thoughts of sampling some wine kept me going until the job was done. Then Unc would disappear into the cellar and only emerge when he needed more sugar for his brew. The wine was made in the cellar, but Unc made his whisky in a homemade still in our big kitchen. Every couple of minutes, a drop of alcohol dripped from his still. Whenever I passed through the kitchen, I glanced over at Unc. Even today, I have the picture embedded in my mind of him sitting, watching his whisky still, reading a newspaper, and listening to a ball game. Unc's thick-rimmed glasses were always perched on the end of his nose so he could glance up at the still and read his paper at the same time, with the pipe held firmly between his teeth. I often imagined him biting the stem off his pipe if something ever went wrong.

We kids knew well ahead of time when Unc was going to make whisky because my mother always gave us strict orders to lock the door when we left the house. We were also ordered not to bring any friends around, "No kits [kids] in the house!" Unc hissed, as this was during the days of the Prohibition. One rainy day, my worst fears were realized. "Why don't you go down the cellar and see if you can help Unc make some wine?" Mom asked. This was like asking me to walk over broken glass in my bare feet! After a while, she insisted, "Go down into the cellar and help Unc!"

Down I went, slowly, step by step, like a condemned prisoner. Unc was in no mood to see me or anybody else, but I had to speak up, "Is there anything I can help you with, Unc?" He turned to me with a piercing look. "Take *dis* open-mouthed stone crock upstairs and *vash* it." This I did. I "vashed it" and "vashed it" and "vashed it," using more soap each time. I figured the more soap I used, the cleaner I could get it. Back down into the cellar I went with my clean crock, hoping for some kind of medal. Mom would be so proud of me. Unc took the crock out of my hands, giving me that same sharp look. Then he raised the crock to his face and stuck his nose in it. Without warning, he put the crock down fast and hit me with the back of his hand, so hard that I went flying across the cellar floor, and when I stopped rolling, I hit the other wall. Crying and hurt, I ran upstairs where Mom met me at the top. She asked what had happened. "I dunno! He just hit me!" I sobbed. When Mom asked for an explanation, Unc replied, "Kits shouldn't be *dat* stupid as to use soap *ven vashing*. No soap in making *vine*!" How did I know that soap would stop the fermentation process? I had gone into the cellar to help Unc make wine, and, in a turn of events, Unc had made me whine!

My maternal grandmother was a pussycat compared to Unc. Both she and her brother, Uncle Leatherjacket, lived with us in Brooklyn. During the early 1930s, my brother and I often teased Granny by clicking our heels together and raising our right hands in a Hitler salute. Grandma always reacted by pointing at us with the bent arthritic index finger of her right hand, and yelling in German, "I will hit you in the eyes and ears until you can't see or hear no more!" Whenever we "kits" complained about not getting a dime to go to the movies, Granny often told us how tough it had been when she was a kid, growing up in nineteenth-century Germany. She and her family were often so hungry that they followed horses and picked up their droppings, searching through them for any corn that the horses had not chewed properly. Then they took home the corn and boiled it up for supper.

Time passed and my stutter disappeared. Then the next catastrophe occurred and it changed my whole life. When I was nine, I broke my left arm in a roller-skating accident. While the 1932 injury to my right arm had been just a common fracture that kept me in a plaster cast for a couple of months, the break in my left arm was a compound fracture of the forearm. During the accident, the bone had penetrated the skin and became infected, and I developed osteomyelitis. This osteomyelitis is just like dry rot and has the same effect as somebody putting a blow torch to your ice cream cone: it melts (the bone in this case).

Now this was quite a while before the use of penicillin, and so there was no effective medicine available to treat osteomyelitis. I was confined to the children's ward at St. John's hospital in Brooklyn where the doctors experimented on me to try and find a cure. In one year I had thirteen operations. During one procedure, they removed four inches of dead bone from my wrist up. The doctors made drainage cuts in my arm and inserted rubber tubes all over to drain out the poison. Some of these tubes went completely through my arm.

When the drainage tubes failed to do the trick, the doctors turned to silver nitrate. Silver nitrate was considered the best remedy for osteomyelitis at the time. It was in a stick form and the doctors inserted it through the cuts, applying it directly to my exposed bone to burn away the infection. When the doctors used silver nitrate on me, it felt just like being covered in cigarette burns because the silver nitrate stick was acidic. I watched with fascination as a light-colored smoke poured out of my arm while the dead flesh sizzled and burned away. Every day, three or four doctors looked on as one of them poked and burned the cuts on my arm. I was their guinea pig. During one consultation, twenty-one doctors surrounded my bed, all were talking in a foreign language: medical jargon.

For three months, I wore a plaster cast on my arm all the way to my knuckles, and when they took the cast off, I couldn't straighten out any of my fingers. So now the doctors fixed some kind of orthopedic device (that reminded me of a tennis racket) to my wrist and hand. Wires attached by turn buckles led to every finger. Each time a doctor checked in on me, he took a twist on the turnbuckles to straighten out my bent fingers until they eventually straightened.

One time, after being confined to the hospital for four months, I returned home feeling as scared as a wild animal, terrified of the outside world so much that I ran and hid on top of an old sink tub in my mother's kitchen, jammed myself into a corner, and cried. The agoraphobia only lasted for a day or so, but the osteomyelitis returned.

A year later, it had traveled through my system and broke out in my right arm between my elbow and shoulder. A large lump appeared, about the size of a golf ball, and I remember my mother taking me back to see the doctor. He lanced the lump. The pus was so concentrated that when the doctor opened the abscess with his scalpel, a quarter-inch ball of yellow liquid shot right over his shoulder. An x-ray showed a large hole that was eating away the center of my bone.

"Don't bump your arm," the doctor told me, "because there's not much holding it together."

It took about a year or so for the bone to heal. Every so often, osteomyelitis flared up and my left forearm became the size of a football. These outbreaks lasted anywhere from a couple of weeks to a couple of months at a time, depending on how well the drainage tubes were working.

Although my father was making good money, he had to drop off most of his paycheck at the hospital each week for my medical expenses. Our family had no medical insurance and I felt bad because my illness was costing him a lot of money; and besides, the doctors didn't know how to cure my bone disease. They finally gave up and advised my parents to take me to a place where I could go in and out of salt water all day. Even at that time, they knew the clean ocean saltwater would help heal any open cut that was infected. And my little spindly body would get exercise at the same time.

So that's what my family did. We moved back to Point Pleasant, New Jersey, where my mother bought a rooming house on Ocean Avenue, close to the boardwalk. She named it Canary Cottage, because my father liked to raise canaries. Year-round, Dad had an aviary on the front lawn filled with canaries.

My mother Christine and father Anthony, in a February 1943 photo, take time off from clearing up weeds in our garden at Canary Cottage, Point Pleasant, New Jersey.

During this time, I kept to myself a lot and became an independent loner, coming home to Canary Cottage each evening just to eat and sleep. And when I did come home, I never knew where I was going to lay my head down. If all the rooms were rented, I always had one of the outside porches to sleep on. I had my choice of sleeping on the first, second, or third floor. That single mattress I had poked away always came in handy for times like these. In fact, I got to like sleeping on the outside porch so much that it became a habit, and I wound up sleeping outside year-round. There were plenty of times in the winter when I brushed snow off my top covers before climbing into bed.

I must have slept outside like this for about five years. This was great and it gave me the freedom to sneak away anytime I wanted. After everybody had gone to bed, I got dressed, jumped on my bicycle, and was gone for a few hours in the middle of the night. No one knew the difference. My mother knocked herself out during the day running her rooming house and my father was working all week in New York. He only came home on weekends.

Even when we lived in Brooklyn, my father had worked long hours, often doing double shifts. He only came home to take a fast nap and change his clothes; so we kids didn't see him much, except for once in a while at the supper table, and sometimes he took us to church on Sundays if he wasn't working at the power house. I can only remember him taking me on one outing. That was when I was six or seven; we fished from a rowboat for porgies in Sheepshead Bay.

Eventually, Pop's health failed and he quit steam fitting after the doctor told him that his lungs were black from smoking two to three packs of cigarettes a day. It was dad's lung problems that helped me resist my cigarette-wielding teenage school pals. Every time my father lit up one of his cigarettes, he would spit and sputter, choke, cough, break wind, and turn blue. This taught me not to tangle with the tobacco weed. When I passed by the boys who were puffing up a storm behind the school, they kept offering me cigarettes. "Go ahead, try one, Frank," they said, pushing one out in front of me.

"What's the matter, Frank? Are you chicken? You must be a baby. We're grown-ups because we smoke." One day, I developed the answer. Because the word "no" didn't work, I said "yes" and they handed me one. I took the cigarette and broke it up into small pieces, dropping the pieces on the ground in front of them.

"Don't do that!" they'd holler.

"You gave me the cigarette. It's mine and I can do with it what I want!" I'd tell them. It didn't take very long for the word to get around. "Don't give Frank any cigarettes because he just tears them up!"

Around the age of fourteen or so, I started venturing into the woods and the call of the wild started to get pretty loud in my ear.

One year, Phil, a friend of mine, and I planned an Easter vacation. We started putting money aside for this trip, which was supposed to last a couple of weeks. It was to be a canoe trip, starting at the upper part of the Manasquan River and leading five miles upstream into freshwater and farmlands. After a while, Phil and I were all set for the spring trip, with our pup tent, supplies, and a canoe. I had planned to sneak my .22-caliber rifle along on this trip, and every time I had extra change in my pocket, I went to the Point Pleasant hardware store and bought another box of bullets. My mother had ordered us not to take guns on this trip, but by the time we were ready to go, I had saved almost a pickle-jar full of .22-caliber bullets.

Me as a teenager.

The day after Easter vacation, we got started on our great adventure. It only took us about a day of traveling to find a good camping spot for the night; most of the area we had paddled through was covered in brier patches and thick brush. Finally, around 4:00 p.m., we came to a spot where there was a nice clearing and big trees. Phil and I pulled our canoe up on the bank and unloaded our food. (I can still see that wooden orange crate full of canned goods.) Toward the end of the afternoon, Phil and I put up our pup tent and were all set to spend the night. We didn't build a fire and just ate cold food out of the can because we didn't know if we were on private land.

After our cold supper, we decided to scout out the area to see if there was anybody close by. "Now that we're all set for the night, let's have some target practice," I said, getting out my rifle. Phil didn't have a rifle so we took turns shooting at pine cones and tin cans, etc. As darkness closed in, we decided to get into our grey canvas pup tent. Phil and I lay on top of our sleeping bags with our feet facing the open part of the tent. I still had my rifle loaded and was waiting for something to move. "Maybe one last shot," I said to myself, resting the rifle between my toes. I poked the barrel outside the tent, about a foot or so past my feet as I didn't want it to be a hazard.

As it grew darker, I decided to put away the rifle for the night. Just as I slid the rifle in, Phil, on a sudden impulse, reached over and pulled the trigger. He said later that he had just wanted to scare me. The rifle bullet punched a hole through the middle toe of my right foot and went whistling up toward the sky. I can still hear the sound that the bullet made as it passed through my toe, just grazing the bone, and the bullet's bent trajectory gave it a loud, whistling effect. If it had hit the bone square, my toe would have been blown off.

It felt like somebody had hit my foot with a sledgehammer. In panic, I jumped up and busted through the top of the pup tent, screaming, "You dumb bastard, you shot me!"

Phil jumped up, and he too burst straight through the top of the pup tent, on the other side, screaming, "Shot you?" Then he looked down at the hole in my toe and turned pale when he saw the blood coming out.

The first thing I thought of was to take my hunting knife and dig the bullet out, like they do in the movies. I couldn't feel anything. My foot was numb up to my ankle. I jammed the point of the knife in and probed around. I could feel something hard, but couldn't pry it out because that was the bone! Then I remembered hearing the bullet whistling toward the sky, so I said to myself, it can't be in my toe. Despite the hole, my toe wasn't bleeding that much so I wasn't worried about bleeding to death.

"We gotta start back," I yelled. "I need a doctor."

I told Phil to carry back everything we could pick up in a hurry. The pain hadn't set in yet, only the numbness. The pup tent, with our two vertical exit holes, wasn't worth saving. I remember putting the wooden orange crate that contained our canned goods in the middle of the canoe as Phil picked up some small things that were lying around. Then we jumped in the canoe for our long trip downstream. I sat in the back while Phil sat up front. I can still hear myself hollering at him to paddle faster as we were running out of daylight. It didn't seem like we were making enough time going downstream. We should be doing better, but there were fallen trees in our way, slowing us down even more. So I got the bright idea of lightening up the ship. "Toss anything overboard that's heavy," I said, throwing the orange crate of canned goods over the side. In panic, Phil threw our alarm clock over the side, and without thinking, I jumped overboard to get it. But when I jumped over the side, we were on one of the bends in the stream, and I remember not hitting the bottom—I kissed the alarm clock goodbye and slid back into the canoe.

"I'll have to say I accidentally shot myself," I told Phil. "This way, you can't be held responsible and won't be prosecuted for shooting me," but we had to think up a story fast.

Now it was almost pitch black. As luck would have it, we had gotten through all of our obstacles: fallen trees, etc., and were more out in the open. "We've gotta hit the first house that has a light on in it," I said to Phil. "Then they can take me to the hospital." After a while, we saw lights in the distance and headed into shore. In the blackness of the night, we found ourselves in high grass and cattails. Phil and I pushed through them for a while until we hit solid ground. Then came a mad dash, with me hopping on one foot.

We thumped up onto the wooden front porch of the first house we came to and pounded on the door. The door opened about six inches and a middle-aged lady poked her head out warily. "Take me to the hospital," I said. "I got shot in the toe!"

She looked at us and looked at my bleeding foot, and shouted, "Go away! How do I know you guys aren't a couple of thieves?" and then slammed the door in our faces. We didn't waste any time telling her where she should go, and made another dash for the next house that had a light on.

Running up on the porch and banging on the door, we got the attention of the people inside. A middle-aged man came out, and we told him what had happened. "Hang on. I'll take you to the hospital in my car, but I just have to get some old newspapers for the floor so you won't drip blood all over it."

"Take the canoe back," I told Phil, as I climbed into the good Samaritan's black sedan.

"I was walking down a steep hill when I tripped and fell. That's when the gun went off and I shot myself through the toe," I told the man.

Fifteen minutes later, the doctor in the emergency room took a big syringe and headed toward the table I was lying on. As he squirted a brown liquid in the top of the hole in my toe and it jetted out the bottom, he made the understatement of the year, "This is going to hurt a little." The brown liquid was straight iodine, and about now, the numbness was over and a searing pain started setting in.

"Holy shit," I said as I jumped up from the table and grabbed my ankle, squeezing it as hard as I could. The pain was excruciating. Thank God it didn't last very long.

They kept me in the hospital overnight. It wasn't long after the words "gunshot wound" got around the ward that I started to get bedside visits from lawmen. The first two were from uniformed local policemen, followed by a couple of plainclothes detectives, and then two state troopers! They all grilled me like I was Al Capone, but I told them the same story and they went away.

Years later, I told my mother (and everyone else) the truth. Admitting that I had been careless enough to shoot myself was hard to do, but at least my cover story had managed to keep Phil out of trouble.

By the time I was sixteen, Dad had retired to New Jersey and gotten himself a part-time job as a summer cop. Now he was "Pop, the Cop!" and the boardwalk became his regular beat. Pop spent his time chasing kids who roller-skated and bicycled on the two-mile stretch of boardwalk. Pop thought that because he patrolled the boardwalk beat, he had the authority to put the fear of God into kids and horny couples. He kept amorous couples' lovemaking to a minimum, banging on the top of their parked cars with his night stick when the windows got steamed up too much. Sometimes Pop got to use the patrol car and rode all around Point Pleasant, handing out tickets to poor unsuspecting souls. His patrol car stories were often more interesting than his boardwalk-beat tales. One morning, he told me about this crazy kid on a black motor cycle that he had been chasing. Pop said that he had seen the kid speeding two or three times and hadn't caught him yet. Pop didn't realize who he had been chasing—it was me on my blue Harley Davidson, which looked black at night!

I was proud of this motorcycle that I had bought with my own money. My independent moneymaking streak had started a long time ago. At around age twelve or thirteen, I retrieved golf balls out of the golf-course pond and sold them back to the golfers who had lost them! Then I got the bright idea of taking pond lilies down town and selling them in front of the supermarket for twenty-five cents a bunch. That went over well.

After the pond lilies, I went crabbing. I used to go with a scoop net (a round net on the end of a pole) around the docks where I would lean over and scoop up the blue-claw crabs as they clung to a piling under the dock. Crabs develop in three stages: hard, shedders, and soft. First they're hard, then they become shedders. Next, their bodies turn soft. Finally, after twenty-four hours, they turn hard again, and repeat this cycle every thirty days. The hard crabs weren't any good except for food. The shedders were the moneymakers. Fishermen bought them for bait. I also sold the soft crabs to restaurants. They used them in soft crab sandwiches.

And after the crabbing, I got into selling bait, mostly sand eels. This venture involved me and a friend buying a twenty-foot-long fine-mesh haul seine net. We used it in the ocean at low tide to catch sand eels—a silver eel-like fish the size of a pencil. Some we would sell to the surf fishermen at a nickel a handful (their handfuls). If the sand eels were plentiful, we would sell them commercially to the rowboat rental stations for $3.00 a bushel.

In the process of netting these eels, I had my first close encounter with sharks. Sometimes low tide came at daylight and it didn't bother us at all to see shark fins in the breakers. Thinking they had gone away when the fins disappeared, my friend and I walked into the water with our net. Because I was the taller of the two, I got the job of pulling the outside part of the net while walking along the sea bottom, about thirty feet offshore. Chasing the crabs away from under my feet, I poked at the sandy bottom with the six-foot pole that I pulled the net with. One time, as I was on the outside part of the net, poking my pole into the sand to drive away the crabs, something big, heavy, and strong hit my pole, almost knocking it out of my hand. It was probably one of the sharks chasing bait. When we got back in to the beach, there was a three-foot round hole in the center of the net.

I was a golf caddy one summer. This job helped pay for my full set of upper teeth. I had lost most of my real teeth due to a couple of accidents: one was a boating mishap where I was standing up in a rowboat and fell face down onto an old wooden beer barrel, driving two of my front teeth straight up into my head. The other happened when I ran into a low-hanging drainpipe under the boardwalk and broke off two more front teeth. I lost the rest of my upper teeth due to the strong experimental osteomyelitis medicine that I was given by spoon instead of by capsule.

In the summertime, before I finished grammar school (at age sixteen), I worked as a mate on some boats owned by my friend, Johnny Chapman, and his father, George. The Chapmans operated three boats out of Brielle, New Jersey. They were the open boats *Chappie* and *Chappie II* and one sport-fishing boat. My disfigured left arm may have kept me out of the service, but it didn't stop me from fishing. On the open boats, my right arm compensated for my left by doing twice the work. I liked teaching people how to catch fish, untangling lines, and being more or less my own boss; the captain gave orders and allowed me to use my own initiative. I knew now that this was what I wanted to do. The only downside was my seasickness, which occurred on each and every trip, but I soon found out how to overcome the effects: by eating more food after each time I threw up.

This open-boat job was only temporary, but I knew that someday it would become permanent. And the opportunity came when I quit high school because they wouldn't let me play football on account of my left arm.

I had one full day of football practice and the coach decided that he didn't like the look of my sliced-up left forearm, badly scarred from years of corrective surgery for the osteomyelitis (it looked a lot worse than it actually was). "We'd better not let you play because something might happen to your arm," he said.

I was devastated at the thought of not being allowed to stay in school and play football. At that time, I was sixteen years old, six feet tall, and 175 pounds, and could outrun the rest of those scrawny little eighth-grade midgets. I think I would have been a big asset to the team; but it was their loss, I told myself, and stopped showing up for classes. My mother said I couldn't quit unless I got a "good job." So I went and I got a good job with the Pennsylvania Railroad freight department. Hah! That lasted just about one year. We had three accidents. Two of them were horrible and I shouldn't be here to talk about them.

CHAPTER 2

RAILROADED TOWARD FISHING

The passenger service had always seemed too tame for me; I wanted some outdoor work that involved excitement, only at that time I didn't realize how much outdoor excitement I was going to be in for.

I must have been eighteen when I first started working as a brakeman for Pennsylvania Rail Road (PRR), out of South Amboy, New Jersey. This is where most of the coal came through, on thousands of coal cars each year, transported to the factories by rail. South Amboy, at that time, had one of the biggest coal yards in the area. Each coal car carried tons of coal: every kind and size of coal that was used in factories and in private homes.

Back then, there were two types of jobs available for anybody working freight for the PRR: yard work or road work. Road work was hard to come by; everybody wanted that job because it was easy. But since I was a newcomer, I only had one road job: riding the hack (a caboose, or house on wheels, it was at the tail end of the caravan, the last car that rides along behind the freight), and that didn't last long because I got bumped. Anyone with seniority could bump a newcomer off a particular job that he wanted. So for the rest of my time with PRR, I worked in the yard with a conductor and another brakeman, moving coal cars around. I spent the rest of my time doing yard work as a brakeman. My job was to move freight cars around. Just like a grocery boy making up an order, I had to assemble lines of coal cars, getting them ready to go on the road. As a brakeman, I used a heavy stick to turn the brake wheel that was on the top of each freight car, applying the brake or loosening it on each car in order to move them around. I rode on the top of the coal cars, standing on a small platform where the brake wheel was located. During the day, I used hand signals to communicate with the engineer. After dark, I signaled to him with a lantern.

I had to connect and disconnect cars whenever the conductor instructed me to. On the railroad in those days, they didn't pay you for the hours you put in but for the danger you were in during your eight-hour shift!

Climbing up and down those slippery steel ladders in all kinds of weather—ice, snow, and rain—especially in the dark while the cars were moving was hairy. One slip could be your last. I remember one guy who did make that fatal slip. He fell beneath the moving cars and thirty of them ran over the top of him before anyone knew what had happened. Afterward, they picked up what was left of his body and put his pieces in a bushel basket.

It happened just before my shift started.

The worst accident I was involved in occurred when we had just finished pushing thirteen empty coal cars to the end of the storage track which stopped just before the Raritan River. The "stop" was a huge block of reinforced cement. The last car had to come to rest lightly against the stop.

That night we had the job of taking care of the empty cars, picking them up, and putting them in storage. After picking up the cars, we had to go through the diamond, the command center for all the tracks, where a switchman was on duty, controlling the direction of each collection of cars. Each time that we picked up empties from different parts of the yard, we were directed through this diamond and switched to our destination. After our thirteen empty cars had been pushed all the way to the end, we left them and headed back to the diamond with our steam engine. It was 3:00 a.m. on a cold January morning. During the ride back, I climbed up on the engine to warm my hands on the fire box. I stood there, between the engineer and the fireman, trying to get warm.

The engineer was looking ahead, with his hand on the throttle. In a muffled voice, he muttered out loud to himself, "Looks like some dumb sonofabitch is backing down on us." He couldn't see any lights, only the dark shadows of cars coming toward us. The engineer blasted the emergency signal on his whistle, four or five consecutive short bursts, then he pulled back on the throttle. The last thing I remember was watching him put his hand on the brake.

Then everything went black.

The next thing I remember is getting up off the cold steel floor and shaking lumps of coal off my neck from the tender (coal box).

"Jump! Jump!" the engineer hollered as he leapt off the engine and disappeared into the darkness. I stood there and wondered why, until I looked out and saw the phone poles speeding past me in the opposite direction: we had collided with another train and were being pushed backward toward the end of the pier. I turned to see the fireman doing the same thing, so I jumped off the engine, not knowing where I was going to land in the pitch blackness. After rolling around in the frozen gravel, I came to a stop and realized the only damage I had was from a sprained ankle.

The dark night was illuminated by the sparks from our engine as it pushed the light empty cars off the end of the pier. That dead-end stop ripped all the wheels off the cars. They flew to the right and to the left, landing in the water. One by one, the cars went over the stop, leaving their wheels behind. The tremendous amount of sparks turned that dark night into daylight as the cars flew up and over the end of the track. It seemed like there was no end to it.

About then, the engine that we had been riding on fell sideways down an overpass and onto the street. It came to rest like a big elephant lying on his side, with steam bursting out of everything. The brakeman and the conductor had been riding on the platform behind the engine and the impact had thrown them at a forty-five-degree angle away from the wreck. Nobody really got hurt. The total tally was a few broken ribs and a twisted ankle.

We found out later that our engine had a head-on collision with a runaway bunch of loaded coal cars, forty-three of them to be exact. Each carried tons and tons of coal. The thing that saved us on impact, when the first car hit us, was that our engine had stayed on the rail. If it had derailed, we would have been rolled over and over by the tremendous force. The switchman at the diamond had been informed of the runaway cars and made a last-second decision to send them to the pier, forgetting that we were out there.

My next railroad accident was small compared to this one, but it put me off the streets for a while. This time, I was riding an empty coal car; we were loading up the four storage tracks where these empties were kept. When the four tracks were full of empty cars, another engine coupled them together and took them back to the coal mines to fill them up again. The engine grabs hold of each empty car and gets it moving fast, then lets go. Meanwhile, someone rides the empty to apply the brake when necessary. It was my turn to ride an empty. They told me I was going all the way to the end of track number 4. Numbers 1, 2, and 3 were filled to capacity so I had a long ride ahead of me and I knew I could probably coast all the way to the end without applying any brake pressure.

The engine gave me a fast push and let me go. I was making plenty of speed going down the slope, but things soon changed. The switchman forgot to throw the last switch. Luckily, I was riding on the back end of this car when I saw the front end turn onto track number 3 and head toward a full load of cars. I said to myself, "It's all over. I'll never stop in time. This is going to be a mess. Maybe another bushel basket case."

I never had time to start applying the brake and I knew it. I ducked down just before impact and hung onto the brake shaft which was under the brake wheel. When we hit, the left side of my face and head smashed into the back end of the car. That was all I remember. They said that after impact, I fell down in the gravel like a sack of spuds. Afterward, the left side of my face was numb for a few years.

After Mom got the report on these bad accidents, she said, "You'd better quit that job before you get killed!" When my mother told me to quit the railroad, I figured, OK, here's my chance. Then I went into fishing full time. Although I didn't know it at the time, this decision would change my life—forever.

After the railroad, I was a regular mate on the *Chappie* boats for a couple of years or so.

When World War Two started, I was eager to join the fight, and so in 1943, just after my eighteenth birthday, I went to New York to enlist in the service. My brother Tony had already signed up for a four-year hitch with the navy. I didn't like the idea of marching around in the mud so I also tried enlisting in the navy. But I got in the wrong line and wound up in the air force enlistment line. They took one look at my left arm and threw me out. Then I got into the long line of men hoping to enlist in the navy—and got thrown out again. There was no sense in me trying to get into the marines so I attempted to enlist for the merchant marine, and lost that battle too. I returned home with my tail between my legs, but at least no one could say I didn't try. Later on, I received a draft card in the mail that read: "4F." This is as low as you can go on the list of broken-down humans.

Even though I didn't get into the service, I had a small taste of warfare near where we lived, right off the beach in Point Pleasant. A small tanker had been heading along the beach when an enemy submarine surfaced and shelled it. The tanker blew up and burnt and some of the bloated oil-caked bodies washed up on the beach. They were almost unrecognizable as human beings. Although that particular area of the beach was off-limits to civilians, I got to within fifty feet of some of the bodies. Another time, I was out on the end of the inlet rock pile when I saw a periscope sliding along the surface like a shark fin. It disappeared about a half minute later. Apparently, I was not the only one who knew about this sub because the next day the marines mounted fifty-caliber machine guns on the boardwalk. It wasn't safe to swim that season, and not because of sharks, but because of the oil-soaked sand. The oil from a sunken ship gets washed up on the beach and stays on the surface in the breakers until it mixes with the sand. Then it sinks to the bottom and forms balls of oil and sand that lie there until an unwary swimmer steps in them and gets covered ankle-deep in oil.

I remember the day the war ended. At that time, I was a mate on an open boat, and when we got back to the dock, a crowd of people was jumping up and down, screaming, "THE WAR IS OVER! THE WAR IS OVER!"

As we backed into the dock, everybody was happy except for one guy, a passenger on our boat, who was grumbling and moaning out loud, "Too bad that the war didn't last another couple of weeks because I'm stuck with ten thousand dollars' worth of black market gasoline stamps!"

PART II

HOW I STARTED SHARK FISHING

CHAPTER 3

THE MOVE TO MONTAUK

One summer, my mother rented out one of her apartments at Canary Cottage to a Mr. and Mrs. Probasco and their daughter Janet. The family was from Allentown, New Jersey, where they owned a one-hundred-acre potato farm, and they had come to stay at Mom's place for a one-month vacation. As I rode home on my motorcycle after a day of fishing, I first noticed Janet as she stood on the front porch and I remember asking her if she wanted to go for a ride: that's how I met my first wife. Her mother didn't like me right from the start, especially after she noticed that I came home from the boat, covered with fish scales.

Once their family vacation was finished at Canary Cottage, the Probascos returned to Allentown, but I continued my friendship with Janet. After I came in from fishing, it only took me half an hour on my Harley to travel the thirty-six miles to Janet's house. Soon, our relationship became serious, and I went out and bought an engagement ring for her from the money I made mating on the open boat *Chappie*.

When I showed the ring to her father and asked for Janet's hand in marriage, he expressed his approval by roughly grabbing my arm and ejecting me from his house, while Janet's school-teacher mother told me that I was not good enough for her daughter as I was "only a fisherman" and had no education. I was also told not to return to their house. Naturally, this made me even more determined.

A 1944 shot of me and Capt. Bob on the Chappie open boat. I'm holding my "shark sticker," a pole with a bayonet attached to the end. My job was to kill the sharks that disrupted our mackerel fishing and get them out of the way.

As I rode out of the Probascos' driveway that night, I hollered over my shoulder to Janet, "I'll be back." The next night, after fishing, I made a special trip to Allentown on my Harley and did one fast, wild pass in and out of the Probascos' long driveway and past their front door. They knew I was there because of the roar from my Harley's loud straight-pipe exhaust.

A couple of days later, my dad answered a knock on the door. It was Janet. She showed up at my parent's house after dark and explained to us what had happened. Janet had told her mother that she was of age and was leaving home. Her mother said, "If you leave this house, the only things you will take with you are the clothes on your back!" So Janet had put on two of everything: two dresses, two sweaters, etc.

My parents took Janet in and gave her a room of her own at the Canary Cottage. On January 26, 1946, the Justice of the Peace came to the house and married us. Shortly after, we had a marriage service at our local church. One year later, Barbara ("Bobbie"), our first daughter, was born. It took two years before Janet's parents relented and finally came over to visit us.

After mating on the *Chappie* for a few years I decided to go out on my own and buy a boat. My brother, Anthony, was just coming out of the service at that time—he had been in the navy during the war—and I talked him into going into partnership with me.

Eventually, I saved up enough money for a down payment on a small boat, the *Osprey*, a thirty-foot round-bottomed clinker-built gasoline-powered cabin skiff that worked some of the time. It was a small private boat that I converted into a charter boat by adding four fishing chairs and some outriggers. I had it coast guard documented to carry passengers for hire and changed its name to the *Cricket*, after my namesake, Jimminy, and also because she jumped and danced around on the waves like a cricket.

Tony, *left*; me, *right*; and our mate pose with one of the first makos we ever caught.

Me and Tony at Hillman's Brielle Basin, with tuna that we caught from our first boat, the *Cricket*.

My partnership with Tony lasted exactly one year
because his wife told him that he had to be home at 4:30
p.m. each day for supper! Well, it doesn't work out that
way when you're in the charter boat business.

Around this time, my father's health began to fail. One
evening in the fall of 1947, Dad returned home early from
his night shift on the police force, only an hour after he had
checked in for his 8:00 to 12:00 p.m. watch. Dad told my
mother that he had a pain in his chest and asked her to call a
doctor. After the doctor examined him, he sent for an
ambulance. The last time I saw my father alive, he was sitting
up in his hospital bed, inside a plastic oxygen tent. He was
warned by his doctor a long time ago to quit smoking because
Dad's lungs were black with nicotine, but he didn't. And now,
after a small heart attack, his lungs didn't work properly.

As visiting time ended, I said, "Goodnight, Pop. See you
tomorrow."

But I couldn't because he died early next morning, on
September 1, 1947, at the age of fifty-eight.

Pop had still been alive when I owned the *Cricket*, and
he had said, repeatedly, "Get rid of that little boat and buy
a big boat with a diesel motor."

This opportunity came when I got to know Bill Zubar.
He owned the dock in Brielle where I had my boat tied up.
Bill was having some boats built down in Virginia.

During the war, he had been a lumber buyer for the
government. On his travels, he happened to go down to
Virginia and saw people building boats out of long-leaf yellow
pine. Bill knew that long-leaf yellow pine is one of the strongest
woods in the States. A lot of people think that oak is a stronger
wood, but you will find dry rot occurs in oak more often.

So Bill had an open boat built in Virginia. It was forty-
six feet long with a flush deck. I liked the boat because it
had plenty of lumber in it. Not speedy, but it was a steady
boat: a work boat. Just before Bill headed back down to the
boatyard in Virginia to make arrangements to have another

of these boats built for his dock (eventually, he had three boats built), I got talking to him and he invited me to Virginia to take a look at his boat.

At the boatyard, Bill introduced me to the builder, Old Man Cockrell. Cockrell was a short yet not too stubby white-haired guy, probably in his middle sixties, and he had been building Chesapeake oyster boats for the last four decades. Cockrell had never built a "sport boat" (charter boat) as he called it. And surprisingly, Old Man Cockrell had never seen the ocean. He had spent a lifetime on the Chesapeake Bay, building heavy oyster boats that would never see the deep blue water. But like Old Man Cockrell would say, the Chesapeake can get "god almighty rough at times," so I figured he could build me a good seaworthy boat.

Once I had seen the lumber they were using and how sturdy the boat builders were putting these boats together, I said "That's for me." However, Cockrell said he could not build me a boat to take out on the ocean because he didn't have any three-inch-thick planks to use. I asked him when he thought he would get the right lumber and Cockrell told me, "Next fall."

"But I need the boat built for this up and coming season," I explained.

"Well, if you want one for this season, I'll build it for you out of the two-inch-thick planks we have on hand now and we'll frame it up heavier. A two-inch-thick piece of long-leaf yellow pine is a lot stronger than any other plank, so don't worry about it. If it falls apart, bring it back and I'll build you another boat."

So I talked Old Man Cockrell into building the *Cricket II*, asking him to make it forty-two feet and heavy-built, with a fifteen-foot beam.

"Why not forty-four feet?" Cockrell asked.

"I can't. Why do you ask?"

Then Old Man Cockrell said, "I got two planks: forty-four feet, twelve inches wide, two inches thick, without a knot in 'um, and I hate like hell to cut two feet off 'um," Cockrell answered.

"I'd like to, but I can't. To meet coast guard regulations, she can't be any longer than forty-two feet," I told him.

The deal was that before he started work on the boat, I had to bring him a deposit of five hundred dollars.

After old man Cockrell and I struck the deal, I said I'd go home and have some blueprints made up. He hollered, "No, No, No!" he said, as fast as I had gotten the words out. "Don't have any of those g-d damn blueprints made up!" (Probably because he didn't work from blueprints, being from the old school of boat builders!)

"When you go home, take a window shade and on one side of the window shade make it forty-two inches. Then make believe that you're looking at the boat from the top, straight down. Mark off where you want the cabin to be—eight inches, ten inches, and whatever you want the cockpit to be. Then," he says, "turn the window shade over and on the other side, and now make believe you're looking at the boat from a side view. Draw the lines how high you want the bow, what the cabin should look like, etc."

So I went home and wore out a couple of window shades until I got the right plan! Then, after selling my motorcycle for five hundred dollars, I rolled up the window shade, put it under my arm, climbed into my Model A, and drove back down to Virginia. Then I gave Old Man Cockrell his deposit and the window shade, and he began work on my boat.

In the meantime, Bill Zubar struck a "deal" with Old Man Cockrell: we were going to bring the *Cricket II* to Brielle where she would be a demo item, so to speak, and we'd talk many other people into having these boats built. So Old Man Cockrell gave me a good deal. He built me the boat, complete, for a little less than ten thousand dollars. To make it a charter boat after we got home, I had to install the bunks, the galley, a flying bridge, the railing around the forward deck, fishing chairs, rod holders, and outriggers.

He supplied all the hardware for the rudder, propeller, and everything under the water line.

There was just one complication: now I was the proud owner of two boats—a boatman's nightmare. So I put an ad in the paper and crossed my fingers.

Three or four weeks later, the good Lord sent me an idiot who came to look the *Cricket* over. When the new buyer showed up, the boat was still over at Bill Zubar's dock, as I had not hauled her out yet for the winter. When he climbed on the boat, the potential buyer walked across the cockpit, from one side to the other, and asked me why the boat rolled so much. I gave him the bullshit excuse that her fuel tanks were empty. He swallowed my excuse hook, line, and sinker and bought the boat. Financially, I came out exactly even and was able to pay back all the money I had borrowed to buy the *Cricket*.

A few months later, I got a postcard from Tiffany Cockrell. It had four words on it: "COME GET YOUR BOAT."

So I grabbed a couple of friends and we drove down to Virginia in my Model A Ford which was loaded with all kinds of nuts, bolts, fuel tanks, and everything else we would need.

When Cockrell told me to come and get my boat, he didn't tell me that I had to do a lot of work on it. The *Cricket II* had been built, but she was not exactly ready. Everything had to be hooked up: all the electric wires had to be installed for the generator and running lights, etc. Then the motor had to be hooked up with its water intake and exhaust pipes. Otherwise, the boat was ready!

Cockrell's boatyard was located in the small Virginia town of Burgess Store, on the west side of the Chesapeake. He was out in the boonies so finding all the material we needed to finish the boat caused many delays. The nearest hardware store was thirty miles away, and if they didn't have what we needed, we had to drive to the next hardware store in Kilmarnock, another hoot and a holler down the road. As a result, it took another three weeks to put everything in working order aboard the *Cricket II*.

Cockrell was the kind of man who would look at you with a twinkle in his eye; you knew he was up to something, but you couldn't figure out what. To him, us "damn Yankees" were gullible. One of his favorite things (that he did to everybody when he was getting ready to launch their boat) was to measure the boat and then measure the width of the railway tracks that detoured around a big oak tree before continuing on to the water.

He knew the boat would clear that oak tree, but he made sure to look worried about it, and always did his measuring in our presence.

"Look, Old Man Cockrell is measuring that big oak tree again," my friend, Joe McGovern, told me as we watched Cockrell scratching his head after running his tape measure out again. Cockrell was very fond of this tree that was about as old as he was and had refused to cut it down when he made the railway.

Cockrell repeatedly told us that he had no winch to lower the boat slowly down the railway track.

"We just cut the string, and down she goes," he said.

There were two things that Old Man Cockrell wanted Joe and me to keep asking ourselves: how fast was the boat going to go down the incline? And would it clear THAT tree?

"If it clears the tree and hits the water, your boat WILL sink. We always let a new boat sink for a couple of days in order to have the planks swell up tight and stop leaking," he said with a twinkle.

Joe and I looked at each other, trying to figure out if Cockrell was kidding.

Then the fateful day arrived. Cockrell asked me if I was going to christen the boat, which I did—with an old beer can filled with salt water.

Now it was time for the launching. Cockrell cut the rope, or "the string" (as he called it) that held the boat up on the railway, close to the boat shed. Down she rolled, *thumpity-thump*, on her carriage, like a runaway freight train. We all held our breath, as the *Cricket II* went whizzing around that big oak tree and splashed into the water, like a crippled duck!

As soon as she was afloat, the water squirted in through every crack and crevice. Old Man Cockrell immediately ordered all hands to man the pumps and keep her afloat. Then Cockrell told us that he couldn't let a "SPORT BOAT" sink, and within two or three hours, the planks had swollen up nicely, making her watertight enough so that only one automatic pump was needed overnight.

Cockrell had "gotten us" again.

That night, Joe and I slept on the boat while she was moored to Cockrell's dock. It would be another three weeks of eating and sleeping on the boat before we were ready for our trip home. All night long we heard loud groaning sounds coming from underneath the boat. It sounded like a bunch of angry bullfrogs. Was this another of Cockrell's pranks? In the morning, we asked Cockrell what those noises were.

"Toadfish," he laughed, and walked away. Toadfish are angler fish—or head fish as they are known commercially. I had never heard this type of fish making those noises before.

Then came our next problem: I owned a Model A Ford that I had paid twenty-five dollars for the year before and I wasn't going to lose it. Loading this vehicle into the newly built *Cricket II* would involve a feat of improvisation and ingenuity.

We began by backing in and tying the stern up against a steep embankment. Next, we ran two planks from the sand to the back of the boat. Then we put heavy planks across the boat, right and left (just like a boardwalk), and then we rolled the car up onto the *Cricket II*. After this, we pulled the car up and onto these cross planks by hand, using a block and tackle. Now we put a jack under the front end of the car and jacked the front up a few inches, enough to slide the planks out. Then we let the front of the car come down. We did the same thing to the back of the car. Finally, the Model A was in the boat.

On our way home from Virginia in 1946. My Model A Ford rode home in the *Cricket II*'s cockpit.

We had a lot of extra trouble on the way back from Virginia to Brielle. Any time that you have a new boat built, you will have many bugs (trouble spots) in it. The newly built *Cricket II* had problems with her generator and electric wiring; we had to lay over in different ports until these minor repairs could be done. The bugs delayed our arrival in Brielle by a week. I knew that when we got home that Friday I had a charter booked for the following day and there was no time to take the Model A off the boat.

The party was a bunch of guys who wanted to do some mackerel fishing. I told them that I still had my car in the boat and I couldn't take them out.

"We don't care about your car, we want to go fishing," one guy said sarcastically.

And another guy piped up, "You must have run into bad weather on your way up here with the car in the boat."

"Yes," I admitted. "The *Cricket II* had encountered some sloppy water on coming up the middle of the Chesapeake."

"Well," he reasoned, "if the bad weather didn't bother anything, why not take us and the car out fishing?"

So that's what we did. The *Cricket II* headed out to the fishing grounds with eighteen passengers and a Model A in the cockpit! These guys had a ball when we started catching mackerel. They sat on the Model A's hood, its roof, and on the carrying box that used to be the rumble seat. By the time we got home that day, I had the only Model A Ford that was covered in mackerel scales and fish blood!

Getting the vehicle out of the boat after we got home was another story. The next day, I called a wrecker to haul the car up and onto the dock. It was a lot harder to take the car out than it had been to put it in because we had to winch the vehicle straight up, about eight feet, and over the flush bulkhead before we could swing it onto the parking lot. When that Model A's wheels touched the dirt, a crowd of people who were watching all screamed at the same time, "HURRAY!" About two years later, my Model A finally fell apart, and I sold it to a Point Pleasant, New Jersey junkyard for ten dollars. I guess that two long trips from New Jersey to Virginia when I was having the new boat built helped wear out that old jalopy.

I fished the new *Cricket II* from Bill Zubar's dock, out of Brielle, for a few seasons before the dock master of Montauk's Fish Shangri-la stepped aboard my boat in July 1951 and invited me to make the move to Montauk. This dock master had made the trip to Jersey, looking for sturdy open boats that could carry many passengers as Montauk lacked head boats in those days. My boat was able to carry a lot more people. Not only was the *Cricket II's* cockpit large, but she also had a railing all around her forward section that could accommodate another twenty passengers or so.

The Montauk open boat captains had more customers than they did boats, especially when the Fisherman Special train brought out hundreds of fishermen from New York City on weekends.

A few days later, I jumped in my car and made a special overnight trip to Montauk on July second. The drive took more than five hours because at that time there were no main highways, and to reach Montauk, you had to drive through all the small towns. I wanted to be there on the docks at daylight to see for myself all the passengers who were left on the dock because of the boat shortage.

Before these customers showed up, I spoke to the other boatmen to get their reaction about my plan of bringing the *Cricket II* to Montauk. They all said the same thing, "Bring your boat to Montauk. We need more boats here!"

As the boatmen received me with open arms and the extra business was there, how could I miss? The first week in July of 1951, I told Janet we were moving to Montauk. So we loaded the *Cricket II* with the few belongings that we had. Then, sometime after midnight on July 19, 1951, Janet, Bobbie (who was now four years old), and I left for

Montauk. Earlier that afternoon, I remember filling the fuel tanks with diesel fuel at fifteen cents per gallon!

It took us fourteen hours to reach Montauk. Since there were no available rooms or apartments, the boat became our home for that season. The three of us took turns sleeping on the floor because the *Cricket II* only had two bunks. When I went fishing, I left Janet and Bobbie to wander around on terra firma until I got back. Because we had no car, we had to walk the mile and a half from Fish Shangri-la into town to go to the post office. Then we had supper at the Shagwong Tavern. Bobbie's little legs got tired on these long walks and so I often carried her on my shoulders.

It wasn't until the following spring that we found an apartment in East Hampton. The next season, we managed to find a small house in Ditch Plains, Montauk. Our final move was from Ditch Plains to Smith's Cottages near the beach, on the old Montauk highway. We lived at Smith's cottages for over twenty years and wound up with three daughters: Barbara, the eldest; followed by Pat, in 1957; and Tammy, who completed our family in 1961.

The *Pelican* Disaster, 1951

I've always said that trouble is something you can't run away from. Some types of trouble can even lead to disaster when a random group of elements combine such as Long Island Railroad's "The Fisherman's Special" train, a good weather report, and plenty of fish waiting to be caught. The Labor Day weekend of 1951 was slated for such a disaster off Montauk.

This was my first season in Montauk at Fish Shangri-la. Fish Shangri-la had been a naval dock for submarines during World War II because of its deep water entrance. After the war, a private company bought the docks and buildings, converting the facility into a fisherman's paradise, complete with all the necessary equipment needed for such a sport fishing Shangri-la: walk-in freezers, restaurants, and a tackle store.

Fish Shangri-la also had about half a dozen open boats, or "head boats" as they are called. These boats took out individuals or groups, charging them $5.00 per head. No reservation was necessary so people just jumped aboard. At that time, coast guard rules and regulations stated that a captain had to have a life jacket available for every person on board; however, the rules did not specify a limit on the number of passengers per boat.

To get a spot on their favorite head boat, many of the weekend fishermen from the city emerged from their local gin mill when it closed at around 2:00 a.m. From there, they went to Pennsylvania Railroad Station in New York City to catch the 3:00 a.m. Fisherman Special heading for Montauk.

When all the seats were filled, these diehards stood or lay down in the aisles for a chance to wet their lines. Among them were ones who passed around the brown paper bag that held the booze bottle. Many were half drunk by the time they literally jumped off the train and rolled onto the gravel at Montauk after throwing their duffel bags of fishing tackle, slickers, and boots out of the train before it had come to a complete stop at the end of the track.

It was amazing to watch these people climb out of windows and leap off the train, pick up their gear, then run to get a spot on a boat. Some pushed and shoved their way out onto the dock, trying to get ahead of the next person. If they were not fast enough to get on board with their buddies before the boat got its load of customers and departed, they were left behind to wander around the dock until the train left Montauk again at 3:00 p.m. on its way back to Penn Station.

The main reason I had been invited to Montauk was that my boat could act as a head boat, carrying a lot of people on weekends; but during the week, I could operate as a sport-fishing vessel, keeping the *Cricket II* in with the other two sport-fishing boats at the opposite end of the dock.

The dock master told me, "On weekends, when all the people come out, I want you to move your boat over to where the open boats are docked. Use the slip on the inside of the L-shaped dock."

This blocked Eddie Carroll's popular head boat, the *Pelican*, from leaving its slip. I had to leave first in order for Eddie to get out. Before the train came in on that Labor Day weekend, Saturday, September 1, I already had a rough count of twenty to twenty-five people on board my boat.

From my flying bridge, I hollered to the dock master as he came walking up the dock that I wanted to go as I did a head count and had enough passengers as far as I was concerned, but he said I couldn't leave until the train came in. The Pennsylvania Railroad had given the dock master a ticket count of around 350 people on today's Montauk-bound Fisherman Special. He knew at the time we would be short of boats and there would be people left behind at the dock, so he tried to squeeze as many passengers as he could on board the boats.

When the train came in and the people started running down the docks, they had to rush past my boat to reach the regular open boats. All the other open boats were full and had left the dock, except for the *Pelican*. At this time, Eddie Carroll had his load and wanted to leave too but couldn't: I had him pinned in because the dock master had told me to stay.

I was still standing on the flying bridge; the motor was running and my mate had one line attached to the dock, awaiting orders to let it go. By now, I had a rough count of thirty to thirty-five people and they were still jumping off the dock and onto the *Cricket II*. In a split second, I hollered down to the mate, "Let it go."

As my boat started to move ahead, I looked back and saw people still attempting to jump on board, but my boat was too far away from the dock.

And I could hear Captain Eddie hollering at the people, "NO, WE *CAN'T* TAKE ANY MORE. STAY OFF, WE'RE FULL!"

But the people kept climbing aboard. By this time, he was overloaded, just like everybody else that day. When the *Cricket II* moved away from the dock, the *Pelican* was able to leave her slip, and she followed me right out.

It was flat calm when we left. There wasn't a breath of air and the local weather forecast for that day was good so everybody expected a fun day's fishing. The fishing grounds lay south of Montauk Lighthouse. On the way out to them, my final count of passengers was forty-two. It was approximately a half hour's ride from the inlet to the lighthouse. Once we had rounded the lighthouse, we headed southwest for another three-quarters of an hour to the fishing grounds. In those days, the fish were all over that area so we had no special spots to go to.

I was five minutes away from the lighthouse, on my way out, when my mate came up on the bridge and told me we had water spurting out the side of my motor box.

The *Cricket II* had developed a leak in one of her saltwater cooling pipes. I didn't want to tell the people we had motor trouble so I stopped the boat right there and told them we would try fishing in this spot.

While everybody was busy fishing, I was busy fishing for a way to fix the leak. As it happened, I was pleased to find out that the leak was only minor and I fixed it quickly with a wooden plug made from a piece of our deck brush handle.

Right then, the wind picked up and started to howl out of the northeast. It blew so fast and so sudden that many customers lost their bags of fishing tackle (and anything else that was loose) overboard. It seemed like the wind was blowing harder and harder by the minute. This was not called for—our weather forecast had been completely wrong. The thing in my favor was that we were catching plenty of fish where we were and the wind was against the tide. When this happens and you are drifting, if both tide and wind are about the same, the boat will almost stand still. Because we were catching fish, I decided to stay right there instead of heading around the lighthouse with the rest of the boats.

By this time, the waves were getting bigger and bigger because the wind and tide were getting stronger. I knew from experience that if these conditions got worse, we would have a real mess on our hands. I also knew that I could not order my customers to go home unless this was an emergency, so I had to get them to tell me that they wanted to go home. Because we had been drifting since we got here, my customers had been catching fish fast and furiously, not realizing that the weather conditions were worsening. In fact, they had already caught half a bag of fish each, mostly porgies and sea bass.

I had to come up with a reason to run the boat into the oncoming waves, showing my customers how bad the weather had become.

My excuse came when I hollered to the customers in the stern of the boat that a lot of the fishermen in the bow wanted to catch more porgies. Then I told them to wind their lines up as we were going to make a move to a spot about five minutes away. I started the motor, put the propeller into motion, and the *Cricket II* wound her way slowly upwind. It took two waves to reach a safe running speed for these sea conditions, but the third wave buried the bow as two feet of green water crashed over it. This wave swept down the walkway, taking with it bags of fish, rods, reels, and lunch boxes, washing everything into the cockpit.

Now that the boys in the bow had had their surprise, the boys in the stern would also get theirs as the wave rolled down, bringing all the debris onto the deck of the cockpit. In the blink of an eye, everybody in the cockpit found themselves in ankle-deep water. Thank God we had enough scupper holes in the cockpit deck to handle this large amount of water all at once. I wasn't worried about this situation because I knew that these scupper holes would drain the water back into the Long Island Sound, but many of my customers who were wading around in the water at this time didn't share my thoughts.

Eventually, their mumbles grew louder and louder, turning into words, "Looks like it's getting rough out here. Don't you think we should start back?"

I gave them my standard reply, "It's up to you guys. You tell me what to do. Take a vote on it."

Most of them said, "We've got enough fish. Let's cut the day short and go home."

So we turned around. Now the *Cricket II* had the wind on her ass. This made for a nice, slow, easy roll of a ride back home. Every once in a while, one of the "following" waves would try to climb over the transom and into the cockpit.

One of the funniest sights I saw on the way home was a tipsy customer sitting on the deck with the back of his head even with the top of the *Cricket II*'s transom, attempting to eat a chicken sandwich made with a whole chicken slapped between two slices of bread. A young blond man in his early twenties, he had been nipping for the entire trip on some booze he had hidden in his lunch box and was oblivious to the laughter of his friends. As he had not worn a hat all day, his hair resembled a road map of Long Island. It was salt-water soaked, matted, and stuck up in all directions. Funnier yet, and unknown to him, all the way home one wave after another was cresting behind him, threatening, within inches, to roll over his head. It was an unforgettable combination.

After we reached the dock at 1:30 p.m., and all the customers had gone, I ran up into the Fish Shangri-la restaurant with my mate to get a hot bowl of soup and a couple of shots of booze because we were both cold and wet. As we were leaving the restaurant, a boatman's daughter who was about twelve years old came running up to me and threw her arms around my waist. Crying and screaming at the same time, she said, "The *Pelican* turned over just outside the lighthouse!"

From what I could figure out, a large wave had hit the *Pelican* on the bow from her right side, throwing lots of water and spray over the boat. Many of the passengers must have panicked and ran to the left side. The next wave did the rest, turning her over. (This is only what I think happened because the captain, Eddie Carroll, never made it back to tell us).

I immediately grabbed a few guys off the dock to help in a rescue attempt and we left as soon as we could. By the time the *Cricket II* got out there, the howling wind had slowed some and sea conditions were not quite as bad. Rounding the point, we saw the hull of the *Pelican*, bow up, bobbing up and down in the water. Three-quarters of her was submerged, like a man-made iceberg.

It was plain to see that any and all the survivors had been picked up by a small fleet of boats that had gone out ahead of us. As we had been one of the last boats to hear about the disaster, we were also one of the last boats to get out there. My next thought was to try to recover the *Pelican*, as we knew there must still be a lot of bodies trapped in the overturned boat, perhaps even Captain Eddie's.

Weeks later, one of the female survivors said that the last time Captain Eddie was seen alive he had been trying to help a passenger stay afloat until help arrived.

The way it looked to me, the *Pelican* was now being driven ashore by the wind and current and the boat didn't have far to go. We needed to put a tow line on the *Pelican* to pull her away from the rocks. It would be a challenge getting a line on the boat because the only thing sticking out of the water was a piece of her bow which bobbed up and down at least ten to fifteen feet.

I told one of my volunteers to walk out on my harpoon pulpit with a tow line and try to make it fast to something, but each time I maneuvered the pulpit over the top of the *Pelican*, whenever the *Cricket II* was plunging down, the bow of the *Pelican* lurched upward and vice versa. After many attempts, we wound up smashing the *Cricket II*'s pulpit against the *Pelican*'s hull; the impact almost tossed our volunteer into the choppy water.

Because the pulpit trick didn't work, I thought of putting a life jacket on one of my volunteers, tying a lifeline on him, and then towing him to the *Pelican* so that he could attempt to attach a tow line from his vantage point in the water. This still did not work. For some reason, I thought that he wasn't trying hard enough to get the tow line on, so I jumped in the water myself and my mate towed me to the upended vessel. When I got there, I discovered why it was physically impossible to make the tow line fast: the *Pelican*'s bow was bobbing up and down so much that it could tear a swimmer apart, and my up-close observation told me there was still no place to make a line fast.

"Pick me up," I hollered to my mate, and he hauled me back in on my lifeline.

The only other way that I knew of was to take our anchor, use it as a grappling hook, and drop it over the *Pelican*'s hull, hoping to catch hold of something to pull on. After a few attempts at this new maneuver, our anchor caught hold of something out of sight for us to pull on. We made the line fast to our stern bit and started pulling very slowly, a little at a time. Captain Carl Forsberg who was running the open boat *Viking* saw what I was doing and came over to help. He had to make his line fast the same way. Everything was going well: two boats, two lines. Slowly, we were moving the *Pelican* in the direction we wanted her to go. After a half hour of this, my anchor tore loose, taking the Pelican's entire port side rail with it to the bottom. It took four or five of us pulling on the rope to get the anchor and railing up to the surface, close to the *Cricket II*'s transom.

I told my crew of volunteers that somehow we had to get the railing off as we needed the anchor again for a grappling hook. Everybody pulled on the rope as hard as they could. Inch by inch, the railing came into view. It seemed like a long time before one of the boys actually had his hands on it, by hanging over the transom and stretching as far as he could. After this, our job got a little easier. A second person now grabbed the railing and started to pull. This railing was not balanced by the anchor because the anchor had hold of it four or five stanchions from one end, so it hung vertically, straight up and down. Soon, three men were lifting the railing. By now, we could see the anchor. A little bit more and we could work it loose and drop the rail.

By this time, everybody was trying to lift the heavy rail straight up to loosen the anchor.

Only one or two men hanging over the outer part of the transom, looking down, could see what was going on.

Finally, one fellah hollered, "I've got the anchor loose. It's clear! Drop the rail whenever you want."

Just as everybody let go, another person hollered, "Look, there's a guy down there hanging on the rail!"

I ran to the transom and saw—eight to ten feet below the water—a fair-haired young man holding onto one of the stanchions in a death grip: his left arm was wrapped around it while his right arm hung limp. We couldn't see his face because it was buried in the fold of his left arm. What I remember most is the youth's fairly long light-colored hair flowing up and down in the surge.

For one split second, we were all in shock. At the same time that we saw the body, we had just lifted the anchor loose and everybody had let go of the heavy rail. It was on its way down and nobody could stop it. In seconds, that heavy rail disappeared out of sight due to poor visibility in the wind-stirred waters.

Now that we had recovered our anchor that was being used as a grappling hook, I ran the *Cricket II* back through the heavy swells to see if we could get another purchase on the half-sunken boat. At this point, just as we got to the *Pelican*, we found out that Carl Forsberg had pulled the other rail off, the same way we had.

He had lost his grip on the *Pelican*; she was free again and drifting toward the rocks. After we made four or five attempts of throwing the anchor over, down, and into the submerged boat, it made itself fast to something and we started slowly moving ahead once more, pulling the *Pelican* away from the rocks.

Carl Forsberg returned from rerigging his anchor and joined us in the towing effort by attaching his own anchor the same way, throwing it blindly into the hull of the upturned vessel. On Carl's first throw, the anchor attached itself to some unknown object.

Soon, both the *Viking* and the *Cricket II* were pulling and making slow headway against the tide. Each of us had to be careful not to apply too much engine power or the anchors could break loose. By the time the two boats rounded Montauk Lighthouse, the ebb tide was at its strongest and it hit us hard. We had to hold our own at this point, hoping we could hang on and that nothing more would break. Here we were, trying to tow a submerged object against the tide and had only a light purchase on it. Despite this, we knew that in the next three or four hours the tide would change and be in our favor, helping to push the stricken *Pelican* all the way into the inlet. My cold, wet, and hungry crew was relieved to come around the lighthouse and enter the calm waters of Long Island Sound.

Everything was going well until after dark when the eighty-three-foot coast guard boat appeared. This vessel had been called on to help in the recovery effort. It took her captain a few hours to arrive from Connecticut where she was stationed full time. At this point, most of the hard work had been done by the *Cricket II* and the *Viking*. All the eighty-three-footer needed to do was make her own tow line fast to the upended *Pelican*. Instead, this coast guard vessel came alongside us in the pitch black of the night (it was somewhere between 9:00 and 10:00 p.m. by now) and turned her big spotlight on the *Cricket II*. Somebody hollered down orders for me to cut my tow line and make it fast to the heaving line that one of the coast guard crew had just thrown into my cockpit. Instead, I screamed orders to my crew to throw the heaving line back.

"Give us your tow line; we have more towing power than you," the captain of the eighty-three-footer ordered.

I screamed back at him, "You dumb bastard, I've got plenty of power, but we can't use it all or we'll tear something else apart and so will you!" Then I told them, "Slide back and make your own tow line fast because we're holding the *Pelican* nice and steady for you against the tide."

Again, the captain of the eighty-three-footer gave orders for his crew to throw us the "monkey fist" (a ball of spliced line which carries over the light heaving line). When the monkey fist landed for the second time in the cockpit of the *Cricket II*, one of my crew, because he was tired of all this bullshit, cut my tow line and tied it to the heaving line.

"There, you sons of bitches, you wanted our tow line, now you got it!" he yelled, throwing all of it overboard. Over 150 feet of three-quarter-inch anchor line slowly sank, still attached to the heaving line that went to the coast guard boat.

It was then I knew there was nothing more we could do, so I went over to the *Viking* and told Carl what had happened and suggested he consider his job finished because the *Viking* could not handle the tow alone. Carl tried to take the tow by himself, but the line parted, like I predicted it would. Meanwhile, the eighty-three-footer backed down to take up the slack out of our line. In doing so, she got our anchor line wrapped up in both her propellers. This put the coast guard vessel out of commission. Now it was the eighty-three-footer's turn to radio in for help. A forty-two-footer coast guard vessel stationed in Montauk came out to assist her.

Carl and I went back to the dock in disgust because everything we had done so far had been messed up by the coast guard. We found out later that the forty-two-footer had put a marker light on the upended *Pelican*, so they could find it again and to prevent other boats from running into this submerged object.

We also found out that the forty-two-footer had hauled in the disabled eighty-three-footer and then went back out to tow the *Pelican* home. By this time, the tide had changed, as it headed toward the inlet, simplifying the coast guard's tow job immensely. That night, they towed the *Pelican* into port.

The next day, nobody sailed. We flew our flags at half-mast out of respect for the *Pelican* and her lost captain, crew, and passengers. After the coast guard had hauled the *Pelican* out of the water, I think that they recovered twenty-one bodies trapped down below decks, but Captain Eddie's body was never found.

I was frustrated when the information the press received got screwed up one more time. All the photos and reports gave the coast guard all the credit with no mention of any other vessels involved. It was wrongly stated that the coast guard vessels were the first on the scene. In reality, they were the last. The only thing that Carl and I got out of this whole mess was a "Thank you" from Eddie Caroll's grateful relatives and some self-satisfaction: we had done all we could. After the *Pelican* disaster, the Fisherman Special weekend passenger service to Montauk was discontinued.

How I Got Started Shark Fishing

When I first moved to Montauk in 1951, I wasn't shark fishing, I was catching the same fish everybody else caught, doing the same thing that everybody else was doing; therefore, I was accepted by everybody else! At the end of the 1951 fishing season, while I was trying to chum up bluefish in September, I accidentally discovered there were a lot of sharks in the waters off Montauk. Some friends and I made an experimental trip one night during a full moon to see if we could catch some blue fish the same way that we did off the Jersey coast; for eight years I had caught bluefish commercially when we fished out of Brielle. The commercial docks there supplied us with all the ground up menhaden (moss bunkers) we needed for chum, but I had to introduce chum to the rest of the fishermen in Montauk because they didn't use it.

To get enough chum, we had to go out and meet the menhaden boats that fished up and down the Long Island coast. I took the bunkers ashore and ground them up at a mink farm in East Hampton. This was the only place that a large grinder was available. No, I never ground up any mink, despite the rumors. In fact, in return for using his grinder, I would bring the mink farmer some shark meat for those little furry critters. We stored the five-gallon cans of ground chum in Duryea's ice house in Montauk. The first night that we fished for blue fish off Montauk turned into a circus: we hooked six jumping mako sharks, but only landed one of them. No one on the boat, including me, knew what we were doing in trying to catch sharks on bluefish tackle. The next night, correcting a lot of our mistakes, we used heavier tackle. Two makos were taken out of the four we hooked. Now our average was starting to pick up. It didn't take long for me to realize that catching a shark was good fun and that it provided delicious shark steaks. I couldn't call this new type of sport "shark fishing," because the word "shark" in those days threw people off. Sharks were considered garbage fish, so I changed the name to "Monster Fishing." If a new party walked down the dock, looking to go fishing, they would asked me, "What kind of fishing are we doing today?"

"We're going monster fishing today," I would tell them. After we finished a day of catching sharks, one of the customers would always say to me, "The only thing that we caught today was sharks, but we had so much fun today, why don't we go shark fishing the next time out?" So that is how I started fooling the public like Barnum did.

According to Montauk charter-boat captains' standards, this is when my credibility as a sane person started to go downhill fast! None of them wanted to go shark fishing because either they were deathly afraid of sharks, or because their boats were not equipped to handle these fish. Besides, their so-called fishing standards would be ruined by throwing out that messy stuff called chum.

One of their stock phrases was, "What customer would want to go out and catch sharks when there is all the tuna, plenty of swordfish, and a lot of white marlin to catch?"

But when our customers showed up on the dock and I asked them, "What kind of fishing would you guys like to do today? There are lots of tuna, and a good chance of a swordfish or white marlin," their answer was, "We know we are going to have action and fun shark fishing—let's go!"

I even made an entertaining routine out of my seasickness. It only took me twenty years to get over being seasick. I even got to the point where I could give a half-minute countdown as to when I was going to toss my cookies. One of my favorite tricks was to find a couple of guys on their knees with the dry heaves, trying to throw up. As I walked over to the side of the boat, I would step in between the two men, and say, "You guys really don't know how to throw up. Watch me, and I'll show you!" Then I took out my upper set of teeth and produced one of my two-inch round "fire hydrant" barfs, just like Linda Blair in *The Exorcist*. Afterward, I would wipe my face clean and start all over again by eating another sandwich. There wasn't a spot on the boat that wasn't barfed on, from the flying bridge down to the cabin. People even tried to fill up my boots, hoping to hide their vomit from everybody, until I put my foot in one and it went *squish*. Their other favorite vomit depository was under a bunk mattress, which I wouldn't find for a day or so. Seasickness or not, my business of monster fishing, or sport fishing for sharks continued.

Everybody laughed at me for being a maverick; everybody, that is, except for Frank Tuma Sr. who owned Tuma's Tackle, one of Montauk's first fishing-tackle stores, down at the dock. "You might have something there with this shark-fishing business," he told me.

It took the rest of them another twenty-four years before they would agree and go shark-fishing themselves. Years later, Frank Tuma's son, who was also named Frank, said to me one day, "I have a slip open at my dock and you can have it for free; if you let me be your agent, I'll take 10 percent. You are the only person I know of who can tell his customers that a pile of horse shit in the middle of the cockpit is gold and they will believe it!" I declined his offer because I always wanted to stay by myself.

So, after the movie *Jaws* was released in 1975, everybody was an instant expert. Their fishing magazine advertisements now read: "We catch sharks and can teach beginners." So I changed my ad to read: "We can teach beginners, because we have taught all the experts."

As you can guess, this did not go down very well with my competitors! There was no competition on my end. I already had twenty-four years of shark fishing behind me before they even got started. In fact, I even told them how to go shark fishing in the book *Sportfishing for Sharks* which I wrote with Bill Wisner in 1971.

Speaking of writers, back in September 1951, when I was lucky enough to catch a 961-pound giant tuna for my customer Hank Brain, literary giant Ernest Hemingway showed up at Johnny Cronnick's tackle store in Montauk the next day. Hemingway had heard of Hank's record fish and wanted to see if there were any more big ones out there. Johnny Cronnick told me that Earnest Hemingway had shown up at his tackle store, searching for a good back harness to fight the big fish with, and so Johnny had shown him one of his better harnesses.

After examining it closely, Hemingway said, "This one will be good," and started for the door with the harness under his arm.

Cronnick said, "That'll be forty-five dollars."

Hemingway, with one hand on the doorknob, said, insulted, "*I* am Ernest Hemingway!"

"I don't care if you're God Almighty, it's forty-five dollars!" Cronnick replied, gruffly.

Hemingway walked back to the counter, dropped the harness on it, and left in a huff Johnny told me.

In a good-humored way, Johnny was the type of guy who tried his best to aggravate everybody that came through his door, but he found his match in me. I got even with him one time after he told me, "If you come in with a shark that you think is a record on light tackle, bring him to the store and we'll weigh him in because I have an official scale." So one full moon, I went out fishing and caught my customer Gerald Stanley a record mako on ten-pound test. It just happened to be 3:30 in the morning when Gerald and I pounded on Johnny's door.

A second-storey window opened and out popped Cronnick's head. "What the hell do you guys want? It's three-thirty in the morning!" he yelled.

"You said if we caught a record mako to bring it down and you would weigh it in. It can't wait till daylight because the fish will lose a lot of weight," I hollered up to him. Reluctantly, Johnny came downstairs and opened up the door to weigh the fish in and I didn't need to say, "I got you."

But paybacks are a bitch and Johnny got his when *National Geographic* needed two surf casters in their photo of the sun rising over the top of Montauk Lighthouse.

"Be down on the beach a half hour before daylight," he told me, "and we'll have our picture taken by *National Geographic.*" I was excited at the thought of being in this famous magazine. We did end up in the picture, but as silhouettes in the distance. The distant distance, that is, and unrecognizable as two figures in a landscape.

Me on the *Sandona* in 1951, en route from Montauk, NY, to Miami, Florida.

Fishing Miami Beach with Capt. Red Stuart

In the early days of my career as a charter boatman, my fishing season ran from May to October, with July and August being my busiest months. Once we got halfway through September, I started looking for a winter job, mostly on boats. In the winter of 1951, I found a job opening as a mate aboard the *Sandona* under Captain Red Stuart. In those days, there were damn few good saltwater fishing guides that really knew big-game fishing. Red was one of them. When I found out that he needed a mate, I jumped at the chance because I knew I could pick up a lot of good fishing tips and tricks from him.

Red Stuart took his boat to Florida each winter after fishing Montauk in the summer. It took fourteen days to make this trip on the *Sandona*, which was reduced to being a ten-knot boat or less on most of the shallow, twisting inland waterway; but out in open water, she moved right along.

The deal was that I rode down with Red and worked on his boat, getting it ready to go fishing. My pay would start from the moment we began taking out charters. We left Montauk on October 3, 1951, and during the trip from Montauk to Miami, I had plenty of free time so I cleaned the cabin from one end to the other, scraping layers of grease from the galley which had not been cleaned in a long time.

Twelve days later, on October 18 at 4:30 p.m., we arrived at the Chamber of Commerce Dock in Miami Beach, Florida. From there, we hauled out for repairs and were up in dry dock until October 31. Red put the *Sandona* in a boatyard where we scraped her bottom and painted the hull. This took almost a month to do—with no pay.

Occasionally, Red would throw me a sandwich and a soda. Meanwhile, my wife Janet came to join me in Miami Beach with our first daughter, Bobbie, who was only four at the time. Janet drove our truck down from Montauk. To help support us all, she got herself a job slinging bagels at

Wolfie's Restaurant. I hope that she didn't have as many problems being a waitress as I did being a mate. Red Stuart was a hard-headed person and awful tough to talk to; for instance, when we came in from fishing on our first trip, I asked him, before he disappeared off the dock, where the soap and brushes were to clean up.

"The brushes are in that compartment over there, but we don't use soap," he said with a snarl.

"How come you don't use soap?" I asked. "How can I keep the boat clean?"

Red told me he didn't use soap to clean the boat as "it would pull the paint off" (and cost money!).

Not satisfied with his answer, I was determined to have a clean boat so I went down to the grocery store and bought my own soap, making sure it was the nonabrasive kind. When Red came walking back down the dock, he couldn't believe what he saw: I had the cockpit full of suds! I felt sure he was going to holler at me, but he never said a word. For the rest of that season, Red was happy because I kept buying the soap out of my money and he had a clean boat.

Another thing that made me mad every time we returned from a charter was when Red's wife jumped on the boat to see what she could find to take home to eat: sandwiches, cakes, etc. I was depending on some of these leftovers to feed myself, Janet, and Bobbie; but Red's wife knew that and she always beat me to the food.

One Sunday morning, I showed up at the dock for work but we had no charter, and when it came to the time of the morning when we couldn't pick up an a.m. charter, I left and went to church with my family. I didn't bother changing clothes because the ones I had on were clean, but I did forget to remove my sheath knife which hung off my belt in my back pocket. As I sat down, the knife handle made a loud clunk when it hit the oak pew, and the congregation members close by turned their heads in curiosity. It was noontime or so when I got back to the dock to find out if we were going to pick up an afternoon charter as Red often did morning and afternoon fishing trips.

When I showed up on the dock, Red yelled, "WHERE THE HELL DID YOU GO?"

I explained to him that I had waited around the dock in the morning until I knew we could not pick up a morning charter then I had gone to church. "I figured we had the morning off," I told him.

"You can have 'em all off if you want!" Red snapped.

I figured I'd better not say anything more.

When we did go out on half-day charters, Red always brought along his big black Labrador retriever, "Duke." The dog was always in the way because the cockpit was small and he just added to the confusion: every time we caught a small fish and flopped it into the boat, Duke chased it around the cockpit. Most of the time, Duke would stand on his hind legs, leaning his front legs in the gunnel, looking for land. The dog did this so much that the hair on his front elbows was worn off. And when we came back to the dock, Duke was the first one off the boat and into the bushes.

I made my first day's pay on November 17, forty-five days after leaving Montauk! My pay for an average half-day fishing trip was $5.00; and if we were lucky, we got a $5.00 tip. And if we were *really* lucky, we would make a couple of dollars in fish money.

When I finished working for Red Stuart that winter, despite the hardships and many other nasty things that happened to me, I did pick up a lot of small pieces of fishing information from him that helped me along in my career.

On days when the *Sandona* didn't sail, I sometimes found time for nonsense at the dock. Close to noontime one day in January 1952, some guy walked down the dock carrying a tank and some kind of mouthpiece. He told me this was what they called "an aqua lung." I think this happened during the first year that the aqua lung came on the market.

I asked the guy if I could try out this new equipment.

"Sure, go ahead," he said and showed me how to strap the tank to my back and breathe through the mouthpiece. As far as scuba diving was concerned, this five-minute introduction was all that I had before hitting the water.

Right there at the dock where I went overboard, it was only about ten-feet deep. It didn't take me very long to venture out toward the big concrete columns that held up the causeway. The closer I got to the columns, the deeper the water became, and the more my head felt like it was in a vise from the water pressure. The aqua-lung guy had not told me how to clear the pressure in my ears. But I was having so much fun watching the fish that I tried to forget the pain.

Up on the causeway there were all these so-called bridge fishermen trying to catch any kind of small fish. I swam out, staying close to the bottom, and hid behind one of the big columns, watching the sinkers and baited hooks come down and land on the bottom. Immediately, a dozen or two small fish attacked the bait and the fishermen on the bridge tried to hook them by jerking up on their rod tips fast.

After fifteen minutes of watching the fish attacking the baits, things got dull so I figured I would liven things up. I waited for a freshly-baited hook to hit the bottom then I swam out from under the bridge, grabbed hold of his line above the hooks and sinker, making sure to take a twist on it just in case he lifted up his rod fast and hooked me. Now I headed out to sea as fast as my little flippers could push me, just like any big fish would act.

After a short time, I noticed that the fisherman was putting pressure on his "fish." And this pressure started raising me off the bottom so I took out my knife, cut the line, and swam back beneath the bridge, clutching a short piece of line, two baited hooks, and a sinker. Then another bright idea hit me. I saw two large groupers, about five pounds each, just resting there. I swam over to them with the hooks and sinker in my outstretched hand. I pushed the bait so close to their heads that it almost hit them, but got no response at all because those groupers were not feeding.

After this, I cut the two hooks off, put the sinker in my pocket, swam beneath the Chamber of Commerce Dock, and climbed back aboard the *Sandona*. Then I took off the aqua lung and walked up the causeway bridge. Everybody on the bridge was hollering about the big fish one of them had on.

As I got closer, one of them said, "That was a diver you had hooked, not a big fish."

"I know a big fish when I have one on, and that was a big fish!" the other guy replied.

When I approached this dock fisherman, I pulled his sinker out of my pocket, and asked, innocently, "Is this your sinker?"

"Yes!" he replied in a surprised voice as I handed him back the sinker. I told him that I had been down there looking for lobster and had gotten tangled up in his line. "I couldn't save the hooks, but I've brought you back your sinker," I said.

"You's [sic] is a good boy," he said, tapping me on the shoulder. I had to turn away as I couldn't keep a straight face after playing that trick on him.

Burials at Sea

When I was fishing the *Cricket II*, we performed five burials at sea that I can recall, starting in the early 1950s with old Eric Seden, a Swedish mate of mine. Eric was in his late fifties when he mated for me between 1953 and 1954, and he had been in pretty good shape except for his asthma which bothered him more ashore than it did at sea. Eric was the oldest mate who ever worked for me, and the most eccentric. He still had his strong Scandinavian accent from the old country and didn't care who was on the boat when he shared salty comments such as "Yesus [*sic*] christ, Cappy, my balls are itching. That means we catch a mako today." And if anyone called him "mister," he would reply in a loud scratchy singsong voice, "No misters at sea and no priests in hell!"

I fired Eric more times than I have fingers on each hand, and he quit just as often: "Yesus [*sic*] christ, Cappy, I quit!" he'd exclaim, throwing his arms in the air in exasperation. Sometimes it was for the most trivial reason such as when I told him he was chumming too heavy. "I was shumming [*sic*] all this time and now I'm doing it wrong. I quit!" One time, we were fishing for a record mako on twenty-pound test, when the angler's line started to touch the side of the boat, Eric reached out with his gloved hand and pushed the line away. This disqualified our fish under International Game Fish Association (IGFA) rules. I hollered down from the bridge, "That fish is disqualified!" In a loud disgusted voice, Eric yelled back, "Yesus christ, I'm disqualified too. I quit!"

He was also very superstitious and would warn me, "Don't throw any old clothes overboard," (the next boat that comes along will see the clothes in the water and think somebody has drowned); "Don't whistle because you'll whistle up a storm," and "Don't turn a hatch cover upside down on deck," (you only find a hatch upside down when a boat is sinking.) One time, we were on our way out to sea, heading around Shagwong Reef, when Eric came up with his funniest comment: "Yesus christ, Cappy, the cows are on the beach," he said ominously.

"What are you talking about?" I asked him.

He replied, "The cows are on the beach which means the wind will swing around and come out of the east."

I looked at Eric like he had some kind of a hangover. "What do the cows on the beach have to do with the wind in the east?" I asked. "The wind right now is out of the southwest," I told him.

"You watch, Cappy, the wind *will* swing around." And sure enough, before the day was finished, the wind *did* swing around and blow out of the east. I thought that this was a freak incident, but after that an easterly wind blew every time that cows from the local dude ranch wandered down onto the beach. I still haven't figured out how the cows knew ahead of time that the wind would change direction and come out of the east.

Anyway, time passed, Eric stayed ashore the following year, and died from asthma complications. In his will, he requested that the *Cricket II* scatter his ashes at sea. I wanted to do a good job and waited until the fall of the year when all the boats would be fishing for striped bass and bluefish around Montauk lighthouse. I picked a date and told the fleet that I was going to have a burial ceremony for Eric at dusk. As we drifted along, the other boats circled the *Cricket II* like Indians around a wagon train as I performed the ceremony. First, I pulled the pin on the copper can that held Eric's ashes and spread them overboard. Then we threw the wreath of flowers and the minister said a few words. By this time, it was starting to get dark and so I tossed a sulphur flare overboard. The first flare did not ignite. After a few minutes, I threw the second flare and it stayed lit. The ceremony was over. I started the motor and we headed home. A few of Eric's friends were aboard for the burial and one of them, Uncle Bud, was up on the flying bridge with me. As he watched the wreath and flare drifting away on the waves behind us, he told me that the first flare was lit now. "If I die, I want to go *exactly* like that," he said.

Ten years later, in the fall of 1965, Uncle Bud passed away and I had to bury him at sea. I did the best I could in exactly the same way that we had done it for Eric. It turned out that the weather conditions were identical, the time of year was the same, and the same boats were there. To top it all, the first flare failed to ignite and the second one lit. Then, on our way home, the first flare ignited. Now the two sulphur flares bobbed up and down along with the wreath, *exactly* the way it was for Eric. Suddenly, someone up on the flying bridge said, "Look! The second flare lit! Just like it did when we buried Eric."

"I don't believe it!" I said, turning to look. Uncle Bud had gotten exactly what he wanted.

It was a very spooky feeling for everybody aboard. A few years later, we buried two more local boatmen. We even hosted a casual burial at sea one time. I was tuna fishing and one of my customers hollered up to me, "How far off are we?"

"About twenty miles," I answered.

"OK, stop the boat," he said, reaching down into his bag of goodies, and pulled out a copper container. He popped the top on it and threw the contents overboard, all in one motion. "OK, he's buried. Let's go," he said bluntly. That was the fastest burial at sea that we ever did.

Some twenty-five years later, I was cutting and splitting logs on my property when a car pulled over and a lady asked if I wanted to cut down a couple of her trees just for the wood. The lady said she lived around the corner and we quickly made an agreement. On the day I got around to cutting her trees down, she came out of her house and asked me, "Did Eric Seden ever work for you as a mate?"

"Yes, he did, but that was quite a while ago," I replied. The woman explained she was a friend of Eric's. And although she didn't exactly say it, I guess she was trying to tell me that she was his girlfriend. One time, Eric had shown her some large glass jars full of half-dollar and silver-dollar coins that he had saved over the years, and told her, "If anything happens to me, dig up the garden."

"Did you dig up the garden?" I asked her.

"No, did you?" (In Eric's will, I had first choice on buying his house for the reduced price of $10,000, which would cover all of his outstanding bills, but Janet had thought the house was too small and told me to turn it down.)

"No, I thought you did!" I told her. To this today, no one knows if Eric's treasure was ever buried in his garden.

How Not to Fly a DC3

In the charter-boat business, you fish everybody from all over and never know where you're going to be invited to next. Most of the invites come during the fishing season, but the one I got from Ralph Ryder[2] came at a good time: in my off season. Ralph had fished with me a couple of times during the summer of 1955. His first trip, on the night of August 3, was a full-moon trip for sharks. Then he wanted to know if we were open on the fourth, which we were, so we fished the day of the fourth too and Ralph caught himself a record mako: 160 pounds on 20-pound test line.

This is when Ralph asked me if I wanted to do another trip on the night of August 4—all this with in-and-out, back-to-back trips and no sleep since August 2. After we came in from Ralph's night trip on August 4, we had to turn around and go back out on August 5 with a different party. This was a long stretch without sleep: three days and two nights straight.

The next time Ralph fished, on August 16, he invited me to go along on a plane ride to Mexico in his private DC-3. He told me that his gear works company was holding a convention in Hollywood so he figured he would travel a little farther and do some fishing in La Paz, Mexico. Ralph told me I was not going to be on the payroll. I would be a guest and should bring some spending money because one of their overnight stops would be in Las Vegas.

On September 20, I left Montauk on the first train and met up with Ralph Ryder's private plane at White Plains, New York. There were eleven people in all making this trip. Once aboard, I noticed that Ralph's private DC-3 had been fully refurbished. They had taken out half of the seats on the port side and replaced them with a snack bar where you could help yourself to a drink or a sandwich at any time. The cockpit area had no doors. It was completely open and everybody could walk up and talk to the pilot and copilot at any time.

Shortly after takeoff, Ralph was standing behind the copilot's seat and he beckoned me to join him in the cockpit. When I got there, he told the copilot to get up and asked me to take his seat. Ralph began showing me the plane's instrument panel. He went through the mass of gauges one by one, but the main one that caught my eye was, in my language, the fathometer (altimeter). I also looked for something that would tell me if she had a port or starboard list, and I found the artificial horizon (attitude indicator) which shows the pilot when he is flying on an even keel. Ralph told me we were doing 180 miles an hour and added, "Grab a hold of the wheel and push it forward, fast, then bring it back fast."

"No," I said as I sat there with my arms folded because I knew what would happen: it would be like jumping over a big wave. But before I could do anything, Ralph had reached over my shoulder, took hold of the wheel, and said, "Here, I'll show you!"

When he pushed that wheel forward and pulled it back, that DC-3 dipped up and down fast. I looked back and saw a mess in the back of the plane: everybody had been walking back and forth with cocktail glasses in their hands, playing cards. Now everything hit the ceiling! About this time, Ralph turned around and roared with laughter, a deep belly laugh, "HA, HA, HA!"

After this little escapade, Ralph disappeared and the pilot had gotten up and walked aft, leaving me all alone in the cockpit. I was looking out of the window, down at the ground, when for some reason I turned to look at the instrument panel. I didn't believe what I saw: the altimeter had dropped from eight thousand feet to seven thousand five hundred and was still descending. Meanwhile, the artificial horizon showed that we were making a right-handed bank.

The only thing I could see to do was take hold of the wheel and pull it back slowly. Somehow, I managed to take the DC-3 back up to eight thousand feet and put her on an even keel. Now the pilot and Ralph showed up again, and the pilot returned to his seat, laughing.

"Hey, you forgot to put this thing on automatic pilot," I told the pilot.

"This DC-3 is not equipped with an automatic pilot," he smiled. They had been testing me to see how I was going to react.

It was then that Ralph told me about the last guy he had played this little trick on. "He just sat there and screamed as the plane started into a downward spin! So you did a good job," he said.

For some reason, Ralph was still laughing. He and the pilot had some kind of private joke going that they wouldn't let me in on. Finally, I asked Ralph, "What the hell is so funny?"

"You've gotten us back up to eight thousand feet and flying straight, BUT, you're going in the WRONG direction!"

I didn't care what direction we were going in as long as we were back up to eight thousand feet and on an even keel! At that point, I figured this was going to be a fun trip now that I had passed the first test in Ralph's initiation rite.

Shortly after, we approached what looked like a small dark-green lake the size of a mud puddle. In the middle of this lake sat a guy in a small outboard, wearing a white ten-cent captain's hat. Ralph tapped the pilot on the shoulder and pointed down at this guy. The pilot looked around and nodded his head. "Yes." Then he shot that DC-3 straight down, aiming at the guy in the outboard!

Sitting in the copilot's seat, I had a bird's-eye view of this poor guy going in circles as he saw our plane coming at him. I felt like I was caught up in a *Road Runner* cartoon! The plane made a high-pitched whine as it dropped sharply, but at the very last second, the pilot pulled back on the stick and the plane swooped upward. I was looking back at the guy in the outboard who was still going in frantic circles as we headed up. I thought he was going to jump overboard. A few seconds went by and I turned my head to look forward.

Now I saw trees dead ahead!

I was sure we would tear the tops out of some of those trees as we went over that mountain. When we cleared them, I looked down and saw I had instinctively pulled both my feet up off the deck—just in case!

The rest of the flight to La Paz was fairly uneventful, that is, it was normal! Our first stop was Indianapolis; we refueled and stopped there for the night. Next day, we flew to Pueblo, Colorado, refueled again, and went on to Las Vegas. Being the last of the big spenders (Jack Benny style!), I spent $5 whole dollars in the slot machines and my aching arm was glad to see the last coin disappear. Next day, we flew to California. That night we stayed in Hollywood and I walked up and down the street where the movie stars get stuck in the wet cement!

That same night, Ralph and the boys went to their convention in Hollywood, which was the main purpose for their trip, while I rested up at a motel. The next morning, we took off again for the final leg of our flight to La Paz, Mexico. On our way there, I overheard the pilot ask Ralph, "How about customs? Should we drop into Texas?"

"To hell with customs, we'll get them on the way back," Ralph said.

Almost in the same breath, the pilot asked Ralph, "How are we going to drop into La Paz Airport? Are we going to come in off the water and hope that we stop before we hit the mountain, or are we going to drop straight in and hope we stop before we go into the water?"

I thought they were saying this just because I was listening and it was supposed to make me nervous, but when I looked down at that tiny airport that had been hacked out of the side of a mountain, I knew they weren't kidding! The pilot took that DC-3 and went around and around and around in a circle, getting as close to the mountain as he could before dropping in. At one point, I felt sure he was going to nick the side of the mountain with his wing tip. When he got ready, the pilot suddenly dropped that DC-3 down, vertically, onto the small runway and landed. Now we had to stop before going into the water. When the plane finally came to a full stop, we did not have much room left!

In the two days at La Paz, we got a good taste of Mexican booze and fishing. We caught two sailfish, one each day, and then we were on our way back home. As soon as we took off, the hedgehopping began. It was then that I found out that the pilot worked in the Aleutians for the government and spent much of his time flying by the seat of his pants. And his copilot was an ex-crop duster! Besides that, Ralph, the owner, liked plenty of excitement! All this led to our hedgehopping on the way home to New York.

Nobody told me they were going to hedgehop, and shortly after we took off, I looked out of the port window and saw a mountain. Then I looked out of the starboard window and saw another mountain. That meant we were flying very low between the mountains!

We hedgehopped across the southwest part of Mexico on our way to Texas. There was one mountain we flew alongside of where we saw people living in caves carved into its side. And another mountain that looked like the Jolly Green Giant had taken his machete and cut away the top, making it flat. Somebody was living and farming on this remote ledge because there was one little house in the corner that had a hand plow alongside a shed and I could see rows of cultivated vegetation.

Later, we flew over a long stretch of dried-out mud plains. The DC-3 was flying so close to the ground I could see the indentation of footprints very clearly, and I asked the pilot, "How low are we, or how high are we off the ground?"

"When you feel that little up-and-down jiggle, you are between fifteen to twenty feet off the ground," he said, smiling.

The only sign of life that we saw out in the mud plains was a horse corralled behind one small house.

I was still sitting in the copilot's seat and could see straight ahead. Even though we were doing 180 miles an hour, it took us a while to get to that house. As we approached it, one man came out of the house, ran around the house, and ran back into the house. He did this three times before we whizzed over the top of him. And his horse was rearing up in panic. If that homesteader had a TV antenna, the DC-3 would have taken it off.

We eventually landed in El Paso, Texas, refueled, and cleared customs. Our second stop was Indianapolis, and then we headed to New York, arriving there at 3:00 a.m. Ralph said that he could drop me off at Montauk by parachute if I wanted. He was serious about this! But I didn't like to make my first jump at night and land on somebody's rooftop, tangled up in their TV antenna at 3:00 a.m.!

I also declined Ralph's kind offer because I didn't want to parachute into the middle of the Montauk Point Air Force firing range, especially in the dark; I might be mistaken for a Russian spy, seeing that this was during the cold war! So I took the first train back to Montauk and got home at 11:30 a.m. This train ride seemed awfully tame after that hair-raising ten-day plane ride to Mexico and back.

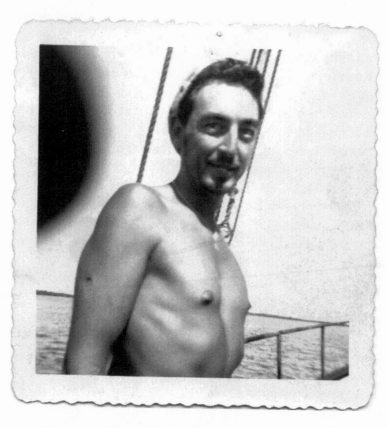

Me as a deck hand on the shrimp boats in 1953.

The Shrimp Boats Are A-comin'

Each winter I got myself a different job to take me through my off season of sport fishing. My jobs on the Florida shrimp boats, like with some of the other boats, came about by accident. I first inflicted this cruelty to my body in the winter of 1953-54 after heading to Florida to visit my mother.

My mother, like my father, had worked her fingers to the bone for us three kids. If my parents had gotten any enjoyment or fun out of this, I could never figure out where or when it was. My parents had never had a vacation of any kind, but were all ready to go to Florida the winter that Dad died. They had even gone out and bought new clothes for their first-ever vacation.

So after my father's death, my mother went out and did things she never would have done while he was alive: Mom started smoking and went on a black coffee diet to regain what she called her "girlish figure." She even sold the Canary Cottage in Point Pleasant and moved to Florida. It was there that she met a guy named Fred.

Because Fred had been a sailor like my father, Mom was taken over by his bullshit and they got married. Then he talked her into buying a bar and grill outside Fort Myers, on the Tamiami Trail.

This bar had been named The Bucket of Blood by the previous owners, in memory of the guy they bought it from who had met his demise there when an irate customer blew a hole in him with a .12-gauge shotgun, splattering his insides all over the back bar! For obvious reasons, Mom did not like the bar's name and changed it to the Alligator Bar.

This bar business was exciting stuff for Mom, and the Alligator Bar became her pride and joy. She had never drunk or visited bars before this and didn't know anything about this business, but Mom thought she could convert all those drinking people into Holy Rollers. It looked to me like Mom's lack of bar business savvy would lead to her self-destruction so I went down there with good intentions to help Mom out because I was drinking at the time and knew how the booze business worked: I was very familiar with booze, bar stools, and shot glasses.

So in the winter of 1953, I decided to spend that off season down South with Mom. Like a troupe of gypsies, Janet, Bobbie, and I were on the road again, driving south in a Ford pickup truck, heading for the unknown. But this time, a friend of ours, Sam Stanley, rode along with us. Sam wanted to stop in on his hillbilly brother who lived near the outskirts of Richmond, Virginia.

To shelter whoever wasn't driving, I temporarily converted our half-ton pickup truck into a camper by making plywood sides and a roof. We also threw a single mattress in the back. It fitted nicely and would make the four-day ride more bearable.

Halfway through our trip, we stopped in to see Sam's brother. Leaving civilization, we drove up into the back hills of Virginia and found Sam's brother in true hillbilly style, sitting on the porch in his rocking chair, smoking a corn cob pipe, with his faithful dog alongside him.

Sam hadn't seen his brother in over thirty years and I was interested in watching their reunion. It was as follows: we drove up, Sam got out of the truck, and his brother asked, "Is that you, Sam?"

Sam said, "Yup."

"How've ya bin?" asked Sam.

"Fine," his brother nodded.

"Is that a squirrel dog?" Sam asked.

"Yup."

Sam asked, "You want to take Frank squirrel hunting tomorrow?"

"Yup."

"I'll bring him around early," Sam said.

So that was a hillbilly reunion? I asked myself.

Next morning, after leaving Janet and Bobbie to rest at our motel, I drove up to Sam's brother's place for the squirrel hunt. The picture had not changed—he was still sitting in the rocking chair as I pulled up and parked my truck.

When I took out my .410 shotgun, he uttered one of his longest singsonglike sentences, "You fixin' to shoot squirrel with that four-hundred-and-ten?"

It was my turn now, and I said, "Yup!"

He grabbed his double-barreled .12-gauge shotgun and off we went into the pine forest where the trees never stopped going up! Soon after we got there, his dog started running and barking around one of the tall pine trees. Sam's brother walked around one side of the tree, looked up, and I walked around the other side of the tree. I could just about see the squirrel; he must have been up there a hundred feet or so.

"See 'im?" he asked.

"Yup," I said, falling into hillbilly character.

"Give 'im a barrel," he drawled.

It was a long shot for my little .410 which didn't have as many pellets in a square foot spread like a .12 gauge does at that distance. I aimed and pulled the trigger, and also did a lot of hoping and wishing.

I was lucky: one of the pellets hit the squirrel and it seemed like it took him five minutes to fall from the tree top and flop onto the ground. The squirrel hit the dry leaves and the dog had him on the first bounce. Sam's brother turned to me in amazement, and said, "That's the shootinest four-hundred-and-ten that ah ever did see!"

He didn't know how lucky my shot had been; one pellet had made an instant friend!

Meanwhile, at the Alligator Bar, good ol' Fred had been telling Mom everything he didn't know about the bar business. So by the time we arrived a few days later, her mind was set. I tried explaining to Mom from my experience about the real world of the bar business. For instance, on the advice of Fred, her shot-glass measures of whisky were only half ounce instead of at least three-quarters to one ounce. I tried to tell Mom that anybody who drank whisky straight would know the difference. I even made Mom a bet that I could show her the difference, and we went to other bars where I drank whisky straight and told Mom whether they were three-quarter ounce or one-ounce glasses. Even after I proved this to her, she said it didn't make any difference because Fred had said she had to get so many ounces out of each bottle.

On January 8, 1956, a scroungy-looking regular, fresh out of the swamps, who only drank one twenty-five-cent bottle of Regal beer per day, started a fight while I was tending the bar. At first, I thought the two of them were dancing together because they were hanging onto each other, and nearby three or four other couples were shuffling their feet around on the dance floor, having a good time while the jukebox played soft music in the background.

The next minute, the two guys fell down, still hanging onto each other. That's when I realized they were fighting. When I saw what was going on, I emerged from behind the counter, armed with a short billy club, only to run into my mother who rushed forward and hung on to it, yelling, "NO, NO, NO!"

The fight stopped by itself while Mom and I were busy arguing over the billy club. I asked Mom to flag this person. She refused and we heard he got knifed a week later in another bar during another fight.

Another time while I was there, Mom refused to cash a worker's weekly pay check.

"Why didn't you cash his check?" I asked in disbelief.

"He would have spent it all on drinks," she said. "I told him to take the money home to his wife."

"The guy is going to drive down the road and spend it at the next bar, anyhow, Mom," I said in frustration. But Mom refused to listen and kept telling me how sorry she felt for the man's wife. As you can see, I couldn't tell Mom anything about the bar business, but I kept trying.

"Mom, you're in the wrong business," I told her, "and there's nothing I can do to help you." After a couple more weeks of knocking my head against a stone wall, I got very disgusted and headed for the fishing docks.

One day, as I was wandering around the docks, I came across Burwell King, the skipper of a shrimp boat out of Fort Myers. I knew Burwell from Montauk where he ran a commercial boat. He was a clean-shaven, soft-spoken pipe-smoking New Englander in his fifties; a calm man who never got excited about anything. Burwell told me he was a crew member short on his shrimp boat and invited me to sign on for the winter.

He also asked if I could cook a little. I said, "*Very* little!" So Burwell made me cook and told me to sit down and make a grocery list for three men for a thirty-day trip! I told Burwell I couldn't cook that well, but he insisted and made out that first grocery list himself. The only item that stuck in my memory was "three ash cans of bread: one white, one rye, and one whole wheat." The ship chandlers knew the order well because they kept throwing the bread into the cans until they were full. I can still see that half-ton pickup truck stuffed to the gills, backing down the dock to unload the thirty-day grocery order on our boat, the *Burwell King*. Burwell said he had always wanted his name on something so it might as well be on the bow of a boat.

We had already taken on our twenty tons of shaved ice, five thousand gallons of fuel, and fifteen hundred gallons of fresh water.

All the groceries were put down the main fish hold, just aft of the wheelhouse and galley for easy access. We had to dig a hole in the flake ice deep enough to bury the food. Burwell's new sixty-five-foot steel boat was in the process of making its maiden voyage, and I was making my maiden voyage as cook.

I'll never forget the day I came home from the fish docks and told Mom that I had gotten a job on a shrimp boat. She asked me what my job was. When I told her I was cook, she developed a large lump on her head from hitting the ceiling. She said, "You, a cook? You can't even boil water right without burning it!"

So I said, "OK, teach me." She politely told me that I could not teach her to fish in a short time either. So Mom handed me this stupid-looking pot that had a locking cover and a jiggle thing on top. Mom said it was a pressure cooker and handed me the instruction book (as I'm writing this, I still have that book in my kitchen drawer). In those days there wasn't much love for pressure cookers because some people had them blow up in their face. It can't happen now because of the safety features that have been added.

This was probably the last time I saw Mom in good health. Years later, in September 1963, she came up to visit me and my family in Montauk and had a stroke in my house during the night. Mom was in a coma at Southampton Hospital for more than thirty days. When she came out of it, Mom was paralyzed on one side of her body, but she insisted on returning to Florida even though Fred had died a year or so earlier. A year later, my mother passed away at age seventy.

But thanks to Mom and her pressure cooker, I got that job aboard the shrimp boat. Captain Burwell decided to make three short ten- to fifteen-day shakedown trips around Key West before heading out for a series of month-long voyages that would last on and off all winter. Our first short trip around Key West went pretty well because Burwell had a lot of patience with my cooking and with the other deck hand who I nicknamed "The Farmer." It's a good thing Burwell knew what he has doing because he was the only one on board who did!

After that first fifteen-day trip of having the galley and stove all to myself because Burwell and The Farmer were afraid of my pressure cooker, I was starting to put out edible meals. We made two or three of these short trips and all went well. Fish wise, the second one was better than the first, and so was my cooking. Our third trip was a real short one because we only got halfway there. We were about twelve to fifteen hours running time from home. The Farmer and I were in our bunks sleeping, and Burwell was on watch, reading a book and smoking his pipe, while the boat chugged along at a steady ten knots.

As he read, Burwell would glance ahead, making sure that there were no boats or debris in our path, and then he would check his instrument panel before getting back to his book as the boat was on automatic pilot.

It was a perfect day; the water was flat calm and the sun was bright. Because Burwell was a good boatman, he was conscious of his surroundings and felt there was something wrong but couldn't put his finger on it. He took a walk on deck, going up one side and down the other, stopping to check things as he went. Burwell thought he heard a thumping noise in the number 2 hold, so he undid the canvas hatch cover and lifted the hatch. That compartment was flooded to the top with water. The faint thumping sound he had heard was that of the pen boards banging back and forth. Pen boards are like pickets in a fence, they separate the four pens (used for storing the ice and shrimp) that are down in each hold.

Number 2 hold was where our groceries were stored. It was a good thing that we had watertight bulkheads on both sides of the fish holds; otherwise, we would have sunk. Captain Burwell knew at a glance there was nothing to worry about because of these watertight bulkheads, so he turned the boat around and set it back on automatic pilot. We were heading home.

Then Burwell came down to wake me up. He said, "Frank, get up. We've got number 2 hold full of water. Wake up The Farmer."

The Farmer and I both got up on deck at the same time. At a quick glance, I knew that with one hold full to the top and the next one empty, we had nothing to worry about. However, when The Farmer looked down and saw King Neptune licking at his feet, all the blood rushed out of his face. He slowly looked around, scanning the horizon for boats or land. There was nothing to see but water. Burwell and I told him not to worry, and we explained why.

After we got back to the dock and put a couple more pumps on, we found out why the *Burwell King* had taken on water. Instead of using a solid bronze propeller shaft, the shipbuilders had used an inexpensive three-and-a-half-inch steel propeller shaft, and then added a two-foot-long half-inch-thick bronze sleeve (or collar) on the shaft, where the shaft went through the stuffing box (a device that creates a watertight area), *but they had not pinned the sleeve to the shaft correctly.* As a result, it slid up inside the boat and let a half inch of water come in all around the shaft. The water filled up the hold immediately. As a result, we spent two weeks in the shipyard, undergoing repairs mainly to replace all the insulation that had been washed away. To add further insult to injury, all the groceries that we had paid for were gone.

Two weeks later, we started our first thirty-day trip to the Bay of Campeche, Mexico. It took three days and three nights to get there from Fort Myers. I could smell land eight to ten hours before we got there; the scent of flowers was so strong I could almost reach out and touch them. When you are out at sea smelling nothing but clean salt air, your nose picks up a new aroma fast. Even when I was up on the flying bridge of the *Cricket II*, fishing out of Montauk, with my nose into the wind, if somebody in the cockpit opened a jar of pickles, or broke open a bottle of booze, the odor always rose up and hit me in the face.

By 1:30 p.m., we sighted land on the horizon and would soon have our nets dragging the bottom for shrimp. As we reached the fishing grounds, it looked like a city of boats, all packed in one five-mile area. There was no sense in our dropping our anchor, so we drifted and prepared our nets for the first tow.

Shrimping is done at night, so the first time we "set in" (put the nets into the water for the tow), it was just about an hour and a half before dark. In that time, you eat and get ready because after you haul back the nets for the first time, there is no time between tows. And now it's time to haul back. The winch lifts our bag up and over the cockpit. The bag—containing up to three thousand pounds or so of fish, shrimp, crabs, sponges, and debris—lands on deck. One of us had to reach under the bag and grab the puckering string that held everything in there. After one good healthy pull, the slip knot would open up the bottom of the bag and the contents spilled out on the deck. Then the net would be made ready again and put over the side to repeat the process.

Now it was a race against time. All the debris on deck had to be taken care of before the net returned from its next haul. We were taught to get rid of all the big things on deck first; for instance, those worthless loggerhead sponges (that each weighed a couple of hundred pounds and had to be split in pieces with our shovels), rocks, automobile tires, and logs, etc.

Next, we sorted through the pile of fish of all kinds, blue-claw crabs (by the thousands), and some shrimp (we hoped). I sat on one side of the pile while The Farmer sat on the other side. Each of us was perched on a six-inch high stool with our feet spread wide apart. In one hand, we each held a flat board (a culling board) that we used to pull our way through the fish and shrimp.

When a shrimp came into view, we dropped our culling board, grabbed the shrimp by the head, dropped it between the fingers of the other hand, and with a twisting motion, tore its head off. When that hand was full of headless shrimp, we dropped them into a wire basket beside us. The "debris" (crabs and good eating fish of all kinds), went to waste because the fish wasn't worth the value of the shrimp and couldn't last as long on ice.

After the first couple of hours on deck heading shrimp, your canvas gloves ooze red with blood—your blood—because the acid from the shrimp eats away at the tender skin between your fingers. Day after day our hands ran red and you knew they wouldn't get any better, only worse.

Almost every night, the wind blew hard while we worked on deck with only a pair of boots, shorts, hat, and gloves. The temperature during the day was as hot as hell. If you were working with a wrench and laid it down on deck for a couple of minutes, the sun made it so hot you could hardly pick the wrench up.

Sleep was for the rich person or for somebody who did not work on a shrimp boat! We averaged three to four hours sleep per day. Every ten days, we had to transfer our shrimp to the next boat that was heading home as the shrimp would not last for the thirty days that we were out there. The transfer had to be made during the daylight hours when we were supposed to be sleeping. On the days when this happened, we wouldn't get any sleep at all.

One day, when the three of us were sleeping, we woke to find two Mexican kids perched on the foot of our bunks, laughing, and saying, "Mucho siesta, mucho siesta!"

We tried telling them that this was no siesta and we were exhausted after working all night, but we could not convince them. Captain Burwell asked the kids what they wanted. They replied, "Bacardi, Tequila: American dollar a bottle."

The boys didn't know any other English besides this, so in sign language, we asked them how they went about bringing the booze to us because during the day we were anchored about five miles off the beach. The kids sat and laughed at us and we laughed at them because neither of us could understand what was going on. Finally, the kids gestured in a synchronous mime that they bought booze by the case, put it in a boat, paddled out to us, gave us the booze, got the money, paddled home, and pulled the boat up on the beach. Then the *"po-li-see-yas"* (police) would approach them for their pay off (the boys mimicked this by rubbing their chests with their wrists, like they were shining a police badge). Even after the police had gotten their take, these ten- to twelve-year-old boys still made a pretty good buck off the American shrimpers. We each bought a bottle of Bacardi from the boys. To them, three bucks was a big sale. Once our transactions had taken place, the two kids jumped into their sixteen-foot-long short-masted wooden dinghy and began their five-mile paddle home in the hot sun.

Another night, we were anchored close to the beach because the wind was blowing too hard, making it impossible to fish. I was busy killing time, trying to catch some small fish that had been drawn under our boat by the deck lights. My concentration was suddenly broken by an old man's singsong voice drifting though the night:

"F——kee, f——kee, five American [dollars]."

As he approached our boat and came into the deck lights, I could see an old man in a dinghy, standing with a paddle in his hand, next to what looked like his wife or daughter.

In a loud voice, he repeated, "F——kee, f——kee, five American dollars."

At this point, I spoke to him in the little Spanish I knew, "Uno momento," (one moment) then I went to get Burwell. "Burwell, come out on deck, you have to see this," I said. Burwell knew a lot more Spanish than I did so he could find out what was going on and perhaps have some fun.

Burwell hollered over to them, "Cuanto dinero?(how much?)"

The salesman in the boat hollered back, "Five American."

Burwell answered, "Mucho dinero (too much money)."

The salesman replied, "Four American."

Burwell repeated, "Mucho dinero."

Now the salesman said, "Three American."

Again, Burwell bargained him down with, "Mucho dinero."

The old man's last and final offer was said in English, "One American dollar."

Burwell slowly took the pipe out of his mouth and said, "Mucho dinero."

This was too much for the salesman, who replied,

"F——ckee youee!" as he paddled off into the darkness in search of another customer on one of the other anchored boats.

During this trip, I had another outbreak of osteomyelitis in my left arm. The forearm swelled to the size of a football and I had to keep it in a sling. Burwell radioed home to Janet and she put a supply of antibiotics on the next shrimp boat headed out our way. It wasn't that big of an emergency to warrant being sent by air drop. I could still work one-handed until the medicine arrived a week later, although it was a challenge heading shrimp and chopping ice down in the hold. Nobody could say that I didn't do my share of the work. My osteo cleared up a week after I had finished the medicine.

I was shrimping in the Bay of Campeche when the Mexicans began confiscating American shrimp boats. They purposely changed their international border lines from time to time and would not publicize this. Therefore, none of the shrimp boats knew how close to shore they could fish before coming under Mexican jurisdiction. As a result, a Mexican gunboat would confiscate any shrimp boat that, according to them, was in violation, taking it into the harbor. The valuable cargo of shrimp would be sold and the crew put in jail. I spoke to some boys who spent time in these jails. They said the air conditioning never worked and the cockroaches were the size of alligators!

When the jail was full, they tied the boats together in bunches, keeping the captains and crew aboard. A boat would be anchored in the bay and the rest tied alongside it. One policeman, armed with a rifle, was stationed on each boat. This situation went on unnoticed by Uncle Sam for most of the winter of 1953. The captured men on the boats grew restless, having nothing to do but drink.

We got in close one day to take a sneak peek and see what was going on, and to discover how many boats they had tied up. Burwell told us we could not get in too close or we would get picked up ourselves. From a distance, we could see clusters of boats.

The events unfolding in the middle of one cluster in particular looked like a scene from a pirate movie. Many of the men looked drunk and disorderly. Some were chasing others around deck.

Later that day, we heard over the radio that one of the men, Dick Stern, from Montauk, was knifed across the chest by a drunken crewman from another boat. The man had chased Dick from boat to boat, clutching a butcher knife. When they reached the last boat, Dick had no place to go but around and around on deck.

Aiming his rifle, a Mexican policeman fired a shot. The man who had the knife fell to the floor, with a bullet in his back.

He died immediately. This event opened Uncle Sam's eyes about what was going on; the Mexicans were told to give us back our boats and set our men free.

The closest I came to being picked up was when we were on our way home aboard the *Burwell King*, carrying a rough total of four thousand pounds of shrimp; some of this cargo was ours, and the rest belonged to other boats who had asked us to deliver it to Fort Myers where the buyers were waiting. Unknown to us, the Mexicans changed the rules again. This time they said that the boats could not fish any closer to shore than ten fathoms. There was one shallow area that big ships had to go around, but us small boats could cut right across it to save time on the way home.

We were taking this shortcut home when I was out on deck, working. As I looked aft, I saw a Mexican gunboat bearing down on us fast.

The handwriting was on the wall: we had a ten-knot boat and they had a thirty-knot boat.

I went to the wheelhouse, poked my head through the open door, and said to Burwell, "I had better put out another plate at the supper table tonight."

Burwell looked up from his book and asked, "Why?"

"Because we're getting company," I told him, pointing toward the transom. I continued pointing toward the transom until Burwell's curiosity got the better of him. He climbed off his stool and poked his head out of the wheelhouse door. Burwell's jaw dropped, and he almost bit the stem off his pipe when he saw the Mexican gunboat gaining on us, with smoke pouring out of its stacks.

There was nothing either one of us could do except stand there and watch in amazement as the gunboat drew closer. When the boat got ready to overtake us, I imagined spending the next six months in a Mexican jail counting cockroaches while our hard-earned cargo was confiscated, but to our surprise, the gunboat captain cracked back on his throttle, the black smoke stopped coming out of his stack, and he made a fast U-turn. The captain must have gotten a radio call of some importance to let us go like that. This was one trip I was glad to see coming to an end. Not only had we narrowly escaped being incarcerated by the Mexican government, but I had lost twenty pounds on this trip—and I was the cook!

I heard of another incident where an American shrimper on his way home was overtaken by a Mexican gunboat. The gunboat, lined with riflemen against the rail, came right up alongside the shrimper and hollered over to them, "Stop!" The shrimp boat's American crew was all drunk, so drunk, that one of the guys on wheel watch stuck his head out the window, and using the necessary hand gestures and phrases, told the Mexicans exactly what they could do with their gunboat. The Mexican gunboat crew could have blown these guys right out of the water but were so surprised that they let them go!

Me with blue shark triplets displaying their teeth.

In the Line of Fire

In the 1950s, when I wasn't dodging Mexican gunboats, I was involved in another risky operation closer to home. Fishing near the Montauk military firing range was so dangerous that the government eventually marked this firing range on the charts. In those days, the charts of Montauk Point, Block Island, and Long Island Sound contained a pie-shaped diagram that told you this was the air force firing range and it warned boats to stay clear of the area during firing practice. This area was delineated on the chart by a line that ran fifteen miles to the southeast and fifteen miles to the southwest, and they always put up a red flag as a warning for boats to stay out.

A small plane towed a sleeve on a long cable for the air force to shoot their 90-mm shells at from the firing range on the beach. The tow plane would fly from East to West, while the artillery went *puff-puff*, trying to hit that sleeve.

The shell of the 90 mm had a timing device in it. If it didn't explode on time or when it struck the target, the shell blew up on hitting the water (or a boat!). Twice, we had a close call with a hot 90-mm shell.

The first time it happened, we were offshore quite a way. The mate and I were minding our own business, trying to catch our customers some fish, when out of nowhere, a hot shell went over our heads and hit the ocean in an explosion of saltwater.

But the second time was the scariest. One day, we were drifting and dreaming to the west of the firing range line, only a few miles off the beach, waiting for a shark to wander into our chum slick. We had John Gnagy, the artist and TV personality, out that day. He was the guy who taught kids of all ages how to draw in his weekly program *The Television Art Course.*

It was one of those hot, flat days when you wish a fish would come along and wake you up. The airplane towing

the target sleeve passed overhead to remind us that they
would be starting their war games soon. Target practice
would begin the next time the plane passed through the
range, but we felt safe because our boat was not in the
firing range. To be sure, I jumped up on the flying bridge to
check our position on the compass. We were clear, out of
the range. No problem. The airplane flew through the range
again to the east and this time the firing commenced. We
saw small puffs of black smoke and could hear the faint
sounds of explosions as the 90 mm struck close to its target.
Then the plane did a U-turn and flew west. We were also
on the west side of the range, but clear of the target-practice
boundary line.

As the plane towing the target headed west
overhead, the guns kept firing and did not stop at the
west boundary line. One of the 90-mm shells did not go
off on time up there where it was supposed to and kept
on coming. It hit the water about one hundred feet from
the *Cricket II*. There was a large explosion as it hit the
water and pieces of shrapnel slid across the surface in all
directions. As the shell made impact, John Gnagy ran half
the length of the cockpit, dove flat on the deck, and slid
along on his face, coming to a stop at the end of the motor
box. I asked him what all that was about and he said he
was hiding behind the motor box for protection from the
shell. I told him he was too late: the shell had already hit
the water.

Some shrapnel came within twenty-five feet of the boat.
One of my terrified customers claimed a piece even hit the
side of the boat before falling in the water, although I
couldn't find any evidence of this.

If the air force was aiming directly at us, they could not
have come any closer. I immediately mashed on the starter
button, put the boat in gear, and spun the steering wheel
west for a fast U-turn. The firing range was to the east so I
headed to the safety of the west.

The ocean was flat, and it left a clear visual of our U-turn wake. Suddenly, we heard the last four or five seconds of a shell's whistle. Up on the flying bridge, I had enough time to say to my mate, Olie Olsen, "I wonder where this one is going to hit?" As I spoke, I turned to Olie and saw him dive head first into the corner of the flying bridge. Just as soon as I had gotten those words out of my mouth, that next hot shell landed on our U-turn spot, right where we had been sitting still.

Once again, I turned to Olie, who was still panic-stricken, and asked, "Did you really think that three-quarter-inch piece of plywood would have saved you?"

Now I continued heading west to make sure the boat was far enough away that they couldn't shoot at us again that day, but there were going to be other days and other shells coming.

That other close call came when one full moon night I decided to go out on an unchartered last-minute shark-fishing trip. I brought along a bunch of friends, including Sam Stanley of East Hampton. Sam was originally from the hills of Virginia, but had spent most of his adult life in East Hampton. Sam had the business smarts to set up an extensive garbage pick-up business. Although Sam spent the rest of his life in East Hampton, he never lost his hillbilly ways; for instance, wherever he went hunting or fishing, Sam carried his .12-gauge shotgun. And you could always recognize Sam walking down the street on account of his pants that were way too loose, but thank God for suspenders!

By late afternoon, we were on our way out. The weather was great and there was still plenty of daylight left as we went around Montauk Lighthouse, heading southwest. We had to stay close to the beach to keep under the 90-mm guns, stationed on the cliffs above us. I was just going to tell the boys that we were clear of the guns and were about to turn the bow of the *Cricket II* in an offshore direction, when there was this tremendous explosion on the beach a very short distance in front of us. The force of that explosion picked up rocks the size of basketballs and tossed them across our bow, splashing them in the water, too close for comfort. If we had been a few seconds earlier on that trip, these rocks would have cut us in half.

Sam had been down below during the explosion. In a rush of excitement, he came out of the cabin, spitting tobacco, and waving his .12-gauge shotgun in the air. He hollered up to me, "Should I give 'em a barrel?"

I said, "For god's sakes, *no*, Sam, no! Put that thing away." Reluctantly, Sam carried the shotgun back into the cabin. I don't know if he had been serious or not, but figured I had better stop him before Sam took on Uncle Sam's air force base single-handedly.

I immediately got on the radio and called the coast guard to report the shelling incident. The coast guard replied using the only two words they know: "Stand by."

I wasn't going to stand by any place; I was on my way out to the fishing grounds! After half an hour or so of research, they called me back to say that it was really nothing and that the air force was *only* blowing up some old ammunition that they had on the beach, and there was nothing to worry about. So I guess, if your boat gets cut in half with what looks like a blast from the Jolly Green Giant's shotgun, it's nothing to worry about!

The Hot Mako in the Firing Range

In my early years of shark fishing, one of our favorite spots for mako was just west of the firing range, a few miles off the beach. Most of the time, if there was no wind the *Cricket II* would drift to the west because of the current in that area. So if we started our drift on the west side of the firing range, we would stay out of the line of fire.

The air force had a sixty-five-foot boat that patrolled up and down, close to the beach, chasing away any small boats that attempted to enter the firing range. On this day, the *Cricket II* was fishing for sharks and drifting merrily along with the currents. For some reason, our drift took us to the east this time. That meant I was heading into the firing range. I did not want to move because we had established our chum slick and had time invested in this spot. Moving would involve the frustrating business of starting all over with a new chum line.

Another hour passed, and we were dangerously close to the western edge of the firing range. I saw the patrol boat coming out and knew he was going to chase us away. We didn't have much time left to fish and I was waiting until the last minute, hoping against hope that one of my customers would hook a fish. Just as the patrol boat got close enough for one of the men to come out on deck and holler at us, it happened: a mako picked up one of our baits and went buzzing straight for that patrol boat with the *Cricket II* in hot pursuit.

The mako jumped fifteen feet in the air, right alongside the patrol boat, so close that it splashed water all over the man on deck! As we sped by his boat, I screamed at the drenched man, "GET THAT BOAT OUT OF THE WAY!"

He was so excited and scared that he put his boat fast in reverse and backed out of the way as quickly as he could. For the entire time my customer was fighting the fish and I was chasing it around with the boat, the crew on the air force boat-patrol boat was avoiding us, watching in disbelief.

After twenty minutes or so, we caught the mako and hung him on the side of the boat. Now the patrol boat figured it was safe to come over and talk to us. I thought the operator was going to holler at us for holding up their target practice. And he must have thought that I was going to holler at him for getting in the way of our fish. As he pulled up alongside us, he said, in a sheepish voice, "Will you please move out of the firing range?"

"Sure, thanks," I answered guiltily.

Another day, when I got back to the dock after fishing, I heard this story about a new sub, the *Nautilus*, which had just been put into commission. She was one of the atomic subs that was built in Connecticut and tested in our open waters off Montauk Point. The navy had just finished installing her underwater radar and sea tests were under way. Out the *Nautilus* went into the deep waters off Montauk, where the local beam trawlers fished, dragging their nets along the bottom. When dragging their nets, these beam trawlers moved slowly ahead to keep these nets operating correctly.

All of a sudden, this local dragger went backward ten times faster than he ever went forward, with water boiling over its transom. Because he was going backward at a hair-raising speed, the trawler captain cut his cables to keep from being swamped. After he cut the cables, he stood there on his aft deck, probably wondering what sort of sea monster had been pulling him backward. As he watched in amazement, the captain saw the *Nautilus* surface behind his boat, all tangled up in his fishing nets and cables.

The next day, a newspaper reporter asked him a bunch of stupid questions. The funniest one being, "Did you know at any time that you had hold of the *Nautilus*?"

His answer was a classic and it was printed word for word: "I knew goddamn well it was not a trolley car!"

Out of the Frying Pan and into the Firing Range

On one of our offshore shark-fishing trips, we had to go out past the firing range, and I decided to slide out on the east side of the range until I got to end. Then I could head east or west. About halfway out, with two other charter boats chugging behind me, the peaceful ocean that we had all to ourselves suddenly changed when an aircraft carrier suddenly loomed on the horizon. The sky soon filled with fighter planes, and out of the deep blue came a couple of submarines. What caught my attention the most was the PT boat bearing down on us at high speed.

Before I could turn to my mate and say, "Wow! Look at this!" the PT boat buzzed up alongside us and came to a stop.

The navy man on deck picked up his loud hailer, and hollered, "Ahoy the *Cricket II*!"

Whenever I can, I enjoy thumbing my nose at these nautical people. "What the hell do you want?" I asked.

Unshaken, he said, "We suggest you clear the area. We are going to have torpedo practice here."

"Where the hell do you want me to go?" I said.

"I suggest you go to the west," he replied.

"I CAN'T GO WEST," I screamed back at him. "If I go west, I will go right into the air force firing range!"

That navy man on the PT boat hollered back, in his flat officer-type voice, "We don't have any authority over the air force. Go west!"

It was my pleasure to spin the wheel and head the *Cricket II* due west, right into the middle of the air force firing range.

I turned my radio on and knew that, when I changed direction, I was going to get a call from one of the charter boats behind me. Sure enough, it happened. "Frank, where do you think you're going?"

"I was told by the PT boat that they are going to start torpedo practice and for us to go west, away from their area. So you might as well do the same thing, or that PT boat will pay you a visit, too." Now, we had a choice: get torpedoed by the navy or shelled by the air force!

So us three boats had gone out of the frying pan and into the firing range, fouling up the air force on direct orders from the United States Navy!

The commercial dragger *Ranger*, iced up on her way home to Montauk in 1961. I was a deck hand aboard her that frozen winter.

Home, Home on the *Ranger*

All my summers were spent sport fishing, but in the winters, I had to get a job on some kind of boat because fishing was the only thing I knew as a profession. I fished on all kinds of commercial boats: long-lining for codfish, working on a scallop boat, working on a beam trawler for lobsters and yellow tail flounder, on private yachts, dock-building—doing anything that was on or around the water.

Every one of these jobs, one day or another, was filled with some kind of danger to life or limb. The hardest thing with any and all these jobs was that of trying to beat the weather. Doing it as fast as I could when the weather was good enough to work outside.

One of the toughest weather-related jobs that I had was in the early 1960s when I was working on the beam trawler, *Ranger*. We had spent almost one week in February dragging the nets over the bottom in local waters. We were fishing for yellow-tail flounders and had enough, about ten thousand pounds, to take to the fillet houses in New Bedford, Massachusetts. This was only about an eight-hour ride by boat from Montauk Point, and it would pay a penny or two per pound more than our local fillet houses in Greenport, Long Island, and it was worth the trip.

When we finished unloading early the next day, we started our eight-hour ride home, figuring we would be home by supper time. The first hour of running time went smoothly, but then the freezing southwest wind started to blow. The sea was not that rough, but as we went farther, it got worse. Freezing spray was sloshing across the *Ranger*'s bow as the heavy wave hit her port side, sending freezing water over most of the boat.

When the spray met the cold air, it turned to ice instantly wherever it landed and stuck to everything. The ice soon began accumulating on one side of the boat more than the other, and it wasn't long before we had a bad list. Leaning harder and harder, the *Ranger* plowed through the freezing waves. By this time we were past the halfway mark in our journey. Captain Dick Stern had his choice: keep on going or turn back. He chose to keep going.

Then we had another thing go wrong: Dick had left his radar set back at the repair shop in New Bedford, figuring that the short inland ride back to Montauk would be a piece of cake.

After four or five hours, the entire wheelhouse was covered in a six-inch layer of ice from the spray. This meant that the glass windows were completely frozen over and were impossible to see out of.

Our emergency lifeboat, a fourteen-foot double-ended dory, was securely lashed on top of the wheelhouse. As of now, there would be no way we could free that dory if we needed it: it was completely frozen to the cabin top. Everybody probably had the same thought in their head: will we make it? But being professional seamen, the words were never spoken aloud. Instead, we had to think of a way to improvise. There's more than one way to skin a cat or deice a window.

I backed out of the wheelhouse and tried sticking my head up and over the top of the cabin to see if there were any other boats in the area, but this was impossible: the cold wind made my eyes water and the liquid would turn to ice as it ran down the side of my face, freezing instantly when it landed on my jacket. We had to see and could not go any farther unless we could. Then I had an idea that was worth a try. I went down below, took the small mirror off the medicine cabinet and brought it topside and into the wheelhouse. I pushed the mirror against the frozen windshield, hoping that the sun, which faced us in our westerly direction, would melt some of the ice.

The sun hit the mirror, reflecting enough heat to melt a small hole the size of a golf ball in the ice. This would take fifteen to twenty minutes of holding the mirror against the glass and only gave me five or six seconds of visibility after removing the mirror.

We took it in turns to do this mirror trick all the way home. When the *Ranger* reached the Montauk Point inlet we laid to in order to scrape off the window so we could see going into the dock. The boat wound up covered in so much ice that it looked like she had a forty-degree list. The *Ranger* could not have taken much more before completely turning over. This was just one more time we had beaten Mother Nature.

Back at the dock, we spent three days using wooden mallets to bust ice off the *Ranger*. All the steel cables that went from the top of the mast down to the cockpit were normally three-fourths inch in diameter, but now they were encrusted in ice and almost the size of a football.

That summer, I spent as usual, aggravating my customers on the *Cricket II*. But winter soon came around again, and I was back on the *Ranger* hoping to make some kind of money to put food on the table for the wife and kids. This time, Captain Dick found out that lobsters could be caught in the net the same way as he caught other fish, but we had to fish offshore in a lot deeper water, closer to the Gulf Stream. The Gulf Stream itself is too deep to fish on the bottom, but Captain Stern fished the edge, where it started to drop off along the sixty—to eighty-fathom shelf. This is where we found most of our lobsters and caught some freaky-looking deepwater fish, including the wolf fish. He was jet-black, long and skinny, and had a big head loaded with long, needle-like teeth.

On flat days, when the wind was not blowing you could see lots of strong tide rips going in all directions. When the wind did blow, especially from the northwest, it blew against the strong tide rips and currents. This was a mess and no place to be, as the waves would be twice their normal size and the holes behind the waves were three times as deep.

One particular trip, which lasted from May 15 to 19, 1961, started out well: we were out there in those rips, dragging for lobsters, until a northwest wind hit us fast. We were caught with our nets down as the weather report on the radio had not predicted this! In order to get up and go, it took from twenty minutes to half an hour to haul the net up from the bottom.

We picked our net up and I thought Captain Dick was going to say we'd be heading home, but instead, he said, "As long as we're out here, we'll set in [drop the net] one more time." Scotty (the other deck hand) and I were not happy about this, but there is only one captain and he makes the orders. So we started another tow, and the wind began blowing harder and harder. Captain Stern decided to cut this last tow shorter than the rest to start our long trip back as the wind blew the waves higher and higher against the tide rips and currents.

The captain gave the order to haul back, and the cables started to turn on the large winches. This time it seemed like we would never get the nets up. Every minute counted: we had to get out of there because the seas were building up faster and faster in those tide rips. Once we had hauled up our net, we just dropped everything on deck and started in. After a few hours of running time, we would be out of the tide rips and currents and into a calmer ocean. Then we could straighten out and put away everything that was loose on deck, but it didn't work out that way.

When the nets came up, we just dropped everything on deck. After checking what needed lashing down, I stood in the wheelhouse doorway, looking aft, watching to see if everything was going to be OK. I gave the OK to Captain Dick and he mashed on the throttle. When we hit the first wave, the *Ranger* was lifted straight up into the air. On its downward thrust, the boat spun, first into a fast right, and then rapidly into a left-handed twist.

If anything was going to move or shift, it would happen now. And it did. The large lobster tank that stretched across almost the full width of the stern broke loose. It had been bolted down to the deck, but apparently not well enough. This tank was filled to capacity with about two thousand pounds of lobster, and water. I watched the tank, which was supposed to have been made fast by the crew in the shipyard, lift up off the deck six to eight inches and ram the starboard side, breaking many of the planks loose from the deck up.

I screamed, "The aft tank broke loose!" Captain Dick pulled back on the throttle and threw the *Ranger* into a drift. As the boat rocked from side to side, everything that was loose or semi-loose was flying around. It took us the rest of the day to tie the tank down exactly where it had stopped, using every piece of tackle we had aboard. We could not afford to let this tank move again, or we would be in bad shape: if it did, it could bust the whole side of the boat out, and we would sink immediately.

For the rest of our trip, everybody had their eyes glued to this tank. We even stopped a couple of times on the way home to make sure that it was still secured. I felt relieved when at last I saw the end of Long Island looming in the distance. Two and a half hours later, the *Ranger* slid into Montauk Harbor, a bit busted up, but we had made it home one more time.

Lifesaver

After another trip on the *Ranger,* and another rough
and wild ride home, the northwest wind was blowing so
hard that Captain Dick Stern said, "We'll never make it
around Montauk Point so we're going into Shinnecock inlet
for tonight. Because we only have half a load of fish to take
to the fillet house in New Bedford, we're going right back
out again tomorrow. Maybe we'll have enough fish in the
[fish] hole by tomorrow night to go to the fillet house."

Shinnecock inlet is not the best, but it's the closest one
to Montauk. The channel going into that inlet changes a
lot. The sand shifts from time to time, making it a dangerous
channel to pass through. With waves breaking on the
shallow spots, sometimes it all looks the same, but Captain
Dick had been in and out of this inlet a few times, so he
wasn't worried about entering it (or at least he didn't show
it). The tide rushes in and rushes out, and if it is going in
the same direction as the wind, there is no problem. But if
the wind is against the tide, this makes for a tougher ride.

As luck would have it, with the northwest wind and
the ebb tide, it was flatter than usual. We got in just before
dark and found a place to tie up, a place that was flush
against a bulkhead. Another dragger came in right behind
us and tied up alongside the *Ranger*. Tying up to one another
is a common practice for all commercial fishing vessels.
Sometimes, when there are two or three boats tied up
together and you want to go ashore, you have to jump from
boat to boat before you hit the dock.

After securing the *Ranger,* it was time to go to the
restaurant and bar to have something to eat and drink.
This was going to be a long night. We had nowhere else to
go except the restaurant and the *Ranger;* and we had no
reason to get back to the boat in a hurry. At around 10:00
p.m. or so, Captain Dick said he was going to turn in for
the night and I said, "I'll be right behind you." In the bar

there were a couple of crewmen from other draggers, who were telling fish stories, and I'm guessing it was around 10:30 p.m. when I knew that I had heard enough of these fish tales. So I decided to turn in too.

I zipped up my heavy jacket all the way to the top to keep out the biting northwest wind, and left the bar. As I climbed onto the *Ranger* and started going below, something made me stop and stick my head up to take another look around.

It wasn't a pitch-black night—there was just enough light so you could see a little. I didn't hear anything so I can't explain why I took that other look around, but when I glanced over toward the other boat, I saw what seemed like a man's hand, hanging onto the side of the next boat. At night, things don't look like what they really are, but I said to myself, "Go and check it out." It was so cold that I had to force myself back up on deck to investigate. The wind cut right through me, but I had to do it.

When I walked across the deck of the Ranger and got closer, I could see there really was a hand with an arm attached, and that a body was attached to the arm! Looking down between the two boats, I could see there was a man hanging on. He was half frozen and only hanging on by one hand when I found him, and the fast, outgoing tide was trying to drag him away. If that happened, his body would never be found.

I reached down and grabbed hold of his hand and started to pull. He responded by raising his other hand that was in the ice-cold water. When I got him up on the deck, he told me he was a crew member who had been crossing from boat to boat when he had slipped and fallen between the boats. The strong tide was pulling against him, and the icy water which had immediately filled his clothes prevented him from climbing back up. He said that he had been holding himself up with both hands when his left hand had lost its grip after becoming numb and half frozen. The man was barely hanging on with his right hand, and the cold waters of the ebb tide were sucking at his body, trying to pull him under, when I arrived.

He said that if I hadn't come along when I did, he wouldn't have been able to hang on much longer. He didn't hear me climb aboard because the rushing water was making too much noise. I asked him if he had screamed for help. "Yes, but I gave that up a while back," he said.

It just seemed funny to me that I had not heard anything. What had made me turn around and take that last look? Every time I bumped into him after that, he would always throw his arms around me and say, "If it wasn't for you, I wouldn't be here now!"

Knowing that you have just saved a person's life is a great feeling.

The New York Sportsmen's Show, 1956-1986

The New York Coliseum, which opened in 1956, excelled in staging huge promotional events such as sport shows. The Sportsmen's Show was a ten-day event held each winter, during the month of February. It had a circuslike atmosphere, and for a couple of years, featured all kinds of live animals, including the famous Budweiser Clydesdale horses that pulled the big beer wagon.

I was introduced to this event by Jerry Rushmeyer who owned Rushmeyer's Inn in Montauk. Jerry specialized in catering to the fishing public; therefore, he invited a choice half-dozen charter-boat captains to help him assemble, disassemble, and operate his twenty-foot-long display of mounted fish, fish photos, and anything else that had to do with fishing. For this work, Jerry rewarded his assistants by allowing them to stand in the booth during the show and hand out their business cards.

After the second year of doing this and advertising Jerry's fishing lodge, I realized I should go about getting my own booth to promote my charter business because the public was reacting enthusiastically to the brand-new sport of shark-fishing pioneered by the *Cricket II* in 1951. The managers of the Sportsmen's Show were very helpful, giving me a free booth. They knew I had a good display of shark mounts and photos, etc., that would attract people's curiosity and interest. I made all my booze money from selling shark teeth, loose or on chains. Anything with a shark tooth on it would sell. I even glued them on a cigarette lighter. One of our best items was a small box of loose, mixed teeth, mostly small. I set this up in the front of the counter with a "twenty-five cents each" price tag on it. The kids would make their daddies buy them a tooth and the fathers thought it was a cheap way of making "junior" happy. What the father didn't know was that before long, the tooth, because of its sharpness, would make a hole and drop out of junior's pocket; then he would have to come back someday and buy another shark tooth!

Every winter, a month before the show, I would sit in my house in frozen Montauk making up shark-tooth necklaces, shark-tooth tie pins, key rings, or anything else I could glue a shark's tooth on.

After I spent two years operating my own ten-foot square booth at the show, I realized I had to have a new gimmick. You always have to have a new gimmick to attract new customers. I had heard somewhere they had a show that featured an angler versus a swimmer contest. This is where I got the idea of using the Coliseum's sixty-foot-long, thirty-foot-wide, three-foot-deep sport tank. This tank was usually used for log-rolling, canoe tilting, and water sports such as duck hunting and fly casting. Bleachers holding up to five hundred or so people would be set up on each side of the tank. My idea was to take anybody out of the audience who thought they could row a boat, and put them up against me and my rod and reel. The managers OK'd my idea and our act was scheduled to run three times per day.

The master of ceremonies would announce over the loud speaker:

"Captain Frank Mundus is here and he challenges anybody in the crowd who thinks they can row a boat against his rod and reel. Captain Mundus says that if your boat touches the other side of the tank, he will give you a free fishing trip."

To the average person who didn't know anything about a rod and reel, this sounded like an easy thing to do, so I didn't have any trouble getting people out of the audience to accept my free challenge. There was always somebody who would jump out of the bleachers with his arms waving, screaming, "I can do it!"

The announcer would ask the person to come up on the stage, introduce the contender to the audience, and the game would begin. I knew the power that I held in my hands, but I had to make it look like a struggle as I held the rowboat back. I even gave the rower a fifteen-foot lead before I started putting a light pressure on him with the reel's drag system. I always waited until the rower thought he was winning because he almost had his boat touching the other end of the tank. At this point, I put a lot of pressure on him and pulled him halfway back. By this time, the crowd was cheering him on. Then I slacked off on the drag and let him get within feet of victory before I stopped him dead in his tracks with one twist of the drag lever. Now, at the height of this drama, the crowd screamed encouragement to the rower. Because this looks like a Mexican standoff, I let the rowboat win by making believe the rower, with all his power, yanked me off the stage and into the pool. This went over great. It must have been something like the entertainment laid on for the old Romans in the Coliseum's Italian namesake. Every time I made believe I got pulled into the water, the crowd screamed with laughter at me, happy for the rower because he had won. Three times a day for ten days, I ended up in the pool. That meant three times a day, I had to work my way through the crowd of people and rush around the corner to get my clothes dry-cleaned between performances.

My act at the show received good publicity from the press. Winners from the audience got a free fishing trip in June, and the Coliseum got good advanced publicity in the middle of the year for the upcoming winter's show.

There was only one little catch to the free fishing trip that I gave to everybody that won. In the spirit of P. T. Barnum, I made sure the trip was only available on a weekday, a time that most people can't get away from work. As a result, only four or five people would take me up on it, and I made sure everybody went on the same day, and invited the press to ride along for publicity. This way, I only lost one day that I probably would have had difficulty booking anyhow.

On one occasion at the Coliseum, a two-man team of professional log rollers and canoe tilters could not resist challenging me and my rod and reel. But not with a rowboat, these Canucks wanted to use their canoes! These Canadians were born and raised in canoes. Even their muscles had muscles! This was to be strictly for fun, no prizes were involved, and no bets were placed. To make sure of a victory, I went over my fishing tackle thoroughly, even putting on new line. I knew I could not use a stand-up harness to fight these powerful boys, so I put together a makeshift fishing chair. On stage, one of my friends would lie on his belly and hold on to the back legs of the chair to keep me from being pulled, chair and all, into the tank.

The Canadian team asked me if I was going to give them the same fifteen-foot head start that I gave the public. I said I would if they used their show paddles. These paddles were half as wide as regular ones and would not dig as deep and as hard as the everyday working paddles. When the Canadian canoeists showed up for the contest, however, they were just as keen to win and had brought their wide *working* paddles. After I saw this, I hollered, "No head start!"

Full of confidence, the Canadians climbed into their canoe and the announcer said, "GO!"

And go they did. With the power they had, I did not know whether I could stop them before they got to the other end of the tank, because with every thrust of their paddles, which bit hard and deep into the water, they were putting tremendous pressure on me. Meanwhile, I had to clamp down on the drag, little by little, hoping I would not break anything, slowing them down until I could bring the canoe to a complete stop. Once I had done this, the game was over and they knew it. This had been the agreement between us and I had won.

Somehow, I still had to finish the act by going into the water. Slacking off on the drag, I let them get almost to the other end of the tank before I stopped them a second time. Now I had to be pulled into the water. I did the same thing that I always did, making believe that the canoeists were too powerful. I hung onto the rod and reel, struggling on the stage, and losing my balance. Then I staggered to the edge of the tank, teetered back and forth (while the crowd went wild with laughter), and fell into the water. When I fell, I had to make sure, because of the shallow water, to land flat on my back to break my fall. After my victory, one of the Canadians was pissed, but the other came over to shake my hand. Both had underestimated the power of the rod and reel and of P.T. Barnum!

I did this act for four or five winters in a row at the New York Show, then one winter I did the same act at the Long Island Sportsmen's show—only my luck ran out. I had decided to make a few changes to the end of the act by making believe I got my tie caught in the reel while the announcer tried to make it look like he was holding me back from falling off the stage. We also had a set-up person in the rowboat, a fellow charter-boat captain on this one occasion. The crowd would think he was an unsuspecting person out of the audience. After I had been pulled overboard, I would walk through the water to where the rowboat was and turn it over. We hoped that this new routine would excite the crowd, especially if they thought my turning the rowboat over was because I was angry and showed poor sportsmanship.

In the meantime, the tank developed a leak and lost about one foot of water over a three- or four-day period. On one particular day, to make matters worse, the announcer held on to me too long, hoping to add more suspense to our routine. But when I fell into the water, I couldn't fall flat to avoid hitting the tank's concrete bottom, and I busted my left elbow. I immediately blacked out from the pain, but the cold water quickly brought me round. As soon as I stood up, I knew my elbow was broken, so I opened a shirt button with my right hand and slid my left hand into this makeshift sling.

Somehow, I still had to finish the act by walking through the water and across the tank to where the rowboat was, turning the boat over (one-handed) for the finale. Nobody, not even the rowboat operator, knew I had been hurt. The joke was on me as the crowd roared with laughter when I turned over the rowboat. I was genuinely angry because of the pain I was in, and ironically, it made the act better!

As I walked into the locker room, everybody hollered and screamed, "Hey, what a great performance that was. We really had 'em going that time!"

The rowboat guy was starting to change into his dry clothes, while I stood in the middle of the room mumbling about my broken elbow. Nobody paid attention. They were still busy laughing and hollering about the success of the act. After I mentioned two or three times that I had a busted elbow and needed a ride to hospital, somebody took me seriously. I spent the next six to eight days in the hospital. That was the end of that show and that act. There were no encore performances!

That spring, I had to refasten the *Cricket II*'s hull planking with my left arm in a sling, and nobody offered to lend a hand to yours truly, Montauk's maverick charter-boat skipper. It's no joke working on your hauled-out boat with frozen fingers in the cold spring of the year. Single-handedly, in all senses of the word, I had to secure the *Cricket II*'s hull planking with size twelve-by-three-and-a-half-inch bronze screws, first drilling hundreds of holes, then driving in all those large screws with a heavy electric drill. But it was my job and I got it done. It was so cold, that I couldn't even give my fellow boatmen a frozen finger as they walked by and gave me the cold shoulder.

Don't Depend on Having a Big Eye

After a few years of union problems, the New York Sportsmen's Show lost a lot of big companies' business. Ticket sales dropped off, forcing it to merge with the Boat Show.

I continued my booth at the show, telling people all about shark fishing and answering a lot of questions. Some of which were even sensible. One day, Frankie Macarena[3], a Montauk charter-boat captain and licensed coast guard instructor, was standing in the back row of people piled up in front of our booth at the Sportsmen's/Boat Show. Because of our extensive display of mounted sharks, jaws, and jewelry, there was always a bunch of people waiting to get close enough to ask questions. Frankie Macarena finally worked his way in through the crowd to talk to me. He approached my booth and announced, "I have a charter, this up and coming season, to go to the Dumping Grounds. I know you've been there a few times," he said. "How far is it from Montauk?"

I looked at him somewhat funny because he was a licensed instructor for people who want to get their captain's papers to carry passengers for hire, and navigation was one of the classes he taught. "I don't know what the exact mileage is, but I can tell you my running time—how long it takes me to get there. If your running time was the same as mine, I could tell you how many hours it would take you to get there, regardless of how far away it is." So I asked him, "What is your running time? I still have to depend on my clock and compass for navigation."

He said he didn't know.

I asked him another question. "In a thick fog, how many minutes does it take you to hit the first bell buoy due north of the inlet? It takes me three minutes. What's your running time?"

He said, "I don't know."

Then I asked, "In a thick fog, how long does it take you, after you hit the bell buoy just outside the inlet, to reach the inner Shagwong buoy? My running time is twelve minutes, what's yours?"

"I don't know," he said.

Then I asked him, "When you round Montauk Point, what's your running time to the Gas Buoy (or MP buoy as it's known on the chart)? My running time is half an hour. It's five miles off Montauk."

"I don't know," he said.

I asked him another question, "How do you operate, if you don't know your running time?"

He poked his chest out and said, "We have radar."

"What would happen if you blew a fuse?" I asked.

"We carry spare fuses," he replied.

About this time I got very disgusted with this conversation and screamed at him in a *very* loud voice, "What would happen if somebody BUSTED a bottle of Seagram Seven into your radar screen and smashed it to bits?"

"We would go home," he said quietly, confident that he had outwitted me. You could hear me all the way across the Coliseum, screaming my final question, "HOW, HOW, HOW COULD YOU GO HOME, IF YOU DIDN'T KNOW WHERE YOU WERE?"

For some reason, Frankie disappeared into the crowd and never asked me another question ever again.

PART III
THE MIDDLE YEARS

CHAPTER 4

SHARKS

The 4,500-pound White Shark, 1964

When the press publicized the 4,500-pound great white shark that I caught off Montauk in June 1964, it gave author Peter Benchley a lot of detailed information that he went on to use in his novel *Jaws* in which the fisherman "Quint" attempts to catch the shark with harpoons, lines, and barrels after trying to bait it on rod and reel, *exactly* the way I did with the real fish. Then we had motor trouble and so did Benchley's fictitious Quint, although Quint's was self-inflicted. By sheer coincidence, Peter Benchley chartered my boat on June 21, 1966, when he was working for *Newsweek* magazine, so he had plenty of opportunity to observe the sharks and me firsthand. However, Benchley's boat ride was two years too late to witness firsthand the capture of the biggest white shark that started it all . . .

It was a cold, damp morning on June 5, 1964, and I was booked for a single day trip by Peter Brandenberg and his three friends, Jerome, Frank, and Harvey. I had already started the *Cricket II*'s 671 diesel motor at the dock for its normal morning warm up. Usually, I let it run for ten minutes or so, then I shut it down and wait for the customers to show up; but this time, they had arrived during the motor's warming up period. It wasn't long before they started loading all their food and drinks aboard, and it looked to me like they had brought along enough stuff for a week. Their ice chest was full of beer and soda and they were still trying to jam more in. This was a familiar sight I saw almost every morning, but I never gave up trying to educate my customers on how to handle food and drink aboard the boat.

After I got everyone aboard and loaded up, we headed out of the inlet. The party was excited, the mate was so-so, and the captain was feeling humdrum: our two-and-a-half-hour trip to the southeast was just another boat ride for me. One of the guys asked me what they could expect to catch today. "It looks like we're gonna catch porbeagles," I told him, "because the water temperature is still cold and the blue sharks haven't moved in yet."

"I've never seen a porbeagle shark," said one of the party. "What do they look like?"

"To you, he'll probably look like a mako. He's got the same body, almost the same color, except that he has a white spot on the lower back part of his dorsal. His teeth are shaped differently, too; just like the mako's, they're long, slender and smooth-edged, but on the base of each tooth there's a small tooth attached to either side of it. Porbeagles are fun to catch and they're good eating," I told him.

Fishing was good that day and by 11:30 that morning, we had caught two porbeagles in the two-hundred-pound class and had hooked our third, but this shark was taking out a lot of line, and I knew I would have to chase him down with the boat to regain it. As I ran across the cockpit, aiming for the starter button, I screamed orders over my shoulder to the mate, "Wind in them other lines and put everything away! Looks like we've got a decent fish on this time."

After I started up the motor, I heard a hollow sound that I've heard before, the one that told me there wasn't any cooling water going through the motor and coming out of the exhaust pipe.

We tried baiting the 4,500-pound white shark first. Note leader wire going into his mouth.

"Is there any water coming out of the exhaust pipe?" I asked.

"No, not a hell of a lot," one of the customers replied.

From past experience, I knew that I could run the motor with no cooling system for about ten minutes with no problem. In that time, we could regain the line we needed on the reel.

When we got back enough line, I stopped the boat and shut off the motor. By now, I was pretty sure that the salt-water intake pump had gone bad. The pump had been working all the way out to the fishing grounds; a blade must have broken off the rubber impeller inside the pump while we were running. I always carried a complete spare pump for such emergencies and I told the party that after we landed this fish, I would change the pump.

As the customer continued fighting the fish, I got ready to change the pump, moving all the junk off the top of the motor box and slid the lid back to expose the motor.

The mate that I had picked up a few weeks ago for this season was an out-of-work jockey who wanted to try his hand at fishing. He didn't have a hell of a lot of meat on his bones, but what he lacked in power, he made up for in enthusiasm. Using a small tin can on the end of a stick, I showed him how to chum, scooping a little at a time overboard to keep the slick going, but I forgot to tell him not to chum when the boat was moving ahead. He was like a machine that I had turned on and forgotten to turn off, chumming happily and rapidly, while the boat continued chasing down the fish. Soon, we had gained enough line back on the reel; I shut off the *Cricket II*'s motor and we coasted to a stop. As I began studying the motor, all at once, everybody started screaming about "a giant of a shark" that had just passed under the boat, almost scraping his dorsal fin on our hull. Meanwhile, the jockey was still chumming as he chattered to the people! I ran over to the starboard side to take a look, just in time to see the fish make his second pass under the boat. He was bigger than any white shark I had ever seen, and in my excitement, I wanted to catch him for a rod-and-reel world record.

The big white shark passes under my boat as I watch with
my mate.

Forgetting all about my broken motor, I ran down below into the cabin to get out the heavy tackle, shouting orders over my shoulder and telling my customers to throw some mackerel overboard to keep the fish interested while I got ready to catch him. We had caught about six hundred pounds of Boston mackerel that morning while out shark fishing, so we had plenty of fish to feed him. As I emerged from the cabin carrying the heavy tackle, everybody was madly tossing mackerel into the air while the white shark swam around, sucking them up like Chicklets.

After getting the angler situated in the fighting chair, I tossed bait into the water: two nice big Boston mackerel. On his next pass around, the white shark picked up the two mackerel without missing a beat and kept zooming in and out of the slick, dragging the leader wire and line behind him, looking for more handouts. It was then that I felt like a kid who had just been caught with his hand in a cookie jar; I knew I had done wrong, trying to catch this fish on rod and reel while trying to fix a broken motor.

I handed the fishing pole to the mate and told him, "Whatever you do, do not strike this fish. Walk him around so he doesn't feel the hook. Maybe I can fix the pump in the meantime."

Moments later, the mate yelled, "He spit out the bait!"

"Good!" I said. "Put that rod and reel away until we get the motor fixed."

Now the questions started. "How long will it take?" one guy asked me.

"I don't know. It depends on how lucky we get."

"What do you mean 'how lucky?'" he demanded.

"This is a gear pump," I told him, "and if the gears don't line up exactly, the pump won't couple to the motor right. Sometimes, I have had to put the pump on and take it off a few times before getting the gears aligned correctly."

About now, everybody really lost it. They were all running from side to side, watching the monster swim beneath the boat.

"How long do you think he'll stay with us?" another one asked.

I couldn't answer this question because there were too many maybes in it. A few times, I heard them asking each other, "If we can't catch him on rod and reel, why don't we harpoon him?" And it wasn't long before they asked me that same question.

"There's no guarantee that once we harpoon him, we'll catch him," I explained to them. Trying to change that pump, with ten thumbs on each hand was not the easiest job with everybody screaming and hollering in the background. As I hurried to remove the old pump, I didn't notice that a piece of the broken rubber impeller had fallen down into the intake pipe when we had shut the motor off. Time was running out, and so was our supply of food for the white shark as we had to continue feeding him heavily to keep him interested.

After harpooning was suggested by my customers a few more times, I said I would try. "But I'm not giving you any guarantee that we'll get him."

I told the mate to go up forward and bring the harpoon, the line, and the barrel into the cockpit. If I was going to harpoon the shark, it would have to be done from here because the fish kept going under the boat where the food was. My mate got four hundred feet of quarter-inch nylon line and an aluminum beer keg and started putting them in place. Then he handed me the twelve-foot-long harpoon pole from the bow. A few times, while we were getting things ready, the shark swam under the boat and the customers began screaming, "HERE HE IS NOW! HIT HIM! GET HIM!"

But we weren't ready yet. I couldn't rush this shot with my hand-held harpoon. We had to be *absolutely* ready. This was no time for a foul-up. I knew we were only going to get one shot at him and I wanted to make sure everything was exact.

Finally, I was ready and stood in the middle of the cockpit like Ahab, holding on to the harpoon pole, waiting. We were just about out of chum when here he came again, hard on the surface, with his dorsal fin and tail out of the water, aiming for the center of the cockpit like a torpedo about to ram us amidships.

I waited.

I knew he wasn't going to hit us. He had to turn one way or another at the last second.

When he made a hard turn and faced the bow, I could have scratched his back with the harpoon dart as I quickly tried to figure out where his backbone would be for a solid shot. When it was time to hit him, he was so close, I couldn't throw the harpoon. I had to slam it in. So I drove the dart deep into his side, using my arm, shoulder, and back to apply more power.

When the fish was hit, he took off fast for the horizon. That four hundred feet of nylon line did not take long to disappear as it sizzled out of its bucket. I threw the red and white aluminum beer barrel overboard and it went skipping at high speed across the top of the water. Then I went back to working on the motor. "Keep your eyes on the barrel and let me know when it's almost out of sight," I told everyone.

I was still trying to change the pump when somebody hollered, "IT'S ALMOST OUT OF SIGHT." I raced to the flying bridge and started the motor. I could only run the overheating motor for a short time. We were lucky enough to come up close to the barrel. Now I shut off the motor and everybody was trying something different to cool down the motor: fanning it, blowing on it, etc. I set a couple of the customers up on the bridge to watch the barrel, which was slowly moving through the water because the crippled fish must have been hit hard with the harpoon dart deep and close to his backbone. In the meantime, I worked on the pump again.

Whenever the barrel began to get dangerously close to disappearing over the horizon, I ran the *Cricket II* up on it again and reassigned my lookouts to continue watching the barrel. This game of "stop and go" happened four or five times until I got the pump changed.

Even the new pump gave us trouble because of that piece of impeller that fell down and was trapped in the intake pipe; it slowed the suction flow of water to the pump. I had to prime the pump four or five times to get up enough suction. Finally, the pump began picking up water. We still didn't have enough water moving through the motor, but now there was at least enough to cool it at medium running speed, which was all we needed.

Now we had the motor back in shape, and I could concentrate on catching the fish. I told the boys, "This time, when we come up on the barrel, we're going to pick it up and start pulling on him."

So we came up on the barrel and picked it up. I told them to have one man to do the pulling. "We don't want too much sudden pressure on the fish or we could pull the harpoon dart out."

They took turns. When one man got tired, the other would take over. With this slow, steady, constant pressure, we raised the fish up close enough so that I could throw the second harpoon in him, and I told the boys, "When I hit him with this second harpoon, you won't be able to hold him. He'll head all the way to the bottom and then we'll have to start the slow process of pulling him up again."

The fish did just that, and we had to start all over again, but this time, we had two harpoons in him and two lines. Now, we had two men pulling, one on each line. I told them we had to repeat the backbreaking process of raising him to the surface until I could hit him with the third harpoon. Each time, it took about an hour to bring him up from the bottom, which in the area where we were fishing, was at a depth of 180 feet.

Once we had three harpoons in him and three guys pulling, each man could put more pressure on him. "Make sure you don't scuffle around and get tangled up in the harpoon lines that's on the deck," I kept reminding them. "When you're pulling the line in, drop it alongside of you and don't move your feet."

You could hear me the other side of the horizon, hollering, "PULL, PULL, PULL!" By now, my customers were starting to fall apart from the exertion: they were not used to this kind of work. So I decided to go down and do some pulling while the jockey took the wheel. Now I was pulling as hard as I could, but couldn't get the mate to steer in the right direction half the time. We were supposed to be heading in the same direction as the fish, at an idling speed.

At this point, I had trouble all around: my customers were wearing down and my so-called mate had never steered a boat before. He didn't know how to counteract the wheel and had the boat going in the wrong direction half of the time. Once we got the fish up again, I knew that I had to be the one who threw the harpoon, even though my arms felt like they were falling off after an hour of hard pulling on the fish.

As I was pulling on the line up in the bow, raising the fish to the surface, I shouted orders to one of the customers who wasn't doing anything, "Get the harpoon ready again!" I also had to tell him how to rig it and where the equipment was located on the boat. His timing was perfect. He had just finished getting everything together and was standing behind me, ready to hand over the harpoon, when we got the fish up high enough for the shot. When the fish was half a pole length beneath the surface, I threw the fourth harpoon. Everybody watched as the harpoon pole went the distance, struck the fish, and came to a stop halfway out of the water. Now we had four darts and four lines on him. Each time I hit him with a harpoon, the fish sounded, peeling off almost all of the line again. Nobody could hold onto the hot line as it sizzled through their hands.

When the fish came to a stop and we could resume pulling, I told the guys, "Everybody pull as hard as what you want. We have nothing to worry about now because we have four darts in him." I also told them all to hold on once I struck the shark with the fifth harpoon. "He shouldn't be able to sound again because we'll have a lot of pressure on him this time and the only thing that he can do now is roll."

That's exactly what happened once I hit him with the fifth harpoon. Everybody hung on and the fish couldn't run anymore. Instead, he went into a roll like all sharks do when they're tired and can't run.

After five harpoon darts and five hours of pulling our shoulders out of place, we had stopped him. Now he was a giant mess: all tangled up in the harpoon lines. We didn't have much trouble putting a tail rope on the shark to tow him home. It took us another hour of untangling lines and putting things back in place before we could start home.

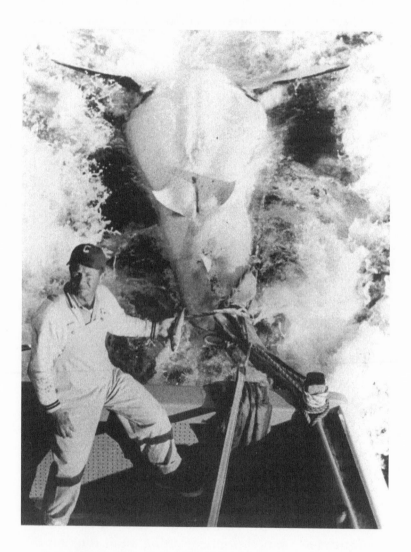

Towing the 4,500-pound fish home. My mate is holding up
a mackerel for scale.

By the time we towed him back to Montauk, it was late in the day. We had started this fight around noontime and it was just about dark when we got in. With no scale or any lifting place, we had to drag him up on the sandy beach just inside the rock pile of the inlet, close to Gosman's Restaurant.

Alex Joyce, a friend of mine who ran a landscaping business in Montauk, was there at the time with his big flat-bodied truck. Alex offered to pull the white shark up on the sand. He put a rope on its tail and pulled until he got the shark half out of the water. Though his back wheels were on the blacktop road, they were spinning, which meant Alex didn't have enough power to pull anymore.

"I'll go home and get my small bulldozer," Alex said. "Be right back."

It didn't take long before a crowd of onlookers gathered, gawking at the fish. A few daring teenagers waded knee-deep into the water, walking out to where the fish's head lay. When I saw this, I yelled at them, "Look out! The fish might still have some life in him!" I had no sooner gotten the words out of my mouth than the white shark showed signs of life and started to roll over. Luckily, the teenagers were able to jump out of the way.

After this, I ran to the boat and got my .30-caliber carbine rifle. On the way back, I loaded the clip of fifteen shots into it. Then I pushed my way through the crowd, saying, "Excuse me, can I get through?" They halfheartedly moved so I could pass. As I reached the shark's head and watched his jaws slowly opening and closing, I threw the first round into the chamber, took the safety off, and started firing into the back of the fish's head. BANG! BANG! BANG! I stood about a foot and a half away from the shark's head while I was shooting, and because it was getting dark, everybody could see the streak of red and blue flames discharged from the muzzle blast. I soon had all the room I needed! Everyone was startled by the gunshots and they stampeded up onto the beach where they stopped, turned around, and continued watching the circus that was going on.

By this time, Alex had returned with his bulldozer which he ran all the way down the sandy beach and then attached a short chain from the shark's tail to the dozer's bucket.

He lifted the bucket and the fish halfway into the air, dragging the rest of the shark's body through the sand, until he had the fish far enough up on the beach. Now it was safe for everybody to walk around the shark and take pictures.

Because it was getting dark, I had to rush and cut out the shark's jaw; otherwise, souvenir hunters would start breaking off teeth with their fish pliers. The mate and I took measurements because there was no scale. We got the length of seventeen and a half feet and a girth measurement of thirteen feet. Basing it on length and girth measurements, I figured out the shark's weight to be at least 4,500 pounds. Many magazines later questioned the weight of this shark, but Dr. Perry Gilbert and other experts verified that a seventeen-and-a-half-foot fish could weigh over four thousand pounds, especially one with a thirteen-foot girth. Even the *Guinness Book of Records* acknowledged this fish as one of the biggest white sharks taken commercially.

My customers were anxious to see what this fish had eaten, so I opened the shark up with a six-inch fillet knife to see if there were any arms or legs in him, but his stomach was empty. He had apparently ejected everything he'd eaten while we had been towing him backward for three hours. That night on the beach, I cut out the white shark's large jaw and it just fit into a wooden fish box that was twenty inches wide by thirty inches long by eighteen inches deep.

This was a good place to store it overnight, locked in the cabin. I could clean up the jaw the next day. (The following season, I had the shark's head mounted by Pflueger Taxidermy of Florida.)

Me, looking through the jaw of the 4,500-pound fish.

After I let the fish lie there overnight, somebody had snuck down the beach and cut the tail off. I was mad because I wanted to have the tail mounted along with the white shark's head and put them on display at the Sportsmen's Shows that I participated in.

My mate, the jockey, must have quit the next day; he didn't show up for work any more: it's a lot harder hanging on to a 4,500-pound white shark than it is hanging on to the reins of a race horse! And it's even harder hanging on to a good mate.

The next day, on my way out of the inlet with another party, I pulled the wooden fish box that held the jaw out of the cabin, and brought it into the cockpit for the passengers to look at. I lifted the jaw out of the box, laid it on the deck, and told my party, as I stepped into the opened jaws, "Look, he's big enough where he could swallow me whole." Then, while standing inside the jaws, I asked two customers, one on each side of me, to reach down with both hands and lift the jaws up, past my shoulders and over my head. After they had pulled the jaws over my head, they laid them, opened, back down on the deck, and I announced to the amazed party, and partly to myself, "That was a dumb trick to do. I wonder if he still has any muscle reaction left in the jaw."

Because I had cut the jaws out hurriedly the night before, some muscle and meat remained, especially down by the hinges that connected the upper and lower jaw. I took out my sheath knife and raked it across the muscle. Suddenly, the shark jaw showed signs of life. The giant "bear trap" began closing; everyone stood there wondering how far it would close, but it stopped midway, then fell open again.

As time went by, all I had left as proof of this fish's capture was the head mount and a couple of black-and-white Polaroid pictures that some little old lady had shot on the beach just before dark. A year later, the mounted head arrived from the taxidermist's in a large, and I say *large*, wooden crate. Now I had to find a place to store it between Sport's Shows and TV appearances, and suddenly, the answer came to me.

The 3,000-pound great white shark that we caught on June 1, 1960, off the bathing beach of Amagansett, Long Island. This fish helped inspire the movie *Jaws'* sensational shark-attack opening scene, off the fictional summer resort of Amity.

Mate Stanley Lennox [*left*] and I alongside the 3,500-pound white shark. We caught this fish on July 5, 1960.

Pete the bartender had recently leased *Salivars'* dock restaurant and bar; he had the room to display the head mount. We struck an agreement: Pete could display it year round at *Salivars* except for times when I needed to use the mount temporarily for the New York Sportsmen's Show and for any TV appearances I might make. And so I struck a deal with Pete, selling him the 4,500-pound white shark head mount and a half dozen small mounted sharks.

Years later, after I retired and had spent several years in Hawaii, I was asked to return to Montauk in 1998 for a month as a fish guide on one of the charter boats. The first morning I walked down the dock, my old buddy Pete, carrying a container of coffee, strolled out of his restaurant. Grinning widely from ear to ear, he handed me the coffee and said, "Welcome back to Montauk!"

Absence makes the heart grow fonder, I suppose. From bum to legend in less than a decade.

Over a Barrel

Back when I was getting started in this wacky business of shark fishing, I thought I had to do what my paying customers wanted: "Your wish is my command, Sahib," so to speak. For instance, when a big white shark showed up in those early days, and the party said, "Harpoon it," I didn't have much choice. They had me over a barrel, so to speak.

One fish that started some controversy was a two-thousand-pound white shark that I had to harpoon at my customers' request (demand).

"He won't take a bait," I told them, after trying to bait that fish time and again.

"HARPOON HIM! GET HIM ANY WAY YOU CAN BECAUSE WE WANT HIS HEAD TO BE MOUNTED AND PUT IN OUR LOCAL BAR," they yelled. Despite their words, I tried to bait him one last time, and then I had no choice: we had to harpoon him. The white shark was harpooned and flopped on the dock. The customers had their photos taken while sitting on top of the fish, and the crowd of head hunters on the dock screamed, "Kill all the man-eaters! A dead shark is a good one! Hurray for Mundus! He's killing all the sharks! It's safe to go into the water."

Even before the movie *Jaws*, out of a hundred people, there was always a small handful that said, "The shark is a good guy. He is cute. He is cuddly. He is loveable and wonderful and wouldn't hurt a flea."

The nuts not only hollered at me from the dock, they even hollered at me over the telephone . . .

One evening the phone rang, and this little old lady asked if she could talk to Frank Mundus. I told her I was "it." In a squeaky voice, she asked if the two-thousand-pound white shark that I harpooned on June 26, 1980, had been attacking the boat. I said, "No, ma'am."

Then she wanted to know why we had killed it. I told her that my customers had wanted it for a trophy and I tried to explain my position in this mess; that I was supposed to try and do what the customer wanted. But there was no explaining this to her. Gasping between words, she screamed:

"YOU'RE NOTHING . . . NOTHING BUT A HIRED KILLER!"

At this point, because I couldn't make the lady understand the situation, my thought was to feed her own words back to her. Besides, my supper was getting cold on the table! So I said, "Yes, ma'am, I'm nothing but a hired killer, ma'am, and if you want anything killed, ma'am, call me up. I will kill anything for money, ma'am. I know you've got my telephone number, ma'am, so give me a call any time you want anything killed, ma'am."

That little old lady got so mad at me twisting her around, that her final words before hanging up were, "I hope you . . . I hope you . . . I hope you get harpooned up the ass!"

She had called up to aggravate me, but when I was done with her, she was the one who probably had to take five Valium before going to bed!

One We Let Swim Away

Everybody has heard stories about the one that got away, but how much truth was there in those fish tales? Were the details stretched? Was the fish blown up to make the story better (as in *Jaws*)? Well, this story is true and it happened on a five-day trip aboard the *Cricket II*, during the last week of June 1977. We were northeast of a place nicknamed the "dumping ground," which is located south of Martha's Vineyard, where the military dumped unexploded ammo after World War II.

The crew was yours truly and his mate, Dickie Bracht. Robert Boggs, the writer of *Monster Man*, was the angler. To complete our bunch of idiots, we had to have somebody to shoot f-11 at 100. This is where Gordon Rynders came in. Gordon was one of the top ten news photographers who worked for the *New York Daily News*; he came loaded for bear, although I told him we were going for white sharks.

And so we loaded up the *Cricket II* with all the things necessary for a four-day trip. To spend four days at sea, sixty miles offshore, with two extra people aboard, takes plenty of preparation. I won't go into the cans of beans and soda department, but I'll give you some idea of the amount of fuel and ice involved—some things are more precious than the food, if you don't think so, then try making that propeller turn with beans! We strapped two extra drums of the precious liquid on board, then put five cakes of ice in a large box in the center of the cockpit, and headed our crab car toward the horizon.

On the first day, the weather treated us like we were tourists; it was flat calm all the way out. We were just about there when we came upon a basking shark, sunning himself on the surface. He was a small one, just under one thousand pounds, but he sure was the right thing to have hanging around in case Mr. White Shark showed up. For some reason, all the sharks like the meat of the basking shark. We harpooned him and dragged him for the last couple of hours. This slowed us down because all of his bulk was in the water.

Gordon got some good shots of the basking shark with his "chicken pole," an underwater camera. The chicken pole was Gordon's own invention. It was a pole with a camera on the other end and it had a trigger and a turning knob which let you shoot the picture as far underwater as you could push the six- to eight-foot pole. Gordon nicknamed it a chicken pole because if you weren't chicken, you would go over the side to shoot your own pictures!

As the *Cricket II* came galloping over the horizon, the sun was sinking on the other end. We picked our spot and camped there for the night. This place would be our home for the next four and a half days. On deck, Gordon was busy with his camera gear, Boggsy "Old Boy" was cutting up bait, Dickie was working on some last-minute tackle, and I was busy chewing on my toothpick, looking into my crystal ball.

We didn't have to wait long before we had our first few blue sharks show up under the boat. This was a good sign because the more blue sharks you have show up, the better your chances are of finding "Big Daddy." As the day drew to a close, we were getting more and more of the blue sharks under the boat; the water was so thick with them, that it seemed like there was hardly enough water for these fish to swim in.

We had to hang the basking shark as high out of the water as we could so the blue sharks wouldn't pick him clean like a bunch of piranhas would. This was a job in itself. The *Cricket II* has a center mast that we pick up our fish with, like the rest of the boats do when they use their gin poles (side poles). The only difference is that our mast is twenty-five feet above the water. This gives us a better height and we can pick up more weight.

So we hauled the shark up as high as we could, but his head and gill plates were still in the water. The blue sharks moved in and started to tear into him almost as fast as chickens pick up corn. There was nothing we could do about this.

If they wanted to make pigs out of themselves, we couldn't stop them. There were so many blue sharks that when one raised his head out of the water to take a bite of basking shark, another blue excitedly bit into him, as if to say, "Get out of the way—I want a bite!" It wasn't the kind of bite you would imagine during a feeding frenzy (something I have never seen), but more like a hickey or a tap on the shoulder; when these blue sharks bit each other on the neck, back, and gill plates, their teeth did not pierce one another's skin. They just made scratch marks.

The blue sharks were fighting so hard toward the end that you could see some of them swimming around under the boat with scratches all over their body from nose to tail.

The first night was perfect. The moon was full and the ocean was flat enough to play marbles on. About midnight, I saw a sight I had never seen before and wished I could have captured it on film. The full moon was lying directly in the path of our slick and it gave me the impression that I was chumming up the man in the moon. The moon illuminated the water so much that almost any fish that came to the surface could be seen. Meanwhile, the blue sharks had bitten their way up to the basking shark's stomach, in spite of how high we had him hanging.

Then the liver broke open and floated on top of the water like a giant marshmallow in your hot chocolate. The first shark tore into the liver only to have it burst into fifteen or so floating pieces as it is so soft. Fifteen sharks hit those fifteen pieces and they busted them up again into more pieces; and so it went on, until the surface of the water, for about a square city block, was a mass of thrashing, eating blue sharks. All this happened directly in the path of the full moon.

The sound effects from all these sharks on the surface splashing all at once, sounded like a heavy hail storm. I woke everybody up to see this amazing event because this was something I had never seen before.

On the second day, the weather had changed somewhat. Gordon walked around with a camera in his hand, waiting for action, while Boggsy sat in a corner, perhaps silently reminiscing about his brush with death aboard the ill-fated Italian luxury liner, *Andrea Doria.*

On July 25, 1956, Boggsy, a young boy at the time, had been a passenger along with his mother and father, when the ship was struck by the Swedish liner *Stockholm.* Although about fifty passengers perished in this disaster, almost two thousand were rescued by the *Stockholm* and the *Il de France*, which arrived shortly after. According to Boggsy, he was in his parents' stateroom at the time of the collision, while his mother and father were up on deck.

The decks were soon awash in the passenger quarters and Boggsy told me that he remembered his mother rushing in to take him up on deck. He recalled the boat listing and the panicked passengers running around. His mother and father were separated in the chaos and placed on different lifeboats. Boggsy and his mother were put into one of the first lifeboats and were later reunited with his father at the dock. Ironically, the *Andrea Doria* went down in about the same area where we were now fishing twenty years later.

The highlight of the second day was cleaning up after breakfast! I had made the boys some ham and eggs, and when we were finished, I went to wash the frying pan by simply reaching over the side and splashing it around like I have done plenty of times in the past. This time was different, however, because I couldn't get the frying pan into the water without three or four blue sharks grabbing at it all at the same time.

The lower end of the basking shark carcass had been eaten up so high during the night that the blue sharks couldn't get any more to eat. So by daylight, they were snapping at anything they could. This frying pan scene was so funny that Gordon shot a few rolls of eight-millimeter movie of it. The rest of our time was spent looking down at all the blue sharks, and as the day wore on, more came. Eventually, we caught four or five blue sharks and hung them overboard for teasers in case a white shark showed up.

To keep all of these blue sharks interested, every three or four hours we would lower the basking shark down to the water's edge where the blue sharks would cut off another six inches or so, just like you would remove slices of baloney. These sharks even preyed on the blue-shark teasers. Every so often, we would have to replace the carcasses as there would be nothing left of them except the tail and tail rope.

Halfway into the third day, Dickie saw what he thought was a small white shark, way back in the slick, under all the blue sharks. We had to gamble and lower the basking shark into the water, in hopes that it would make the white shark come close to the boat and feed.

With all those blue sharks, it was impossible to get a bait down past them. The trick is to try to get the white shark as close to the boat as you can, then drop the bait right into his mouth. Dickie's white shark turned out to be a red herring, or rather, a dusky shark. We got a good look at it when the fish came up close to the boat.

It was close to 2:00 a.m. the next morning when Boggsy Ol' Boy was on deck. Like an ocean-going shepherd, he was feeding his flock of blue sharks. We had all taken our turn on watch, chumming and keeping the blue sharks interested. Now everybody else was in the sack, doing what we do best, when I heard Boggsy say, in a clear loud voice, "Frank, he's here. Here he is!"

I jumped out of the bunk and spun around to look out into the cockpit. I saw Boggsy standing there with the chum ladle in his hand, his outstretched arm frozen into position. The worried look on Boggsy's face told me the whole story, the same story I have seen on other people's faces when they come in contact with a two-thousand-pound fish. Before I could get one boot on, Boggsy said to me, "Wait a minute, wait a minute, I might have been seeing things."

"No way," I said to him. "You saw him; I could tell by your reaction; Cecil B. DeMille couldn't have taught you how to act any better. He *is* there."

In a flash, I could foresee the drunken fire drill that was going to take place in the next few seconds. And I made sure I was already on my way out of the cabin before I lit the fuse that set off the panic bomb. As I emerged from the cabin, I hollered, "Let's go, Dickie. He's here! Get Gordon up." Seconds later, Dickie and Gordon were rolling around the cabin, fighting for their clothes, while Gordon was trying to figure out how he got into this mess in the first place.

When I got out on deck, Boggsy was still mumbling something about how it might all have been his imagination. About that time, I looked over the side to see Boggsy's "imagination" making another pass under the boat. Turning to Boggsy, I said, "Here comes your imagination again!"

The fish was a white shark in the two-thousand-pound class and he was in no hurry to go anyplace; the blue sharks knew this also. The blue sharks' behavior—in particular their slow body movements—signaled that these fish were unafraid of the white shark because they knew he wasn't hungry. They continued to swim around, picking up pieces of the chum.

Because of its large girth, I guessed this white shark was a female. Most male white sharks are thin, but every once in a while, you'll find a heavy one. The blue sharks continued to let her swim in and out. This proved to me that she was not hungry and that they were unafraid of her. I have seen a lot of these big brutes emerge from nowhere, pass under the boat, and disappear again just like they were phantoms. Some white sharks are so big and so slow that you can't see them swim at all when they are not hungry; plus the fact that they don't make a sound and don't leave any footprints! Well, not the footprints that you are familiar with; but if all of a sudden you see this large whirlpool effect on the surface without seeing a fish, there's no doubt about it that there is a white shark down deep that almost surfaced and then went back down again in a hurry. The churning mass of water left behind is what I call a footprint.

It's a funny feeling to have a fish that big pass right under your feet. The cockpit of the *Cricket II* is deep, and when you are on deck, you're only standing about six inches above the water. Sometimes you get the feeling that the dorsal fin, as high as it looks, will cut one of your feet off as it glides beneath the boat.

All night long, the white shark came and went. And all night long, she refused to eat any of the blue-shark teasers we had hanging from the boat. Meanwhile, the blue sharks continued chewing on these dead sharks. From 2:00 a.m. till daylight, the white shark stayed with us. Most of the time she was barely visible, hanging back in the slick, out on the edge of the deck lights.

We had a large bait ready, thirty pounds of blue shark fillet, but couldn't throw it over the side on account of the hungry blue sharks. Without warning, she appeared and came zooming in with her pectoral fins outstretched. We thought she was hungry and I threw the bait overboard. In seconds, four or five blue sharks were chewing and eating it. I quickly pulled the bait up before we hooked a blue shark with it.

The white shark was gone.

We were down to our last can of chum and our last hour of fishing: we had a long trip home ahead of us. If I hadn't had a party waiting for me at the dock, we could have stayed longer. It was shortly after daylight that she really put on a show for us, kind of what you would call a grand finale. We could have harpooned her at this time, but from the start, Boggsy and I agreed that if we found a white shark during our trip, it would be a rod-and-reel fish or nothing at all. No harpooning.

She came straight up from the deep, and headed toward the blue shark that we had hanging from the stern cleat. The white shark was in no hurry. She very casually opened her mouth and grabbed the blue shark by its middle. All in the same, slow movement, she turned the blue shark sideways and looked straight up at us, with the blue shark's head sticking out of one side of her mouth, its tail sticking out of the other, like a dog with an oversized bone. The way she was lying there motionless, not even blinking one of those beady black eyes, was creepy.

If that fish could talk, she would have said, "If I were hungry, all I have to do now is bite your blue shark in half." The muscles in the side of her face were barely flexing. Then she shook her head slightly and spit out the blue shark, like you would spit out a chicken bone, as much as to say, "I told you I was not hungry."

Now she turned toward the bow and headed for the bottom. The only damage that she did to that 150-pound blue shark was to barely puncture its skin with her three-quarter-inch-wide teeth marks.

Everybody stood and watched that beautiful beast swim away for the last time. I could have cheated and harpooned her, but why? The game was played fair and square by both of us and I had lost. I was just thankful to have had the chance to play the game and I hope that someday you too will be able to say that you let a big one swim away.

Peter Gimbel and the Shark Cage

My first introduction to the explorer and adventurer Peter Gimbel was in the mid-1960s at Gosman's Dock in Montauk when he walked up the dock and asked me about the shark cage that my customers and I had invented. Pete was young and wiry-looking; and after talking to him for five minutes, it didn't take me long to figure out that he was highly intelligent and very knowledgeable about diving. Although the name Gimbel rang a bell, it wasn't until a while later that someone told me Pete was related to the Gimbels of department-store fame in New York.

I told him the shark cage was up behind my house if he wanted to look at it; the cage had been there for a year and was buried in weeds. It had been made of tubular steel bars for ease of transportation, but was now gathering rust. Some of my customers who wanted to take underwater photographs of sharks asked me if it was feasible to build a shark cage whose top, when dropped overboard, would be held at water level. The cage would hang off the side of the boat so they could step off the boat and into it.

"Sure," I said. "Why not?" and I drew a sketch on a piece of paper and handed it to them. A month or so later, these customers showed up on their next charter with a cage on a trailer. We suspended the cage from the starboard side of the *Cricket II*, and when we got to the fishing grounds, we lowered the cage into the water with our block and tackle, holding it at water level.

This first shark cage and all the cages thereafter had many of the same features that my prototype had: a square cage with a hatch on top. The cage was good for what they wanted, but it was big and clumsy and hard to transport back and forth on their trailer. Therefore, after a few trips, these customers wanted to know if they could store the cage in my backyard.

One year later, I dug it out of the weeds for Peter Gimbel. Pete said that the idea was good, but my cage needed many minor modifications, as did the first airplane or automobile.

The first time Pete used the cage, when it was tethered to the boat, he commented that it moved up and down too erratically, making it hard to take pictures. On Pete's next attempt to modify the cage, he brought out two thirty-gallon oil drums and strapped them on top of it. That didn't work either because he still had an unsteady underwater platform in his cage to stand on for picture taking.

Pete's next step was to clamp on two hand winches, which held fifty feet of cable, inside the cage. The cables were secured to the oil drums on the surface. Now Pete could lower the cage down to a depth of fifty feet. He thought that by going down fifty feet, the depth would smooth out the bumpy ride; however, the cage was still attached to the surface and its occupants would be at the mercy of the waves lifting and dropping.

We also attached two ropes to the cage so it could be adjusted in and out of the chum slick to wherever the sharks were. But this still was no good.

Undeterred, Pete said he was going home to build a lighter smaller cage that was big enough for two photographers. Next season, he showed up with a cage made of welded aluminum tubing. And for buoyancy, he had poured Styrofoam into the six-inch aluminum pipes that went all around the top. Pete's new cage had a hand-operated air box on the top that could be filled or dumped to allow the cage to go up and down just like a submarine. He had also added air tanks to the corners of the cage to supply this air box. For any emergency, Pete had a thirty-five-pound block of lead for ballast. For a swift ascent, the lead block could be dropped through a hatch in the bottom of the cage.

All that season, Pete and his diving partner, Mike, made many trips with me on the *Cricket II*, testing the cage in all kinds of weather. Pete was a perfectionist and was still not happy with the manual air control because it required continual monitoring. Only one photographer could take pictures while the other had to constantly attend to the air-control system. It had taken Pete four painstaking years of research to get this far with the cage.

Rising to the challenge, again, away he went that winter and returned the following season with an automatic control for the air box, operated by twelve flashlight batteries. Now the cage could be taken down to any depth and held there automatically, while both photographers concentrated on their work. Pete and Mike could even leave the cage for fifteen minutes or so and it would stay at the depth where they left it.

After Pete had tried out the shark cage quite a few times and was happy with it, he detached the safety lines. It was now free floating, able to rise and go down under its own power. Finally, after five years, the cage had been perfected.

Now Pete wanted to swim outside the cage to shoot some sixteen-millimeter footage of it. He came up on the flying bridge one day, on our way out to the fishing grounds and said, "I want to try something new today, Frank, and I want your opinion of it."

I had known Pete for five years and he had always asked my advice regarding particular situations. He had never given me an argument or an order. If my answer was, "No, I don't think you should try that today," he would ask, "Can you give me a reason?" Sometimes my answer would be, "No. I just don't feel right about this particular thing." With that answer, Pete would say, "OK," and walk away happy, trusting my instincts.

"I know you want to try something new, Pete," I answered.

"How do you know?"

"You've got a two-man cage down there in the cockpit and three divers. The way I look at it, you want to swim outside the cage, don't you?"

"That's right," Pete said. "Do you think that the sharks will bother me?"

"I don't think that the blue sharks will bother you at all," I said. "The best way to find out is to put you overboard with only your wet suit on so you can swim around the first blue shark that comes up to the boat." I told him to stay as close to the boat as he could so that I would have a good shot at the shark with my .30-caliber carbine.

"My only concern is if I moved my hand in the direction of the blue shark to protect myself and you shoot simultaneously, would you accidentally shoot me in the hand?"

I reassured Pete that I had been doing a lot of testing, shooting at blue sharks on the surface, and watching their reactions.

"First, I threw a beer can or rag soaked in fish blood into the water; then, when the sharks got close to it, I dropped a .30-caliber bullet three to five inches in front of the shark's nose, and the concussion from the bullet hitting the water would make the shark come to a complete stop. Then it would go to the right or to the left. If I tried to hit the shark for a one-shot kill, I had to hit its backbone. If I missed the backbone, the shark could spin around in circles and possibly hurt somebody."

Soon, our first visitor showed up, a small blue shark. Pete went overboard in his wetsuit and snorkel, and stayed close to the boat like I had told him to do.

The blue shark came up slowly, straight toward Pete. Pete raised his hand and waited until the blue shark was close enough to touch. Then he slowly lowered his hand, took the blue shark by the nose, and gently turned him to the left. With his right hand, Pete reached out and took hold of the blue shark's dorsal. Now the fish was facing away from Pete, he let it go and watched it swim leisurely away. After a minute or so, the shark returned and continued nibbling on the chum.

"You were right," Pete said, as he climbed back on board. "Those blue sharks act like puppies."

We were both satisfied with the results of this experiment. Peter Gimbel was the first man that I know of who purposely put himself in the water to see what a shark would do. Later that day, as Pete stood next to me in the *Cricket II*'s cockpit, I proved to him by shooting in front of a blue shark that was swimming on the surface, how I could make a shark stop dead in its tracks and turn to the left or right when I dropped the bullet in front of its nose. Nowadays, when you are watching TV and you see sharks swimming around divers, you might think nothing of this until you asked yourself the question: Who was the first man who intentionally went into the water with sharks to see what would happen?

Fishing with Pete Gimbel that last season was hard on my nerves: I carried the full weight of responsibility for Pete's personal safety. In all kinds of weather, the cage would go overboard; and every day, Pete got braver and braver, with more and bigger sharks. My job was to follow the air bubbles from the submerged cage. I was stationed up on the harpoon pulpit, armed with my .30-caliber carbine, directing the boat right, left, or straight ahead, while my mate Dickie steered the boat at idling speed.

When the cage began rising to the surface, I stopped the boat so that the cage could come up in front of me. This gave me a forty-five-degree angle where I could see everything that went on. The only time I could protect Pete when he was swimming around outside of the cage was when he came to the surface. Only once, out of all the times Pete and his buddy went down in the cage, did we have a close call with the sharks.

On this particular day, August 25, 1965, it was flat calm, and I could see down deeper than in rough weather. We tried counting the amount and kinds of sharks swimming around. It was a mixed bag of large blue sharks, some in the three-hundred-pound class; half a dozen small blue sharks; and three or four duskies in the five-hundred-pound class. There were also some small brown sharks and a small tiger shark. Pete was swimming around in this mess, when all of a sudden a three-hundred-pound mako shark breached clear out of the water between the cage and the boat. Seconds later, Pete stuck his head out of the water and announced to me in a very calm voice, "Mako in the slick, mako in the slick!" But before I could answer, Pete went back under.

There was very little wind that day and the underwater current was slow, making it hard for Dickie to maneuver the boat and keep it in position when the cage came to the surface. I was standing on the pulpit when the cage surfaced. As it came up, so did Pete. He was outside it, facing my right side, about two and a half feet from the cage.

Mike was still in the cage. All at once, three large blue sharks appeared. One headed straight toward Pete. I wasn't worried about this one, because Pete had seen it and was getting ready to hit it in the face with his Plexiglas camera casing like he had done in many similar situations.

The second shark was coming in from Pete's left-hand side, and I knew he could not see it because Pete's peripheral vision was restricted by his face mask. The third big blue shark was also coming in fast, directly behind Pete.

All this went through my mental computer, and I only had six to eight seconds to react. I knew Pete was concentrating on the shark that was headed straight for him. I hoped that in one or two seconds Pete would drive that blue shark away by smashing him in the face with his camera casing. I only had time for one shot and had to shoot at the shark that was coming up on Pete's back in the hopes that Pete, on hearing the shot behind him, would spin away from the cage, see the second shark, and hit it in the face, making a double play, so to speak.

When I took the shot, the bullet had to pass close over the top of Pete's head, then hit the water under the blue shark's nose. If Pete had a coffee cup on his head, I would have blown it off. Everything worked great and according to plan. Pete smashed the first shark in the face. I shot, Pete spun to his left, saw the second shark almost up on him, and smashed it in the face too. Pete continued his circle and made another circle for safety's safe, scanning the water for more sharks, before putting his thumb up, signaling, "Job well done."

Meanwhile, Mike opened the trap door on top of the shark cage and stuck his head out of the water. He had not approved of my tactics. In a loud voice he said, "Watch out where you're shooting. You almost hit me!"

I lost my cool for the first time in five years, and screamed back, "Would you rather be shot or bit?"

He replied, "I'll take my chances on being bitten, anytime!"

"You'll never get bit inside the cage. If you wanna take your chances on being bit, you have to get your ass out of the cage!" I yelled. That was it. I realized I had blown my stack. Pete was calm and relaxed. He had appreciated where that bullet went. After they had both climbed aboard, Pete and Mike were standing there, shoulder to shoulder, drying themselves off with towels, when I walked over to Pete and told him to tell Mike that there would be no stray bullets.

"The next time I squeeze one off, you will have a dead shark to take pictures of," I told him.

Mike turned to me, in a sheepish way, and said, "Oh, I was only kidding."

Then I turned to face Mike and told him, very slowly and seriously, "I am *not* kidding."

The next day, we only had three big blue sharks in the two-hundred-fifty- to three-hundred-pound class. We flopped the cage into the water and both Pete and Mike jumped overboard and climbed into the cage. After a while, Pete signaled to me that they had run out of sixteen-millimeter film and so they were coming back aboard. Just at that time, one of the big blue sharks made a pass between the cage and the boat. I took my .30-caliber carbine and made a backbone shot. That big blue shark hardly wiggled. He just sank, very slowly, down past the cage with blood oozing out, right past Mike's face. When they climbed aboard, Mike couldn't help himself, and said to Pete in astonishment, "Did you see that? He killed that big blue shark like he said he was going to do with just one shot!" Mike hadn't thought I was capable of dropping the bullet exactly where it was supposed to go.

That season, Pete made a short documentary that he named *In the World of Sharks*, which he used for bait to chum up finances for a bigger project, the ninety-nine-minute documentary *Blue Water, White Death*. After he had completed *In the World of Sharks*, Pete rented a small movie house in New York and invited many people in the movie business to come and see his underwater documentary.

He wanted to prove what could be done with a new invention, the shark cage. *In the World of Sharks* proved to be a success, and Pete went on to codirect (with James Lipscomb) *Blue Water, White Death*. (Years later, I heard that Pete had offered to direct the movie *Jaws* after he had been approached by Universal and asked to be a technical advisor. Pete declined the job of advisor when the studio turned down his proposal to direct the film.)

Before they began filming *Blue Water, White Death*, Pete visited me sometime between December 3 and 9, 1967, at the Presbyterian Hospital in New York where I was an inpatient. I had been admitted for a punctured inner ear and was undergoing a series of tests.

During his visit, Pete showed me his expense account and told me his backers had given him the green light to go any place he wanted in search of white sharks. "Where do you think we should go to find these white sharks?" Pete asked me. "Durban, South Africa might be the place for you guys to start." I said, and mentioned that in doing the book *Sport Fishing for Sharks*, Bill Wisner and I had done a lot of research work and we had been corresponding with fishing clubs in Durban, South Africa. They had sent us photos of white sharks that they had caught right off the rock pile of an inlet down there.

Pete invited me to go down to Durban with him that winter to help him with the movie, but I couldn't because that was when I had to fish my other boat the *Cricket III* out of St. Maarten in the Caribbean. I had just started a new fishing operation with the *Cricket III* and I had no one else lined up to run the boat and take care of it. So Pete went down to Durban for a month, only to find blue sharks, duskies, and no white sharks. At that time, whaling was still permitted off the coast of Durban, so Pete "rented" (or rather, bought) a dead whale in the hope of raising a white shark, but even that didn't work.

In the spring, Pete returned from South Africa and told me that he had bad luck down in Durban; whether or not it was the wrong time of the year for white sharks, he didn't know. Pete brought his entire film crew to Montauk on March 11, 1969, and they shot 1,200 feet of film while he and I sat beneath the head mount of the 4,500-pound white shark that hung in our local bar, *Salivars*; and we talked about all the white sharks that had been caught, and lost, by the *Cricket II*.

This little scene was going to be the ending for *Blue Water, White Death*, unless Pete got some more funding to try and find a white shark on the Great Barrier Reef of Australia.

As things turned out, he did get more funding, and Pete went to the Great Barrier Reef with Stan Waterman and

Ron and Valerie Taylor, in the hope of finding those elusive white sharks.

It wasn't until after the movie that I got a chance to sit down with Pete again and ask him some questions. One important question was "How long did it take you to raise your first white shark off the Great Barrier Reef?"

He said, "It took us twenty-eight days." Pete went on to tell me how he simulated his own dead whale by having whale oil and blood flown in. All that time he had spent chumming up sharks with me on the *Cricket II* was put to good use, and it was gratifying for me to watch the Taylor's footage of white sharks swimming around Pete's cage. I knew these underwater shots and those of the white sharks feeding on the surface would keep audiences on the edge of their seats because this was some of the first widely-shown footage of great white sharks. *Blue Water, White Death* was released in 1971.

Pete's next adventure was a visit to the North Pole where he tested some new wetsuits for the government by swimming under icebergs and chasing seals around. When he returned to his home in East Hampton, Pete told me that the water at the Pole was very clear and very cold.

Then on August 5, 1963, sponsored by the National Geographic Society, he became an expedition coleader with G. Brooks Baekeland. Their group, which also included Peter Lake and Jack Joerns, intended to parachute out of a chopper and walk down a mountain in Cordillera Vilcabamba, Peru.

No one had ever made the 10,500 feet ascent to the top of this mountain; a couple of expeditions that had started the climb from the base of it had disappeared completely. So Pete and Baekeland attacked the problem in their own innovative way. Pete said that the crew had made sixty-seven practice jumps to perfect their technique before going on the expedition. Their adventure included the descent on foot and an exploration of the surrounding terrain. It lasted eighty-nine days and became a twenty-eight-page photo story in the August 1964 issue of *National Geographic*.

I lost touch with Peter over the years and later found out that he had contracted cancer and died at the age of sixty in July 1987. This planet lost a really good human when Pete left it. He was a fearless, intelligent underwater pioneer.

Tag, You're It!

'Twas at the beginning of the 1960s that I got mad at the government because they were giving out tags for tuna and marlin but none for sharks. So I decided to get all of my customers to write to their members of Congress and make as much noise and stink as they could to get a shark-tagging program started; I thought it would help to find out more about these critters: for instance, where they went to, how far they traveled, how fast they got there, and how long it took them to reach maturity and reproduce.

After a lot of bullshit, the government finally set up a shark-tagging program in 1961. Located at Sandy Hook Laboratory, New Jersey, it was headed by National Marine Fisheries scientist John ("Jack") Casey, and was known as the "Apex Predator's Investigation." An army of volunteers including scientists, commercial fishermen, and sport fishermen such as yours truly, tagged and released a variety of shark species. Marine Fisheries Biologist, Wes Pratt, joined the program in 1968, and Wes told me that the first shark was tagged in 1962, and that in 1966, the research operation relocated to Narrangansett, Rhode Island, and was eventually renamed "Apex Predator's Program." As I write this, Wes and Dr. Nancy Kohler (the present program chief) are busy pulling up my old tag records to discover how many sharks I tagged and released from 1962 through 1991.

When I was tagging sharks, the National Marine Fisheries Service (NMFS) would send me a package of consecutively numbered M tags. Each tag came with an ID card. This numbered card was a blank form that asked for the shark's sex, species, weight, length, and the location where it was tagged. It matched the number on the tag that we stuck into the fish. The card had to be sent to the NMFS address enclosed. This information was collected and saved until someone caught the fish with that tag number.

The *M* tag had a stainless-steel dart head that was attached to a three-inch piece of monofilament. On the end of the mono was a watertight Plexiglas capsule that held the number of the tag and where to send it. The person who caught the fish also had to submit his or her name and address. They had to measure the length of the shark, and if possible, weigh it or give an approximate weight, report the fish's sex, and describe the health of the shark, plus where and when they caught it. These statistics would be compared with the original tag information in the NMFS data banks. Both parties would then be notified of where the fish was tagged and recaptured, how much it had gained in size and weight, and what distance the fish had traveled in that time period.

The tag's dart head is inserted by the tagger into any meaty area of the fish's back, but the fish had to be positioned directly alongside the boat before it was tagged. The shark can be free-swimming close to the boat, or caught by an angler and pulled to the side of the boat. The tag is usually on the end of a six-foot pole so the tagger can reach the fish, and is a harmless device. It probably feels to the shark like a splinter in your finger would feel to you.

According to the National Marine Fisheries' statistics, "Between 1962 and 1995, more than 128,000 sharks of forty species have been tagged and more than six thousand sharks of thirty-two species have been recaptured as a result of the Cooperative Shark Tagging Program (CSTP)" and a 1990 report (which I found on the Internet) from the scientific journal *Discovering Sharks*, pages 87-90, by Jack Casey and N.E. Kohler, stated that the recapture rate for sharks is "approximately 4 percent."

However good this low recapture rate looks for sharks, the truth is that the other 96 percent are not swimming around out there. They are probably lying dead on the ocean floor after having had a hook tear up their stomach lining. If these sharks had been hooked in the *jaw* by volunteer taggers using the Japanese long-liner hooks, I know that there would have been a higher rate of recaptures.

This has been my theory all along: a gut-hooked fish will not show up as a recapture. As far as I know, there has never been National Marine Fisheries (NMFS) documentation of a recapture tag from a gut-hooked shark. The exception would be if the shark is recaptured very shortly after he has been gut-hooked. At this point, he would only be in the hospital, not the morgue. The few tags that the *Cricket II* sent swimming away were on fish that were hooked in the jaw, and our return rate on those few tags has been high.

Just to give you an example, one day, when we got back from a day's fishing, I flopped six blue sharks onto the dock. The customers had finished taking their photographs and the mate was sharpening his knife, getting ready to cut the sharks up, when along came one of those neophyte private boat owners, who had just gotten one whole season of fishing under his belt, and if you let him talk long enough, he would tell you everything he did not know. As he approached the dead blue sharks, he said, "It's no wonder there aren't any sharks left out there," with a self-righteous smirk on his face.

"Why is that?" I asked in a calm voice.

"Because you kill them all!" he said, starting to get excited.

"How do you figure that out?" I replied, raising my voice slightly.

"Because you just killed six and they're lying right there," he shouted back.

About this time, I thought I'd try to educate this person and tell him the fishing facts of life, so I asked, "Were you out there fishing today?"

"*Yes*," he said, "and we tagged *twelve* blue sharks and let them swim away," the guy growled back at me in a know-it-all tone.

"So you tagged twelve sharks, but only about two out of the twelve will survive and be caught again. So you killed ten and I only killed six. But the six that I killed will be utilized: three for the customers to take home and eat, and three for us to use as bait. If there are a hundred boats like yours fishing on one day (and that is a low estimate for the Montauk fishing fleet), and you all kill ten blue sharks because you tagged twelve, that comes to one thousand sharks killed in one day out of one port. If you would all use the Japanese long-line hook, the Gamakatsu, or a circle hook and hook the fish in its jaw, then you can say you tagged twelve fish and that twelve will live to be caught another day," I told him.

Unconvinced, his comeback was, "The hook will dissolve in his gut because the shark has very strong stomach acid."

My final answer sent him away, "The hook will dissolve in the shark's stomach, but how about the long tear that the stomach got when the mate pulled the struggling fish close enough to be tagged? That fish will die before the hook disintegrates."

With this, he gave up and walked away, shaking his head, like a lot of them do when the truth hurts.

My solution (and recommendation) to save as many of these sharks as possible is for the taggers to use a hook that will slide up from the stomach and fetch up in the jaw. The best hooks for this are Mustad's conservation-friendly circle hooks. Nine out of ten times, these hooks will slide up from the insides of a fish and lodge in its jaw and this shark will live to be caught again. As far as size is concerned, you should use a hook that matches the size of your bait. For instance, if you were using a half-pound fish for bait, you would not put the biggest hook that you have in that fish, you would use the smallest hook. But you can use a ten-pound bait with a small hook. Just remember, you can always catch a big fish with a small hook, but it's hard to catch a small fish with a big hook.

Back in the early days of the tagging program, scientists were still learning about sharks, trying to figure out the age of a shark or how long it took them to reach maturity. Every once in a while, one of my customers would ask me, "How can you tell how old a shark is?"

"Cut 'em in half and count the rings," I wisecracked. I said this for years and then it happened: One September, my mate Dickie and I were fishing the Babylon Tuna Club in the United States Atlantic Tuna Tournament (USATT), over at Point Judith, Rhode Island. Every afternoon, when all the boats came into the dock, Jack Casey and his boys from Narrangansett were there examining any and all sharks that were brought in. One day, I was on my boat when Dickie came running down the dock, breathless, and yelling, "Frank, Frank, you've gotta come see this!"

"See what?" I asked.

"Jack Casey is cutting the sharks in half and *counting the rings!*"

"You've gotta be kidding me." I jumped off the boat and ran up the dock to where Jack was cutting up sharks. I found out from Jack that he was counting rings in the high part of the fish's back, close to its head. Sure enough, my stock answer (that I thought was a joke) was no joke anymore. The scientists were cutting them in half and counting the rings!

My chicken-dance routine filled in the gaps between fish.

Magic and Voodoo

I really didn't get that crazy all by myself. I had lots of help from my customers (that is another reason I call them idiots). In the late 1950s, you could find the Cricket II drifting all by herself in that big, blue ocean. This was mysterious to a lot of other fishermen. "Why are they drifting out there? Are they fishing for sharks?" In those days, if you saw a boat drifting, the captain had either stopped for lunch or his vessel had broken down.

Catching sharks was my gimmick, but on the days that we didn't produce sharks, I had to invent more gimmicks to keep the customers happy. My motto was: "Keep the customers amused or keep them confused."

My friend, Gordon Rynders, was one of the first customers to help me get the nonsense started; he created the "chicken dance," supplying me with our first prop, a beaten-up yellow rubber chicken.

If we had a slow day and hadn't seen a shark in a while, I took the rubber chicken by its scrawny neck and jumped and danced around in the cockpit, doing my version of an American-Indian dance. Gordon had access to the *New York Daily News'* sound archives, and he made me a recording of an authentic American-Indian dance to which he dubbed in the sound of real chickens clucking. So I played this on my cassette recorder as I dangled the chicken and danced around on deck. It got to the point where my regular customers would say, "Hey, Frank, it's about time to do the chicken dance, isn't it?"

One morning, I found a dead chicken in our fish box on the boat. It had been put there by an unknown idiot who had fished on the boat *Wahoo*—captained by Roley Clark—which was moored next to us at the dock. Both Chip Edwards (the *Wahoo's* mate at that time) and Roley Clark told me that they did not know anything about the guy except for the fact that he had put a live chicken in their fish box. When they had reached the fishing grounds and opened up their fish box to take out some chum, a live chicken jumped out of the box and flew overboard. I later found out more about this guy from my customers that morning, who happened to be five off-duty New York City cops. As we were leaving the dock, the chicken man appeared and lit an M80 (a very heavy firecracker) and threw it toward my cockpit. Luckily, it overshot the boat, landed in the water on the other side, and blew up. Immediately, I hit the throttle and we got out of there, fast. Soon after, one of my customers came out of the cabin and hollered up to me on the bridge, "Who the hell was that guy?"

"I don't know," I said. It was then that my customers told me that they were all off-duty cops and had been sleeping in their car, waiting for me to come down to the boat, when they had been woken up by gunfire. Moments later, they had seen a man coming over the sand dunes with a smoking .38-caliber pistol in one hand and a dead chicken in the other! The off-duty cops immediately closed their eyes and made believe they were sleeping because they didn't want to arrest him. If they had booked him, they would have had to take him in to police headquarters in East Hampton and lost their day's fishing.

A couple of weeks later, Chip Edwards told me the rest of the story about the "chicken man." Chip found out that the man had shot and killed his father-in-law over the $100,000 in cash that the old man had stashed away at his house. The chicken man took the money, put it in a black garbage bag in a box, and mailed it to a friend in East Hampton to hide for him. When his friend saw all the money, he got scared and didn't know what to do with it. Finally, he threw the bag in the East Hampton dumps. Not long after, the FBI arrested the chicken man and found out about the money. They shut down the dumps and pulled the landfill apart, piece by piece, until they had recovered all the cash. This happened in 1971, and as far as I know, the chicken man is still in the coop.

My regular customers knew that if my chicken dance didn't work, my next line of attack was the skull-and-crossbones ritual. For this, I carried a piece of white chalk and drew a skull and crossbones on the *Cricket II*'s dry wooden decks on days when we had no drift and no fish. I couldn't do the skull-and-crossbones gag on a rough day because the decks would be wet.

After drawing a three-foot-round skull and crossbones on the deck, I would wait for a short while. If no shark came up the slick, I jumped up and down on the skull a couple of times. If that didn't work, after a while, I erased one of the eyes with my foot. Then another eye would go, followed by the nose or the mouth.

If we raised a shark after erasing the eye or nose, this was our signal; and the next time they came, these customers would ask me to "do the skull and crossbones." And one guy would always tell a newcomer, "Wait 'til he does the chicken dance. That'll get us a shark," or "Wait 'til he draws the skull and crossbones on the deck and rubs out the left eye. This is sure to work." Of course nobody actually believed in any of these rituals, but all this nonsense helped pass the time on a slow fishing day.

I also discovered that I could always get people to laugh. When I laughed, so would they. If I walked up to a fisherman whose mistake had cost us a fish, I would never have a straight face. I always smiled and laughed when I approached him, and in a joking tone, I would explain his mistake. This way, it was funny and everybody would laugh; then he would not get embarrassed about his mistake. I found this worked on about 95 percent of the people.

Whenever a party climbed on board the boat, I always had a habit of asking who the boss man was: the big-shot guy everyone always bowed down to, who is never called by his first name. He gets this treatment every day at his job, so when I call him by his first name, "Charlie," "Mike," "Tony," or whatever, he likes this. Once in a while, I even pat him on the back. If he catches the fish, I even give him a bear hug or a handshake, much to the horror of his flunkies, who consider this an outrageous act. For instance, in October 1974, a year before the movie *Jaws* was released, we were making the *American Sportsman* TV program with Peter Benchley. After he had caught a two-hundred-pound swordfish, I yanked the pole out of his hand, kicked him lightly in the ass, and said, with a laugh, "You are supposed to catch sharks, you idiot!"

One of my customers came aboard one day and told me, in hushed reverence, "That guy over there is the big boss for Western Union and we've got to catch him a fish."

So I knew, right then and there, that my usual nonsense was going to go on all day with this fellow human. It did, and then we were on our way home. Everybody had caught a shark and the boss man had a drink in his hand. The time was right for me to turn on my stereo speakers that were hooked up to a cassette player. I put on my favorite calliope (merry-go-round) music and watched as the big boss man started tapping one foot up and down to the rhythm of the music. Then I cranked it up louder and sat down beside him. Suddenly, one of his flunkies came along and pushed his head between us to holler, "FRANK, ISN'T THAT TOO LOUD?"

That backfired because his boss man shouted back, "FOR CHRIST'S SAKE, SHUT UP, CHARLIE!"

The boss was having fun; this is what he was supposed to do. This is what we are all supposed to do.

Fishing Blind

For nonfishermen, a definition of fishing blind is when you put your bait down out of sight, and you don't know what you are going to hook. One of my most unusual charters was that of a blind man fishing blind. Vinny was a man in his early thirties and in good physical condition. He had lost his sight in World War II, and my job was to catch him a mako on spinning tackle for a fishing-magazine photo story. When Vinny climbed on the boat for the first time, he sat on the transom and asked me for a foot-by-foot description of the cockpit. So I told him and he walked slowly around, measuring things off.

Later on that day, Vinny asked me if I wanted a beer and a sandwich. "What kind of beer and sandwiches do you have?" I asked. He named the different kinds of sandwiches and beer. Just to test Vinny, I asked for a roast beef and a Budweiser. He returned with my exact order.

"How did you figure that one out?" I asked.

"You have eyes, but you can't see," he laughed. "The roast beef is wrapped in foil, the chicken is wrapped in paper, the Budweiser is in cans, and the Miller is in bottles."

Vinny sat there, holding his spinning tackle, with his bait in the water where I had put it. Later on, as I walked past, looking down, I saw his bait, and forgetting that he was blind, I said, "Vinny, drop your bait down another fifteen feet. It's too close to the surface." Vinny put his spinning reel in free spool and dropped the bait down to where I wanted it. It was then that I remembered that he couldn't see. "How did you figure out that your bait went down fifteen feet and out of sight?"

"You have eyes, but you can't see," Vinny said again. "At every turn, I can feel the line coming off the reel and that is two and a half inches." Vinny didn't have eyes, but he could see more than I did.

Toward the end of the day, Vinny had a chance at two makos, but both of those fish jumped and spit the hook. As he wound in his empty hook, I told Vinny that this was not his fault. He reached down the leader wire and sadly felt the hook. After that, Vinny put his pole down and sat to one side—he blamed himself and didn't want to fish anymore. I went over and sat down beside Vinny, and whispered in his ear, "If it was your mistake, I would have given you a kick in the ass like I would anybody else. Now, get up and go back to fishing." You could see the smile spreading across Vinny's face because I wasn't giving him the baby routine.

CHAPTER 5

IDIOTS

Why I Called My Customers
Idiots/Idiot Magnet

People ask me for my definition of the word "idiot," so I tell them to look it up in the dictionary. It comes from the Greek word meaning: "private person, layman." My boat is a private-charter boat that takes out the laymen. The modern meaning of idiot is: "person in the lowest class of feeblemindedness; very foolish person." This fits my description of the word because the head idiot lures his feebleminded fellow idiots into going shark fishing! And so I call my customers idiots because they are idiotic enough to climb on my boat and go out fishing with me.

When we first started shark fishing, if you went out for anything other than sharks, many of the boat captains called you a fisherman, but if you went out for sharks, they called you an idiot. When the people who fished on other charter boats asked their captain if he would take them out shark fishing, the captain's answer would be, "If you want to go out and catch that garbage, go out there with that idiot Mundus on the *Cricket II*."

When the charter party climbs aboard my boat, I ask them, "Who is the head idiot?" In my estimation, the head idiot is the person who got all the other idiots together, and it is a high honor to be the head idiot because there can only be one of them, just like there can only be one president.

I wanted to call the *Monster Man* book that I wrote with Robert Boggs, *Idiots I Have Known*, but Boggsy was afraid that this would insult the public and decrease book sales. In my eyes it is an honor to be called an idiot. Anybody that gets insulted by this name tag does not have a sense of humor. I have been called an idiot for a long time, and I must be, to have taken all those other idiots out fishing.

Those over-intelligent, over-educated people who are educated beyond their intelligence are the ones I don't bother calling idiots: they're well beyond the idiot stage, so I call them "intelligent nuts." Seeing is believing, and I tell you, I've seen 'em in action on my boat, displaying their over-education. The word "Why?" is the only word they know. One particular over-educated person asked why when I told him to throw his lure into the water! It would be an insult to call these people idiots: an insult to my idiots! Even my idiots know what happens when they throw their lures into the water.

My Idiot Magnet

On the way home from a fishing trip, during the early years of my shark-fishing career, one of my mates came up to me and said, "You must have an idiot magnet because it looks like all the idiots are attracted to you." It had been a tough day for this mate, idiot-wise.

I responded by looking up at the top of the mast. This made my mate ask, "What are you looking at?"

"I'm looking for our invisible idiot magnet. It must be up there some place," I replied.

We talked and joked about this idiot magnet so much that I had to make one and hang it in the mast. This idiot magnet was made of two-inch wide Plexiglas and was a quarter-inch thick. It was bent into the shape of a horseshoe or magnet, and we painted it black, with white lettering, to read: "IDIOT MAGNET." Frank Borth, the cartoonist who did all the illustrations for the book *Monster Man*, drew a hilarious cartoon of the *Cricket II*, complete with idiot magnet hanging from the mast, attracting all kinds of idiots from every direction.

Whenever any customer made an idiotic remark or did something foolish, the mates and I pointed up at our idiot magnet. The customers' eyes followed the flight of our pointed fingers, then they would see the idiot magnet and laugh.

The Idiot Who Talked To Sharks

As I have said before, white sharks are unpredictable, and so are the idiots who fish for them. You never know what either one of them will do, or how they will do it.

On one trip, we had our usual bunch of tourists out shark fishing, when up came a white shark of around 1,500 pounds or so out of nowhere. Now the usual drunken Chinese fire drill started: the mate began pulling in all the regular light tackle and put it away so he could bring out the heavy fishing tackle to try and catch the white shark with.

Sometimes, I give one of the customers a small job to do. It makes them feel important and helps us out. So I told a customer: "Stand here and chum. Ladle that chum heavy over the side to keep him interested." We always chum halfway up the starboard side, from the middle of the cockpit.

While all this is going on, my job is to make up a big bait, so I'm usually on my hands and knees, sewing together all the small fish to make a big bait. I was almost underneath our chummer, working on the bait, when he began talking to the white shark, in a slow, calm singsong voice, "That's it. Open up your mouth. Here's another ladleful of chum. How's that? Taste good?"

The man was moving in slow motion as he ladled the cups of chum over the side. I did not know what to think. Was he crazy? Drunk? Fooling around?

After I got the big bait put together, I picked it up off the deck; because it was heavy, around fifteen to twenty pounds, I could not pick this bait up by the leader wire. So, all in one motion, I used two hands to scoop up the bait and swung it over the side, dropping it quickly. As the bait was on its way to the water, I saw this white shark lying there vertically, with his head out of the water. His mouth was open and he had chum all over his face! Now I knew this guy wasn't kidding. The shark was eating the chum as fast as the guy had been dropping it into his mouth. When the big bait hit the fish in the head, I know I spooked him because the shark turned quickly on his side and swam away, never to be seen again. I stood there in amazement: fifteen pounds of bait had scared away a big, tough, ugly white shark.

Man over Surfboard

The weather was good to us, the fish were good to us, and believe it or not, the customers were good to us too. It was just one of those unbelievable days. We were on our way home, about six-seven miles off the Montauk Point Lighthouse. One of the party was still awake and he was up on the flying bridge with me, in the middle of a fish story that I had heard over and over again.

He had his nose poked into my right ear, but I was looking straight ahead. By now, I was using the lighthouse as a guide and didn't have to look down at the compass—and then I saw something in the water, almost straight ahead, a shade to the left. As we got closer to it, to me it looked like some kind of a buoy, but there wasn't supposed to be a buoy anywhere around here. This thing came to a point on the top, and now I saw that it was moving!

When we got closer, I could see that it had arms! It had hands! Sure, I said to myself, it was a man lying flat on a surfboard! He had his clothes neatly piled up in front of him and covered with plastic. From a distance, his bundle of clothes had looked like a buoy. The man was lying face down, looking at a built-in compass on his surfboard.

My customer was still telling me his fish story, when I said to him, "Excuse me for interrupting you." He stopped and I said, "Look straight ahead and tell me what you see."

He turned and looked, and said, "My god, it looks like a man on a surfboard!" With that, he jumped straight up into a standing position alongside me.

By this time, I had pulled back on the throttle and slowly came alongside the surfer. He looked up at us, and I said, "How are you doing?"

"Fine," he replied, smiling. "Where is Montauk Point from here?"

I tried to keep a straight face, and said, "Straight ahead. We can see the lighthouse from up here. You can't see it yet because you're too low to the water." Then I said to him, "We're heading in to Montauk if you want a lift."

"No thanks," he said. "That would be cheating."

"Sure you don't want a lift?" I offered one last time. He refused my help again, and I wished him good luck as we pulled away.

By this time, I thought the guy who was on the flying bridge was going to have a coronary.

"Why didn't you pick him up?" he demanded.

"He refused assistance," I said. "There was nothing I could do."

"Why didn't you call the coast guard?" he persisted.

"The coast guard couldn't do anything, either," I told him as he looked back at the man on the surfboard. "That man is the captain of his vessel," I told him, "and he refused help. No one can remove him from his vessel regardless of how small it is. That's the marine law," I said, still trying to make this fact sink into his head.

We found out the next day that the man was attempting to set a record by traveling from Boston to Miami on his surfboard, lying face down and only paddling with his arms. He would pull up on the beach at night time wherever he could. That night, he hit the beach at Amagansett. The light westerly current had pulled him off course by about five miles. I also found out that farther down the line, he had gotten into some kind of scrape or fight in the Carolinas and had wound up in jail for a couple of weeks. Now he had to go back to Boston and start all over again. And would you believe, he did make it all the way from Boston to Miami on his surfboard, but I never found out how long it took him.

Tokyo or Bust!

Most of the time, the summer trade winds blow out of the southwest off Montauk Point. The southwest wind slides up the Long Island beaches until it hits the end of Long Island and strikes the high cliffs at Montauk. This causes heavy gusts as it rips around the Point, yet it can be flat calm five miles or so offshore.

We were on our way home from a fishing trip, and rounding Montauk Point. My cocaptain, Teddy Feurer, was at the wheel as it was my turn to take a nap. I was sound asleep in the bunk down below, lulled by the steady hum of the *Cricket II*'s motor, when all of a sudden, Teddy pulled back on the throttle. Figuring something was wrong, I immediately sprang out of my bunk. When I stuck my head out of the cabin, I saw a young Japanese-looking man standing in the water, hanging on to the side of the *Cricket II*. At first, it looked like he was walking on water. As I took two steps in his direction, I saw the man was standing in a small plastic boat and he began climbing into the *Cricket II*'s cockpit.

"What the hell's going on?" I hollered up to Teddy. Teddy was laughing so hard that he could hardly answer me. So I jumped up on the flying bridge to find out what was going on and where this Japanese guy had come from. Teddy had seen the whole thing and it wasn't very hard for him to figure out that the man had been in trouble. He told me that, apparently, the guy had been playing in his plastic kiddy boat close to the beach and got caught by a gust of southwest wind. He was pushed offshore, away from the lighthouse, so far that he couldn't paddle back.

"If I didn't pick him up, he would never have made it back in that little plastic boat," Teddy said. I didn't have to ask Teddy what we were going to do with this guy because in another half hour we would be back at the dock. I watched the man as he started to let the air out of his stupid kiddy boat. Teddy and I were waiting for him to give us some kind of explanation, but the man said nothing. He continued deflating his boat and began folding it up. It was about then that we figured he couldn't speak a word of English.

By the time we hit the dock, the Japanese man had let all the air out of his plastic boat, and he stood there with the neatly rolled-up boat under his arm. As soon as the *Cricket II* got close enough to the dock, he jumped off. The last we saw of him, he was running down the dock. I just hope he wasn't headed back to the Point!

Portrait of the Artist as an Idiot

I soon found out that my idiot magnet worked overtime, even during the off season. One winter's day in the late 1970s, my phone rang. The man on the other end said he was an artist who was inspired by me to paint a picture of a white shark. He told me he was from Australia and was now here at the Montauk Motel and would very much like to meet me. Because he didn't have a car, I drove into town to pick him up at the Shagwong Tavern. I did not know what this man looked like, but just like in all the best the spy stories, he said he would know me when he saw me from photos that he had seen.

When I walked into the tavern, there was about a half dozen men standing at the bar. One of them immediately put his glass of beer down on the bar counter and walked over to shake my hand. He was a thin clean-shaven man in his forties, and his unruly hair was flecked with grey. After he finished his beer, I drove him up to my house and we sat and talked for a while. And so began a bizarre adventure, full of twists and turns that even had me confused.

He began by telling me all about this painting he was working on which would be finished soon. The man even explained the technique and materials he was using to paint the picture: no brushes, just soft *Q-tips,* and water paint. Once it was done, he would give it to me. This artist asked for $10.00 because he said he was waiting for money to arrive by mail. I gave it to him as I dropped him off at the Montauk Motel, just behind the post office in town.

The next day, he called to say he had gotten his money and wanted to pay me back my ten dollars. So I drove down to the motel. The man gave me my money back and began telling me about one of his sculptures, a marble bust of the mayor of Shelter Island, that he was supposed to deliver to him; somehow, it had gotten lost since his move to Montauk. The artist thought the garbage men might have taken it away in one of the empty cardboard boxes that he had left outside his motel room. I wanted to help him find it and contacted the garbage collector, who said he had picked up garbage from the Montauk Motel yesterday, and had taken it to the town dumps. I drove the artist to the dumps and asked the bulldozer operator to spread out all of yesterday's garbage so we could search through it for that marble bust. This was a cold day and my feet were freezing as we trudged through the semi-frozen garbage and fought off the sea gulls. A couple of hours went by and our search ended in a bust, but not a marble one.

A week later, the artist gave me that painting. It was an accurate rendition of a white shark swimming through the kelp, with a seal clenched between its jaws.

This watercolor painting was in a nice frame and all ready to hang up on the wall. After that day, the artist disappeared and I never saw him again. In the meantime, I had hung the painting in my house. Then a friend of mine, Paul DiAngelo, came to visit. I showed Paul the painting and told him the story about the disappearing artist. Paul looked at the painting and said he had seen it somewhere before, perhaps in a sports magazine. I said, "No, you couldn't have. It's an original work: the only one of its kind."

Paul said he'd look through the piles of magazines he had at home and would let me know if he found it. On Paul's next trip to Montauk, he brought me a sports magazine that had a centerfold-spread photo of that same painting. I researched the sports-magazine artist's name and called him, asking if he had made any copies to sell. He said there had not been any copies made. He had done the painting and the magazine had taken a picture of it for their publication. The mystery deepened.

Where did the guy in Montauk come from?

Who was he?

Where did he get the painting from?

Where did he disappear to?

I think, sometimes, that we are better off not knowing everything. Only one thing is for sure: my idiot magnet still works overtime!

Blood, Harpoon Guns, and Ajax

The name Mundus has become synonymous with sharks over the years, and in the eyes of some dock rats, normal people, and enterprising salesmen, it has also become synonymous with blood, harpoon guns, and a few other things, including (for a short time) a household cleanser.

Some time in 1975, after the movie *Jaws* was released, two guys in their early twenties, dressed in fancy city clothes, walked down the Viking Dock to where the *Cricket II* was tied up. Each had a big grin and an armful of cardboard boxes. They rudely broke into a conversation I was having with one of my intelligent idiot customers on the dock, who I just had out fishing. As they got closer, I could see the white boxes they were carrying were about six inches square and had red lettering that said "Dried Blood."

"Do we have a deal for you, Captain Mundus," one of them said. "Here is some dried blood for you to use and catch lots more monsters with," the other guy said. The fast deal they wanted me to make with them was this: they would give me all the dried blood that I could use for this fishing season, and if I put my name on it, saying how great it was, they could sell it to the other fishermen and would give me a twenty-five-cent return on each box they sold. I suggested that they leave a dozen or so boxes and I would test it out on the sharks, and told them to check back with me in a couple of weeks to see how things were going.

For some reason, when they walked away at a much slower pace than when they had arrived, the two young men had lost their smile. They had probably thought I was going to jump right into the deal and endorse their product, which was in a plastic bag, secured by a tie-wrap inside the box. There were no instructions on how to mix it, or how much to use. The only writing on the boxes was those words "Dried Blood." Don't ask me what this stuff really was, but when I dumped it into a bucket of seawater, it was so finely ground that it went airborne, covering me and my customers and every inch of the cockpit! After that first encounter, we were very careful to pour it slowly into the water, stirring it constantly. I didn't dare use this product without adding it to our regular ground-up chum. We called the dried stuff "hamburger helper."

After a couple of weeks of confusing the customers with this red powder, and not having had a decent mako jump into the boat to get at it, the blood boys returned for my report, and hopefully, my signature, saying I would sponsor the stuff. By this time, I had another thought. I told them I would try it for the rest of the season and keep accurate records, using the stuff every other day. If, at the end of the season, my records could prove we caught more fish on the days that we used it, then and only then would I recommend it to the other boats for their use. By the end of the season, I could not see any difference in the amount or size of fish we caught, so I told the men that I did not want to make money off a product that was not going to work. My reputation was worth more to me than a couple of bucks.

Another time, I was fumbling around on Gosman's dock, while my mate, Dickie, was scrubbing the *Cricket II*'s cockpit down. Dickie's normal procedure was to dump half a cup of liquid Ajax into a bucket of water, and then sud down the whole cockpit to loosen up the fish slime and blood stains. I was standing behind the boat when a man walked down the dock, took one look at Dickie and the cockpit full of suds, and asked me, "Is that your boat?" I said, "Yes, why?" He asked, "Do you use Ajax?"

Ajax was written all over this guy's face, so I told him what he wanted to hear. I said that we used Ajax and that liquid Ajax was the best because it cuts through all the fish slime and blood. It took me a couple of minutes to finish telling him how good it was. Suddenly he said, "I'm with Ajax." I made sure to have a surprised look on my face when I said, "Oh, are you?" Now I waited for some kind of a sales pitch, but never got it. What I got was the complete opposite. The man just asked me for one of my business cards because he said he was going to send me some liquid Ajax. I watched him as he walked down the dock, and I shook my head, mumbling to myself, "One wasted business card," because I never thought I would see anything.

Two or three weeks later, a big truck pulled up on the road that was right behind the boat. The driver got out with papers in his hand, and hollered to me, "Who's Mundus here?"

I said, "I am. Why?"

He said, "I have a drum of liquid Ajax for you. Where do you want it?"

Cautiously, I asked him what the charges were. He said, "None." Then I asked him what the freight charges were. Again he said, "None. Everything is paid for. Where do you want the drum?" I said, "Just drop it right where you are. We'll handle it from here." It was a thirty-gallon drum, so it wasn't that hard for Dickie and me to move. We put the drum of liquid Ajax in my backyard and I brought a bottle of it to the boat whenever Dickie needed some.

For the rest of that season, I kept looking over my shoulder, waiting for the Ajax man to show up and demand some kind of a payoff; but this never happened.The next spring, and the spring after, a drum of liquid Ajax would mysteriously appear by truck. Three years in a row we received a thirty-gallon drum of liquid Ajax, absolutely free. On the fourth year, nothing happened in the spring: no liquid Ajax arrived, but it was toward midsummer when Mr. Ajax walked down the dock again. He asked, "Do you remember me?" I said, "Yes. You are Mr. Ajax!" I couldn't thank him enough for his thoughtfulness. He told me not to worry about it, but he had some bad news for me. Mr. Ajax informed me that he was retiring and couldn't send me any more drums of liquid Ajax. What he had done was to fill up the trunk of his car with regular plastic bottles of liquid Ajax. He gave me these as a going away present and apologized again that he couldn't get me anymore. I waited for him to ask me for something in return, but he never did, so I offered him a free trip on the *Cricket II*, and he refused because he didn't go fishing. I even asked him if he wanted a shark jaw that I had fixed up. He said, "No, not really." I insisted that he take the jaw even if he gave it to a friend. Eventually, I managed to force it on him. I felt awkward, stupid, and very surprised to have somebody give me all this free merchandise and not expect a penny in return.

Every once in a great while, you will find somebody who wants to do something for you and asks for nothing in return. It's just when you think that everybody is out there to screw you that something nice like this happens. Just when I thought it was safe to walk up and down the dock again, along came someone with another shark-catching device for me to test. This happened long before the movie *Jaws*. In those days, it seemed like there was always somebody coming down the dock, wanting to give me something to try out: this time, it was a harpoon gun. Actually, it was two harpoon guns, because this happened twice! Each device varied slightly in its design. I have field-tested just about anything that had to do with catching sharks, and harpoon guns were no exception. The harpoon gun developed from the line-throwing gun used by big ships to pull two ships close together, for instance, when they needed to refuel at sea. The harpoon gun would throw a very light line onto the deck of the other ship whose crew would tie a heavier line to it, then the first boat pulled back the heavy line that had just been attached and made it fast. Now the other boat could put this heavy line on a big winch and pull the two ships together.

One of the guns I tested resembled the harpoon gun used by the character Quint in *Jaws*. The first gun used a light charge and the harpoon line was coiled around a stick, which was pushed into a tube under the gun. When the loading stick was removed, the line stayed coiled within this tube. The second gun used a .45-caliber blank cartridge for a heavier charge and the line was coiled around a wire-tube basket fastened underneath the gun barrel. Both guns had winged harpoon heads and similar breaking points. When a slight pressure was applied to the harpoon heads, such as an attached barrel that was being dragged through the water behind a shark, this pressure alone was enough to bend and break those folding harpoon-head wings and the harpoon shaft would slide out of the fish. (Believe me, I have done this so I know that Quint could never have had that barrel chase.)

I tried out the first harpoon gun on the boat at the dock after the company representative had shot it, reloaded it, and handed the gun to me. Both of us took turns shooting at a beer can floating on the water, fifteen to twenty feet away from the boat. The gun seemed accurate enough as the harpoon shaft slid into the water, about half a foot away from the beer can. Everything looked good and I agreed to test it out at sea. The sales rep reloaded it once more and I stored the gun away on the boat. A few weeks of fishing went by and I hadn't had a chance to try out the harpoon gun.

One day, when it was flat calm and we were drifting and dreaming, waiting for a fish to come along, I remembered the harpoon gun. This would be a good day to try the gun out and show the customers how it worked. I asked someone to throw a beer can off the *Cricket II*'s stern while I stood alongside one of my customers, who sat in the fighting chair in the middle of the cockpit. Taking aim, I fired the gun from where I stood. Everyone followed the flight of the harpoon head, which traveled toward the beer can like an arrow until, in the flash of an eye, the harpoon head came to an abrupt stop and changed direction. That thin nylon harpoon line acted like a huge rubber band, pulling the harpoon head back at us at the same speed it had left the gun. Before anybody could get out of the way, the shaft came tumbling through the air and hit me on the high part of my leg. The good news was that when it hit me, it didn't hit point first! The shaft struck me sideways and fell to the deck. The only thing I got out of it was a bruise. A few inches to the right and the dart would have hit the customer seated in the fighting chair square between the eyes.

I always hate to be the bearer of bad news, but I had to inform the company that their product might impale its users like cocktail olives. The company told me that this could never happen and they had test-fired it numerous times. I gave both guns the thumbs down and returned them to the manufacturers, along with my field-testing reports. If my report was wrong, the harpoon guns would be on the market today, so where are they?

Bonnie and Clyde

You've all heard the joke about the guy carrying a machine gun in a violin case; well, on August 9, 1988, we picked up a last-minute charter from a guy on the dock, "Charlie," a well-spoken man in his forties. Charlie and his girlfriend were both dressed in white nautical clothing: white boat shoes, white slacks, and white shirts. They wanted to go shark fishing, so I told Charlie that I had an opening for an overnight trip the next day. That night, I called my son-in-law, Dale Greene, who is married to my youngest daughter, Tammy, and invited him to ride along. Dale had always wanted to ride along on a shark-fishing trip as an observer, and on this trip, he was about to see something he would never forget.

At 7:00 p.m. the following day, Charlie and his girlfriend walked down the dock. He carried a violin case, and his girlfriend carried a small cooler. As Charlie handed me the violin case, he said, with a grin, "Hang on, it's heavy."

I still didn't know what was in this case. It could have contained anything from a frozen elephant to a contraband chicken! In my business, I think I have seen most everything, and nothing, I thought, would surprise me. However, on the way out to the fishing grounds, Charlie opened up his violin case and showed me what was inside: an authentic .45-caliber submachine gun that was used in the prohibition days! Alongside it lay the round clip that held one hundred shots. This was a real "Elliot Ness special." Both Dale and I saw the tommy gun at the same time. I don't know what was going thorough Dale's head, but I fell in love with this piece of metal. I picked it up, just to say that I had held a submachine gun, and it fooled me because of its weight. After watching *The Untouchables* on TV and seeing how fast those TV gangsters swung these guns around, I now realized they couldn't have been using the real thing. Charlie told me he had chartered the boat especially to see what his tommy gun would do to a shark. He had already found out what it would do to an automobile. Charlie and his friends had gone to a junkyard with an impressive-looking video camera he had rented. They told the junkyard owner that they were making a scene for a TV program that involved shooting up an automobile and would pay him $100 an hour for his trouble.

"Which car do you want?" the junkyard owner asked enthusiastically.

Charlie picked out a blue convertible that was on top of the pile. The junkyard guy took his large fork lift, picked the car off the pile, set it on the ground, and stood back, eager to earn a fast one hundred bucks. Charlie took aim and put one hundred rounds into that automobile in a few seconds. After observing the damage, he paid the surprised junkyard owner $5 because it had only taken a few seconds to demolish the automobile! Charlie's next project was to demolish a shark.

As usual, we got to the fishing grounds around midnight, and it was flat calm: good weather for the fisherman, but lousy weather for shark fishing because we would have no drift and sit in one spot; but like the man said, "You can't have everything." I knew Dale was going to stay up because this was all new to him and he didn't want to miss anything, so I told him to wake me up the minute something happened. I didn't want to miss any of this action either. Around 3:00 a.m., Dale came down in the cabin and woke me up: we had a shark on and Charlie was in the process of catching it. I asked him how he was going to shoot the fish and he told me he would hand the rod to someone else at the last minute. I told Charlie I'd take the pole and see if I could guide the shark in for a good shot, but I didn't have to because the 150-pound blue shark came right to the surface. We could see him well in our deck lights. The shark's dorsal fin was slicing through the surface of the water when Charlie returned with his gun. He walked to the side of the boat and took the safety off.

Firing from his hip, Charlie didn't have to aim; he could follow the trail of bullets as they hit the water. It was all over in a few seconds. Charlie hit the shark with one hundred shots, killing it and blowing the leader wire apart. The fish didn't move a muscle: it just sank with a grin on its face.

Charlie and his girlfriend were happy. They had done what they had come out to do, and as I headed back to bed, I saw them sitting on the motor box, celebrating with their long-stemmed glasses of champagne. I later nicknamed them "Bonnie and Clyde." Next day, they returned home— across numerous state lines—with the machine gun tucked safely away in the trunk of their car.

Of Dock Rats and Gawkers

The worse type of idiots are the dock rats and gawkers. The "dock rats" are people who keep coming back and back and back, asking me the same stupid questions again and again and again; whereas the tourists ask sensible questions and believe my answers. The gawkers are the ones who just stand there, get in your way, and won't move. I ask them to move because I'm putting a fish on the dock and they just stand there and look at you.

I remember one incident where we had returned to the dock with a small mako shark, and I was standing at the cutting board, cutting the shark's jaw out for my customer who had a vacant wall at home to hang it on.

Nearby, my mate was cutting the mako carcass into steaks for the party to take home and eat. We were soon surrounded by a mixed crown of dock rats and tourists. Some people were asking sensible questions: and some were not. After about half an hour of me answering the same questions, everybody should have known them by heart; I know I did, and I was tired of answering them!

My patience was wearing very thin when a man-and-wife dock rat team hit me with another volley of questions that I had just finished answering within their earshot. Then came their pièce de résistance: two last questions whose answers were obvious to almost everybody else, except themselves.

The first, from the male: "What is that you are cutting out, a shark's jaw?"

"Yes," I grunted.

His second question: "What are they going to do with it?"

I grunted back: "Hang it on the wall."

Then the woman echoed, "What is the mate doing, cutting up steaks?"

"Yes," I grunted.

Then she asked, "What are they going to do with those shark steaks?"

I didn't grunt this time. Instead, I turned around and calmly screamed at her, "HANG 'EM ON THE WALL!" One other time, a female dock rat was standing on the dock with her video camera grinding away. As I jumped off the boat and onto the dock, heading for my truck which was fifty feet away, she hollered to me, "Stop! I want to take your picture. Stop! I want to take your picture." I paid no attention to her, climbed into the truck, and put it in first gear. She ran up the dock after me, still hollering "Stop! Stop! I want to take your picture." As I drove away I screamed back at her, "If that thing doesn't take moving pictures, throw it overboard!"

As long as you have a boat and a dock to throw the fish up on, you're going to have dock rats and gawkers. Once I had to stop a near knockabout Three-Stooges-style fistfight between my mate Dickie and a male dock rat. We returned from a fishing trip with a few sharks that we were going to drag up on the dock. There were too many people in the way, so I told Dickie to jump up on the dock first and put the crowd-control safety ropes up. So Dickie jumped up on the dock, took the dock's water hose, and began wetting down the dock so that the fish blood wouldn't stick to it. This one dock rat refused to get behind the rope. He was in his early twenties, pretty well-dressed, with an arrogant attitude and he wanted a free front-row seat for the fish-gutting process. As Dickie waved the hose back and forth, washing the dock down, this dock rat refused to get behind the rope despite the fact that Dickie had asked him to about half a dozen times. I was in the process of stepping off the boat when an infuriated Dickie took the hose and squirted it across the guy's chest. The angry dock rat screamed profanities at Dickie and started moving quickly toward him with clenched fists. At that point, I jumped between Dickie and the dock rat and screamed at the guy, "What the hell's the matter with you?"

"Your mate squirted me with the hose!" he screamed back at me indignantly.

"If you don't get behind the ropes, you're gonna have to contend with me too!" I screamed back at him, and added: "I don't know what you're hollering about." The few drops of water Dickie hit him with had dried up by now. The dock rat looked down at his clothes and saw that all the water spots had disappeared. Then he sheepishly jumped back behind ropes. Before we had crowd-control ropes, the dock rats would stand as close as they could to me while I was cutting up a shark. "Move back a little," I would tell them, "because you're gonna get splashed with blood." And sure enough, as I was cutting a shark open they would get splashed with blood.

Once in a while they will ask me a good question. A lot of the tourists who have seen me walking around in a short-sleeved shirt look at my left arm that is full of scars and pot holes, and ask, "Did a shark get you?" and I always answer them with the truth, "No, a shark didn't get me. I broke my arm when I was a kid." The look on their faces tells me they don't buy it. They want to continue believing that the scars came from a shark bite. I try telling them that if a shark did get a hold of my arm that bad there would be no arm. Another question they ask is, "How many fishermen on your boat got hurt by sharks?" My answer is, "Our accident rate over the past forty years or so has been two broken ankles and three fish hooks in the hand, but don't ask me how many close calls we've had." The two broken ankles occurred as separate incidents and didn't really have anything to do with fishing.

The first happened when an angler decided to try and beat a wave. He ran from the cockpit, heading for the cabin just as the big wave was about to meet the bow head on. His buddy was sitting on an outside bunk. As the angler reached his buddy, the *Cricket II* went up and over the wave while he was still running and in the air. When the boat got over the wave and came to a stop, so did the airborne angler, but only for a moment, then his knee slammed into his buddy's ankle, breaking it. Luckily for us, we were only a short distance away from the dock.

The second broken ankle occurred when a good friend of mine, "Uncle Bud," and a few other friends decided to go out with me on a last-minute full-moon trip. Because this was one of our first trips of the season, we did not have all the necessary equipment on the boat. Each of us grabbed whatever we thought would be needed. Uncle Bud asked if we would need the harpoon. I told him no as this was a night trip. Unbeknown to us, he did bring along the twelve-foot wooden harpoon pole, putting it on the pulpit without tying it down. As the weather was flat calm, I did not know the pole was there because it didn't roll or move until we got to the fishing grounds. We had caught a few sharks. Now it was Uncle Bud's turn. As he was fighting his shark, the fish decided to swim up and around the bow. Walking the fish around the bow with his rod and reel was no new trick to Uncle Bud.

He had done this many times before, so I wasn't worried, but when he walked up on the pulpit, Uncle Bud stepped on the loose harpoon pole and it rolled out from underneath his foot, causing him to fall and break his ankle. Some of my customers had a lot more closer calls, and so did the crew and I.

Most of the danger in shark fishing lies in the final act of landing the fish. After an angler winds a shark up to the swivel that attaches the line to fifteen feet of leader wire, his work is done and ours begins. The mate's job is to pull the fish up with his gloved hands handling the wire leader. One mistake by him can spell disaster. A lot of mates on other boats have gotten into trouble with leader wire, becoming entangled in it. There have been plenty of fingers lost this way. As the mate pulls up the fish, my job is to gaff the shark, using a flying gaff: a detachable hook on a rope which is temporarily fixed to a six-foot pole.

Out of all the close calls that my mates and I had messing with these monsters after the angler had wound one up to the boat, I only remember one bad incident that happened on July 28, 1971. It was a hot summer day and Dickie was drinking a lot to cool off, but unbeknown to me, he was drinking more booze and less soda. Because I didn't notice any difference in Dickie's actions or reactions, I continued doing what I usually do: taking care of the lines and changing the baits in high hopes of something coming up our slick.

BINGO! A decent-sized mako hit. The usual fight between angler and fish went on and the angler won. Mr. Mako was brought up to the *Cricket II*'s transom and was swimming from one side to the other. Now it was Dickie's job to take hold of the fifteen-foot leader wire and pull the fish close enough for me to jam the flying gaff in.

Dickie was supposed to drop the loose wire overboard while I hung onto the flying gaff rope and the thrashing fish. Finally, Dickie had to slide a tail rope onto the shark's flapping tail and then the game was over. But it didn't happen that way. This time, when Dickie was throwing his arms around, hanging onto the leader wire, I lifted the flying gaff up even with the top of the transom; when I began swinging the flying gaff down toward the water, Dickie's whirling right arm struck the sharp point of the gaff head.

"OW! You got me!" he hollered.

I felt the gaff go *CLUNK* and stop as it hit bone. Good thing it stopped there; otherwise, it would have gone right through Dickie's arm. Dickie did not stop pulling on the wire as he had the fish almost up. I planted the flying gaff into the mako, behind the dorsal, and when I spun around, I saw a six-inch jet of blood shooting out of Dickie's arm.

About now, my customers went wild. One loudmouth know-it-all jumped around, screaming in my ear, "PUT A TOURNIQUET ON! PUT A TOURNIQUET ON!"

I politely told him in a loud voice, "SHUT UP AND GET LOST!"

After telling Dickie to sit down on the motor box, I placed my thumb ahead of the cut and searched for a pressure point to stop the bleeding; finding one, I applied pressure to his arm and the flow of blood slowed down to almost a stop. While all this was happening, Dickie calmly sat there like I had told him to. Then I asked Dickie to put his thumb where mine was and continue holding pressure on the artery.

Meanwhile, Mr. Mako was still thrashing around on the flying gaff. I got some assistance from my customers, and together, we put a tail rope on him. Time wise, our day's fishing was just about over, so we cleared up everything, hung the mako, and started for home. When we reached the dock, Dickie was walking around with the big clumsy bandage I had put on his arm oozing blood.

"GET OUT OF HERE AND GO SEE THE DOCTOR!" I yelled to make him listen. I had already called my doctor, telling him what happened and mentioned that Dickie was on his way to the office. Before long, Dickie returned to the dock with a small bandage on his arm, and he told me there was nothing Dr. Livingstone could do: it was a clean cut that would heal by itself. Dickie was lucky that it had been a clean cut. In a few days, he was back to normal again. I had been more worried about Dickie's accident than he was. His injury had been no gaffing matter!

Mr. Banks of America

Mr. Banks and his friends were one of the nicest African-American parties that ever chartered the *Cricket II*. He and his fellow fishermen were true sportsmen. When an entire charter party can go home laughing even after a bad day of fishing or after losing a big fish, this proves it to me.

I will never forget the first trip Mr. Banks took on my boat. It was during the 1960 fishing season. By 10:30 a.m., we had caught our first 150-pound blue shark, and as soon as I had it hanging up by its tail, Mr. Banks turned, and said to me, "Head this thing for Brooklyn."

"What do you mean, 'Head this thing for Brooklyn'?" I asked.

By now, Mr. Banks was jumping up and down with happy excitement. "I want to get this shark hung up in front of my social club before dark. So let's get back to the dock as soon as we can."

Back at the dock, we lost no time, as Mr. Banks's friend, Mr. Beeler (who at three hundred pounds, looked like a retired, straight-faced wrestler), effortlessly picked up that 150-pound blue shark and threw it into the trunk of Mr. Banks's shiny black Cadillac.

I told them it would mess up the car. "You'll never get that fish smell out."

Mr. Banks looked at me with a twinkle in his eye, and said, "That's all right. This is my fishing Cadillac. I have two Cadillacs. The good one is home!"

I found out later that he had even removed the back seat so he could carry bags of fish home for giveaways.

A couple of years later, he sent Mr. Beeler to the New York Sportsmen's show to pick up me and my mate, Gus Rule. Mr. Banks wanted to show us a good time while we were in New York, so he and Mr. Beeler took us on a tour of Harlem. Gus and I still wore our work shirts with the lettering "Monster Fishing *Cricket II*" and I didn't want to embarrass Mr. Banks because I knew we were going to end up in some fancy places. But it didn't bother him. He replied, "If they don't let you in, they don't let me in!" And so Mr. Banks and Mr. Beeler took us on our tour of Harlem. Gus and I were probably the only two white guys at that time who ventured that deep into Harlem. At all the nightclubs we visited, everyone respectfully addressed our guide as "Mr. Banks," and never "Charles."

After our tour, we stopped in at his social club which was lit by a five-foot-long neon sign over the doorway that said BANKS'S SOCIAL CLUB. I found out that membership to this exclusive social club was restricted to people who paid the $100 membership fee for a key to the front door.

When Gus and I walked inside, we noticed a small bar with six stools on the right-hand side of the room. Past the bar, on the left, was a brass hand rail that led downstairs to a complete .22-caliber shooting gallery with ducks and all! You paid $1 to the man at the shooting gallery for ten shots, for this you got a ticket which was redeemed for a free drink upstairs at the bar. So as far as the law was concerned, Mr. Banks didn't sell booze: he gave it away!

After Mr. Banks had shown us his bar and shooting gallery, we had a tour of the rest of his building. In the back was half a dozen coin-operated pool tables. Upstairs was divided into different rooms, and when we walked up to the second floor, I noticed that the first door, facing us, had a four-inch jagged hole in it, just above the door knob. To me, this hole looked like a shotgun blast.

"That hole has all the earmarks of a shotgun," I said to Mr. Banks. He looked at me in surprise (like I wasn't supposed to know) and I could see his answer on its way, so I threw in another question, "Did you get him?"

Mr. Banks's smile turned into a light laugh as he said, "Don't know, he jumps out da winda. Now, whatever gave you the idea it was a shotgun hole?"

I answered him like Sherlock Holmes might, "Because you have a shotgun standing in each hallway corner and I don't think they are there for bird hunting."

As we walked outside again, I saw that Mr. Banks had a steel frame attached to the front of his building so that he could hoist and display his large game and fish. He was known in the neighborhood as a big game hunter. Mr. Banks told me he once shot a 1,450-pound bull moose. He also bagged bear and deer that he hung outside. The *Daily Post's* "Believe or Not" column even gave him a write-up. They showed a photo of Mr. Banks leaning out of a second-story window, over the top of a hanging 450-pound dusky shark he had caught on my boat. They said the fish hung from his fire escape, but Mr. Banks had no fire escape, it was his big-game frame!

And on September 1, 1964, Mr. Banks finally caught his elusive big tuna. For four years, he had climbed off my boat, saying, "That's OK, Captain Frank, if we didn't catch him today, we'll catch him on the next trip."

He was never discouraged or disgusted, a true sportsman. That sixty-year-old fisherman once spent five hours and fifteen minutes in the fighting chair, catching a 620-pound tuna. This was a record, and the longest time we had ever spent on a giant tuna. The fish had been hooked on the outside of its upper lip. The hook didn't bother that fish at all and the tuna was able to swim anyplace he wanted for the next five hours.

After the fish had been weighed in at the dock and all the photos had been taken, Mr. Banks borrowed my truck to tote his trophy home. He headed for Harlem with the iced-down tuna's tail sticking out two feet past the tailgate. At this time, giant tuna were not worth anything at Fulton Fish Market so I knew Mr. Banks couldn't sell it.

I just had to ask him, "*What* are you going to do with that fish?"

"I'm going to hang him up in front of my social club."

"How are you going to display this tuna in front of your social club in this September heat?" I asked.

He looked at me, smiled, and said, "A friend of mine is going to *IMbarm* [sic] him."

The following week, on our way out to the fishing grounds I asked him curiously, "How long did you have that fish hanging?" Mr. Banks looked cautiously over his shoulder to the right and to the left, before answering quietly, "We has [sic] him hanging three days."

"What did you do with the fish afterward?" I asked.

"We dumps [sic] him in the river," he said, in a quiet voice. I imagined this fish being laid to rest Mafia-style with concrete slippers in the murky East River.

The following season, when I was out shark fishing, I heard my customers talking and realized their conversations were all police related. There was no doubt about it. These men were cops. They were discussing different cases, and one man brought up the story about "The guy who had a giant tuna hanging for three days from his fire escape in Harlem last September."

I moved closer to listen. "It took us three days to get an injunction against him to take the fish down. He said it was embalmed, but he couldn't embalm the flies!"

I busted out laughing and told this cop that the giant tuna came from here, right off these decks!

Some time later, Mr. Banks borrowed my truck again, this time for a 350-pound swordfish that he had caught while shark fishing from the *Cricket II*. Before we hit the dock, Mr. Banks had asked me a lot of questions regarding the fish. His first question was, "How heavy is this fish?"

"Three hundred and fifty pounds," I told him.

"Not heavy enough," he said, marking down the weight on his writing pad as "450-pounds."

"What kind of tackle did we catch him on?"

"Fifty-pound test."

"Not light enough," he said. "I'll make it thirty pounds."

"How far out were we?"

"About twenty miles."

"Not far enough," he said, licking his pencil. "I'll make it thirty-five."

He anticipated all these questions from his friends, neighbors, and onlookers. And when he returned my truck the following week, I asked him, "Did you have all the answers on the swordfish that you took to Harlem?"

"No," he said, laughing. "Mr. Beeler got stuck on one question. Some little old lady asked him, 'Wassat thing out in front of his face and wassit made outa?' Mr. Beeler bullshit his way out and told that little old lady, 'That's a *sward* an' it's made outa *swardfish.*' That little old lady walked away happy."

Mr. Banks fished with me throughout the 1960s, but his grand finale occurred when he chartered the boat for one week on June 11, 1978. It all began a week earlier with a mysterious phone call from a man who called to tell me he thought there was a white shark off Atlantic City. This anonymous tipster even gave me coordinates: "He's up the river, past the Atlantic City bridge, inside the inlet." The caller added that he'd found a couple of broken-off teeth in the bow of a small boat. When he described what these teeth looked like, I said the teeth had to have come from a white shark. I told the man to put out a few baits on a string, with no hook, "And call me back the next day."

Next day, the man called back and told me that the bait was gone. I told him to rebait and call me the following day. On the third day, he called me back and said the bait was gone again. This coincided with the time that Mr. Banks had the boat chartered, and I casually mentioned to him what was going on.

There was no hesitation on his part. "Head this thing for Atlantic City!"

"We can't. I've got a couple of charters for next week," I said.

"Can't you put them on another boat? I'll charter you for a full week and pay you day and night."

He also told me that if we did catch the white shark, "There's a $10,000 bonus in it for you."

Mr. Banks could be very persuasive. I moved my charters around and started making arrangements to go. Then I called up the man in Atlantic City and asked him if he could get a white goat that we could use for bait: white shows up better!

"The goat will cost you $35."

I agreed and told him to meet us with the goat when we got there.

Somehow, Jerry Kenney, my "friend" from the *Daily News*, found out about this escapade, and the next night, he gave me a jingle on the phone. "What's the story about this white shark in the river off Atlantic City?" Jerry asked.

I knew if I didn't tell him what was going on he would hear it from someone else and get it all screwed up. So I made Kenney give me his word that once I gave him the scoop, he would not print it until it was all over; in return, he would get the exclusive on this story. He agreed and I gave him the facts.

The next day, Mr. Banks, Mr. Beeler, Dickie, and I left for Atlantic City. When we got there, somebody showed us the *Daily News*. Kenney's entire article was all about Mundus going to Atlantic City with a charter to catch a white shark that was up the river!

This was a royal pain in the ass because now everybody

knew about our plans, from the bridge tender to all the local fishermen, and even the Bay Constable, who stopped by us to ask questions when we were anchored just inside the bridge. Cars were stopping on the bridge as people asked the bridge tender, "Has Mundus caught that white shark yet?"

When we pulled into the dock to get fuel and supplies, the man was there with our white goat on a rope. I had brought along a canvas and spread it out in the cockpit to catch the goat droppings. But because Kenney had told everybody about our plan to use the goat as bait, the whole thing turned into a circus. There were people on the dock, with tears in their eyes, offering the goat apples and cabbages for his last meal. "How could you feed this nice white goat to a shark?" some of them asked.

We were anchored out there for five days and tried different spots, intending to put the goat in the water if a white shark showed up. But we never saw our fish. Then the goat broke away one evening when I was sleeping. He had gotten to the end of his rope, so to speak, chewing it off. By the time we knew he had escaped, the pesky animal had walked up to a couple of my poles that were in the holders and ate the monofilament fishing line.

I was asleep in the cabin when the goat trotted down and nuzzled me. "What the hell—Hey, the cussed goat's loose!"

After five days, Mr. Banks, Mr. Beeler, Dickie, the goat, and I headed back to Montauk with our tails between our legs, wondering whether there had been any truth to the white shark story. Had it all been a cleverly-planned hoax? Or was there a white shark in the area? I never did find out.

Whatever the truth, Mr. Banks was not disappointed in losing, and was glad to have been able to play the game. When we got back to Montauk, I staked the goat out in the middle of the lawn at West Lake Fishing Lodge, and left him there munching happily; then I resumed my normal fishing routine. Next day, I found out that Eddie Miller, the owner of Westlake, had gotten my goat (in every sense of the word) . . . and sold it for $35! But I had the last laugh. Later on that season, when it came time to pay Eddie Miller my dockage bill, I deducted the $35. Now I had gotten Eddie's goat!

Dornfeld the Showman

When we had plenty of sharks in the 1970s, the *Cricket II* only had to go a short distance offshore, so I mostly did day trips; therefore, we had plenty of time for nonsense. After a three-quarter-of-an-hour boat ride to the fishing grounds, it usually took only an hour to get the chum slick set up. That gave the people a couple of hours of nonsense. Because there were so many sharks, my regular customers knew they had plenty of time to play practical jokes on one another or on me and my crew. All this nonsense and plenty of action made for a memorable and exciting day.

One of the best actor/aggravators to hit anyone's funny bone was one Lenny Dornfeld. At that time, when Lenny was fishing with us, he held one of the highest positions at Tuscan Dairies in New Jersey. Dornfeld was a superb impersonator and prankster, pulling off quite a few of our best tricks, both on the boat and dockside. One was "The Indian Mongoose," but his two funniest were "The Return of Frankenstein" and "Catching a Live Mermaid."

Dornfeld's Indian mongoose trick was simple yet effective. This was the first of his tricks that I fell for hook, line, and sinker.

One day, I found myself in New Jersey so I dropped by Lenny's office. Dornfeld was busy behind his big mahogany desk. To pass the time, I started roaming around his office, which was so big that I was afraid of getting lost!

The first thing that caught my eye was a wooden box, about two feet long and a foot wide. It was placed on Dornfeld's large leather couch. My eyes were immediately drawn to the stenciled printing on both sides of the box:

Danger! Indian Mongoose

As I walked over to it, I could see that the box consisted of two sections. The first was closed off completely except for a mouse hole on one side. This led into the opened part of the box which had a screen across the top. Sticking out of the mouse hole was half of an animal's furry tail.

I was still looking at the box, trying to figure it out, when Lenny came across the room. "Have you ever seen an Indian mongoose before?" he asked.

"I have seen regular mongooses in the Caribbean, on the island of St. Maarten, but how come the tail looks so different on this one?"

Dornfeld told me he didn't know but that I should tap on the box "and he will come out into the opened section." I tapped on the box like one of my idiot customers would, but nothing happened.

"Here, I'll show you," Dornfeld said. He walked over to the box and began tapping on it. While he tapped, Dornfeld started turning the box so that it faced me. All of a sudden, the top flew open and this thing hurtled through the air and hit me square in the chest! It was only an ordinary fox tail, but for two seconds it sure had me worried.

Lenny had another box made up especially for me to use on my customers and on people roaming the docks. We would wait until six or eight people had gathered there looking at the box before I would spring it on one of the female tourists in the exact same way that Lenny had done to me. You could hear the woman's screams three miles away as the "Indian mongoose" hit her right in the middle of her cleavage! I played this trick on each new crowd that showed up, sometimes up to eight times a day. I even took my "Indian mongoose" pet to Johnny's Tackle shop in Montauk and scared his wife half out of her wits when it flew out of the box, hit her square in the chest, and fell onto the counter top. "Get that thing outa [*sic*] here!" she screamed and ran in the back room. I was laughing so hard on my way out that I could hardly see the front door.

But like I said, the best nonsense was supplied by our friend Lenny Dornfeld. Some of my customers always had to be the first in as many things as they could and Lenny was one of them. After we had gotten to the fishing grounds one day, he said,

"Frank, did you ever have a person ride a unicycle around the motor box while you were out here shark fishing?"

"No, why?"

This must have hit his funny bone because he turned to my mate, Teddy, and said, "OK, Ted, bring it out!"

For this occasion, they had stashed away a unicycle in one of the hatches down in the bilge. After Teddy had brought the unicycle on deck, one of Dornfeld's friends climbed onto this thing and rode it all around the cockpit without falling while the boat lurched from side to side.

Another time, in 1974, while we were drifting and dreaming, waiting for a shark to show up in our chum slick, Lenny asked me if I wanted to do a little acting.

"What do you have in mind?" I asked him.

"Can you make a box the size of a coffin out of plywood?"

Lenny said the box had to be made out of old beaten-up plywood so it would look like it had been drifting around in the ocean for a long time. "The box will have to be premade so we can slide the pieces onto the boat on the morning of a charter without anybody thinking 'box,'" he said.

"OK, no problem." I made up the box in my garage and took it apart again. The date was set for the following Saturday because there were always plenty of people around on the weekends. To set the stage up good, I told

Johnny Likey, one of my former mates, to visit all the local bars and restaurants that morning and just ask one question:

"Did you hear anything about the box that Mundus found drifting offshore today?" So Johnny traveled the dockside and spread the word. And soon, that word spread like wildfire. Everybody was asking the same question: "What's this I hear about Mundus and the box?" and nobody knew the answer.

On our way home from the fishing grounds, we started assembling the box. It was made of old plywood like Dornfeld had specified. Now he added the final touch, in Spanish, with a can of orange spray paint: *PELIGRO* (danger)*!*

Now it was time for me to turn on the radio and spread some disinformation! Everybody in Montauk knows that, as a rule, I never, ever, turn on my ship's radio; and that when I do, it is for something very important. I made believe I was talking to another boat that was out of range to the people on shore: "Yes, a big box. Don't know what's in it." This message was probably picked up by a lot of people.

As we approached the inlet, Dornfeld had put on a complete Frankenstein costume, exactly like the Boris Karloff version, that he had rented from a professional costume company. And he climbed into the box which was now fully-assembled on top of the motor box. I got a big kick out of driving the eight penny nails into the top of the box because Lenny was screaming, "Don't nail me in too good. I have to get out fast because I have claustrophobia!"

After we had nailed him in, we only had a fifteen-minute ride back to the dock. There must have been a couple hundred people assembled when we arrived, and every other person had a camera ready.

Lenny Dornfeld all dressed up for his Frankenstein-in-the-box gag.

People were also up on the rooftop of Westlake Fishing Lodge, hoping to get better pictures of what was in the box. We had to push the crowds back when we got ready to lift the box off the boat. We lifted the box off with my winch and boom and placed it on the dock.

About this time, you could hear a pin drop.

Now it was time to open the box. I jumped on the dock with a wrecking bar and a hammer and drove the wrecking bar under the lid to pry it up. The sound effects were perfect because the nails were squeaking as I lifted the lid. I promised myself that I was not going to run after I opened the box because I was afraid it would look too phoney, but when I started to pry open the lid and bent it back, the squeaking sound effects of the nails added to the eerie atmosphere. When I opened the box and looked inside it, I dropped the lid and ran, anyhow, through the crowd, yelling, "Oh my god!" (I just couldn't help myself!)

"Frankenstein" slowly got out of the box and started walking toward the crowd. His groaning noise, outstretched arms, and stiff-legged walk sent the crowd into a panic, running all over the parking lot. There was a small girl, about three or four-years-old, who had tripped and fallen down during the stampede. She just happened to be in Frankenstein's path. He picked up the screaming girl in his arms and walked across the lot to the bar at Westlake Fishing Lodge. There, he slowly lowered the child to the floor, and she ran screaming back to her parents. Dornfeld's Frankenstein prank only lasted five minutes, but for the people on the dock who had been there all day, the suspense and the grand Frankenstein finale must have been well worth waiting for.

To Catch a Mermaid

The following year, in September 1975, Dornfeld staged a second stunt: he would catch a mermaid. In the early part of the season, he had told me that we should catch a live mermaid. Dornfeld even told me on what date we would perform this fabulous feat. The time was set. The actors were ready. Now all we needed was the audience for the show. Weeks ahead of time, I began spreading the story that on a certain date the *Cricket II* would catch a live mermaid. Whenever I came across a Doubting Thomas who said this could not happen, I made a twenty-five-cent bet. (As everybody knows, this is the highest stake I have ever wagered.)

Dornfeld rented a Hollywood-style mermaid outfit and made arrangements with a modeling agency to hire a well-built female for the job. It would be an easy enough job to bring the girl on board—there was nothing unusual for one or two girls to go along on a shark-fishing charter with the men. And so it was on Dornfeld's Sunday charter, one day in August.

We had caught our usual half a dozen blue sharks, had our fun and frolics, and started home to display our catch of the day to the people on the dock. To show our mermaid off better, I made a swing seat to go across the armrests of our big fighting chair that sat in the middle of the cockpit. This way, she would be sitting up higher for everybody to see. I put two holes in each side of the seat so we could insert ropes and pick her up with our boom and tackle when we got back to the dock.

The ocean was good to us. We had plenty of sunlight and a calm, rolling sea. As we started home, the "mermaid" climbed into her costume, an outfit which extended from her belly button to beyond her feet. For more authenticity, I had saved a real swordfish tail and hand-sewed it onto the bottom of her costume after we had tied the girl's ankles together.

She sat topless on the seat, with her two-and-a-half-foot-long black hair streaming in the breeze. We made sure to come as close as possible to the other boats on our way home so the mermaid could wave to them. I knew that they would immediately get on their radios, and the news would soon spread around the docks like wildfire.

Going in through the inlet was another funny sight: the surf fishermen on both sides of the rock piles screamed and pointed at us as we headed in.

The mermaid had left the top part of her costume off, displaying her natural features (so to speak), as the *Cricket II* ambled around the other docks so that the occupants of boats tied up at the dock and other people could plainly see our catch. She had wanted to remain topless when I backed the *Cricket II* into the slip at Westlake Fishing Lodge, but I said no, and handed her the bra top. After all, I didn't want to get arrested for inciting a riot!

There were always a lot of people on the dock waiting to see what the *Cricket II* would bring in, but on this day, the crowd was thicker than fleas on a hound dog's back. The mermaid sat waving to the people, while we hooked her swing seat ropes up to our boom. We lifted her straight up and then swung her in over the dock. She was suspended four feet over the dock so that her tail was just touching the planking. I let the enthusiastic crowd photograph her for twenty minutes or so before we took off the tail and untied her feet so she could climb on the boat and change back into her clothes.

Dornfeld also played tricks on members of his own party. One of his favorite fall-guy employees was Santo Sacca. Santo, or "Santa" as I called him, is a quiet, good-natured man who had never been shark fishing before Lenny took him out on an overnight trip with us. Santa was very enthusiastic about his invitation from Dornfeld, and asked Lenny ahead of time what he could do to help out on this trip. Lenny told Santa that he would find out what his job would be during the trip. Santa's eagerness to help had put a bug in Dornfeld's ear and the wheels started turning.

On this particular overnight trip, it was dark. There was no moon and you couldn't see your hand in front of your face: a perfect opportunity for Santa's initiation to shark fishing, Dornfeld-style. When we reached the fishing grounds, shut off the motor, and started to drift, Dornfeld led Santa up to the bow and onto our twelve-foot-long pulpit, which extended past the bow and over the water.

Santa took this all in his stride, trusting his boss completely. I was watching as Dornfeld pushed Santa ahead of him up on the pulpit, telling Santa, "This is what you have to do." Handing him a flashlight, Dornfeld explained, "You have to look for sharks, and as soon as you see one, holler."

Then Dornfeld took a ten-foot piece of rope and tied Santa to the pulpit rail! Poor Santa, he must have looked like a ship's figurehead up there, suspended six feet above the water that he couldn't even see, swaying with the movement of the boat. The flashlight that they gave him wasn't even bright enough to find a shark in the dark!

What Santa didn't know was the fact that the chum was drifting out from the cockpit, and chances were that if there were any sharks, they would come straight up the chum slick and head toward the cockpit, not the bow.

Twenty minutes or so went by, and we didn't hear a peep out of Santa, so I told Dornfeld, "You'd better bring him down before he has a heart attack up there in the dark!"

Reluctantly, Dornfeld went up in the bow to untie Santa, and in a few minutes, the two men emerged from the blackness of the night and stepped into the cockpit deck lights. Santa, of course, thought the whole thing had been the usual procedure for shark fishing at night: until I told him differently!

Poor Santa, he took a lot of nonsense from Dornfeld. Another time, Santa was in the process of catching a fish, using stand-up tackle while walking around the cockpit, when Dornfeld got the bright idea of cutting Santa's pants' belt. Dornfeld knew that Santa was at his mercy because he had to keep both hands on the fishing pole.

Meanwhile, Dornfeld snuck up behind him. With one swift slice, he cut the belt in two, and Santa's pants fell down around his ankles. This was a funny sight: Santa trying to hop around and catch that fish! To my amazement, he eventually worked his feet loose, climbed out of his pants, and wearing just his undershorts, finished catching the fish. A good trooper!

After Dornfeld had worked his way through a vast supply of victims, he couldn't find anyone else to go fishing with him. In fact, when the *Monster Man* book was published in 1976, Dornfeld had me autograph two full cases (a total of 120 books) to read: *To another one of Lenny's victims.*

CHAPTER 6

LIFE'S PROBLEMS

In the mid to late 1950s and onward, my drinking problems started to become serious without me addressing the situation. I would come home, fall into my easy chair, and sleep. "Get up and go to bed!" Janet would tell me angrily, frustrated by my years of drunkenness. The drinking never affected my daily fishing routines and I never took money from the charter income. Customers bought me drinks, and whenever I could, I made a little extra pocket money for my booze. The alcohol eventually started to take its toll on my health, and I had three health warnings from the "man upstairs" that booze was raising my blood pressure. On the rare occasions when I wasn't boozing or fishing, I was having close calls with the "grim reaper."

My Drinking Days

It seemed like all the important fishing information was located inside a gin mill. So I had started hanging around bars in Jersey when I began my fishing career there. I'm not trying to tell you that all charter boat captains are drunkards or hoboes, but you might think it seems that way, reading this. In those early days, most of the time I was lucky if I had a dime to split a beer with someone. My family and I went through some tough winters when we didn't know where our next meal was coming from, never mind my next beer. A lot of times, I would buy all my fishing tackle on credit at Point Pleasant Hardware Store as each season began. After I had sailed a few charters in the summer, I could pay for my tackle in full, then resell it in the winter time for grocery money.

There were a couple of winters in the late 1940s when Janet, Bobbie, and I were so badly off that we moved into an apartment which we had to share with a fellow charter-boat captain and friend, Joe McGovern, and his family. We split all our expenses down the middle. This way we only had to heat one building and had one grocery bill. Joe and I tried everything to make grocery money, including working on the docks and unloading fish from the commercial boats for a dollar an hour. These commercial boat captains would often give us fish to eat.

Joe and I took the fish and sold it to the neighbors, using this money to buy food. Sometimes, after a storm, we went down into the surf and picked up sea clams that washed up on the beach. Joe and I brought the clams home and opened them up, taking out the best parts; then we went around the neighborhood, selling the clams for thirty-five cents a quart.

We found even more ways to get food for the table: a bakery truck used to deliver bread and cakes to the houses, and we would swap the driver some fish for bread. During the fishing season, when Joe and I didn't have a charter, we fished commercially for mackerel. We used Joe's thirty-eight-foot boat the *JoAnne* and left my first boat, the thirty-foot *Cricket*, back at the dock. This cut our expenses down quite a bit.

In those days, I was sober all winter because we didn't have enough money for booze. The only booze that you could find was at somebody's house or at a party where it was free. In fact, the booze didn't flow very freely until after I got to Montauk in 1951. One of the reasons I joined the Montauk Volunteer Fire Department was for the parties they held in the winter time. I made history at one fire department party because I got so drunk that I fell backward into a large tub of boiling water filled with corn; everybody thought my ass would be covered in blisters for years.

Next morning when I woke up, I was in hot water with my wife! Janet asked me how my clothes got wet, as they were all in a pile by the radiator. Not knowing the reason, and fishing for an excuse, I was saved by the bell when our telephone rang. It was a local charter-boat captain, calling to ask how I was. He told me over the phone what had happened the night before. Armed with a watertight alibi, I hung up the phone and turned to Janet, saying, "You wanted to know why my clothes were wet? Somebody pushed me into a tub of boiling water."

As a father and family man, I never took any house money or charter money away from my family for booze. My drinking money was always the extra cash I made on the side from fish money and tips. In the winter when we weren't fishing, the booze money came from a piggy bank that I had put away from the money I made on the side. I always had $5.00 a week for a bottle of cheap bourbon. That bottle had to last me the week out. If I had a party to go to, all the better. This way, I could drink their whisky and leave my bottle in its hiding place. Joining the Montauk Volunteer Fire Department and belonging to the ambulance squad brought in plenty of drinks each winter. If they had a party, I volunteered to be part of the clean-up committee because I could almost always get a couple of bottles to sneak out with. As the years progressed, there were more charters, more money, and more booze. Then came my St. Maarten drinking. When I took the *Cricket III* to the Caribbean, the whisky there was almost free. A bottle of Johnny Walker (a fifth) was $3.50. A case (twelve bottles) of Mount Gay Rum was $9.00, and so on, and I always brought home two cases of bourbon to start off the Montauk fishing season. One of my drinking buddies was my mate, Dickie. Dickie was with me for fourteen years. We each had our private bottle of booze on the boat, under the chart table (like W. C. Fields once said, "A little whisky for the cold once in a while don't hurt").

In the mid-1960s and 1970s, Dickie and I would have a few drinks before our party got to the boat. Then we'd put our coffee cups, filled with bourbon and coke, up on the flying bridge. This was our ration until we got to the fishing grounds. Sometimes it was our ration until we got back to the dock. If one of us had too much to drink, the other one would tell him. This way we tried to keep everything running smoothly. When we got back to the dock, it was a different story! If Dickie and I caught fish, we were happy and went to the gin mill to celebrate. If we didn't catch fish, we went to the gin mill to cry in our beer. Either way, it was drinking time back at the dock.

The drinking stopped suddenly just before I started doing the overnight trips. It ended by choice, after another brush with death on July 13, 1976.

That morning, I woke up and felt my heart pounding like it was going to come out through my chest. I went down to the dock to greet my party for that day, knowing that I would not be able to take them out. Not wanting to alarm them about my condition, I used bad weather as an excuse to reschedule their charter. Then I went home and a friend of mine called Southampton hospital for me.

The hospital told him to bring me in immediately. When we got there, many of the doctors recognized me because I was a volunteer with both the ambulance squad and the fire department, and we had brought in a lot of "customers" for the doctors at Southampton Hospital over the years. They put me in a wheelchair and I was whizzed right by the admitting desk as the doctors hollered over their shoulder, "We'll get you all the information later. We've got to get Frank upstairs now!"

I was placed in the intensive care unit for two days before they got me straightened out. A doctor explained that I had developed high blood pressure and a lump in my blood had become lodged in a heart valve. They had to thin the blood and get things back to normal. This took a few days, but I had to stay in there for a week for observation. On the way out, I had questions for the heart specialist. He was a white-haired little old guy who was sitting across from me with small round glasses perched on the end of his nose.

My first question concerned food. "Are you going to put me on a special diet?"

"No. You did not have a heart attack, but you should lose some weight (I was about 250-pounds at the time.)" My next question involved booze. He said I could drink all I want, but that I should not drink to "excess." My answer was: "You don't know who you are talking to. How can you say that I can have all I want to drink without going to excess?"

The doctor calmly replied, "The hospital door swings both ways. If you drink heavy, you'll be back."

"My last question is a three-lettered word," I told him. "S-E-X. What do I do about this?"

About now, he straightened up in his chair, cocked his head back, looked at me through his little round glasses, and said very slowly, "I don't know whether you're an all-nighter or not, but I do know that if the body wants it, the body will accept it."

So I said, "That's it. I've had my last drink." I did it all by myself, and didn't go to none of them doggone meetings!

Years later, a friend of mine was going to one of these meetings, and I went along, just for a joke, to see what went on. I sat in the second row and there were about fifty people at the meeting. One by one, these people stood up, said their name, and described how they were fighting the demon drink.

Soon it was my turn. I stood up and said, "My name is Frank Mundus and I haven't touched a drop of booze in six years. I keep my house well-stocked with booze. When my friends come in, the booze is there for them if they want it. Whenever I have a sore throat, I can gargle with the booze and spit it out and never swallow it."

I thought I'd done well by having the booze in the house all this time and not touching it, but one little biddy, who was sitting not too far from me, screamed like she had something caught in her throat, "WELL, I CAN SEE THIS IS AMATEURS' NIGHT TONIGHT!" That was it for me. I said no more. That was the first and last meeting I ever attended.

Although I got out of the bottle, I couldn't get my mate Dickie out of it. I tried everything, every day, but knowing how I had been and how he was, I knew it would be a tough job. Dickie was my longest-serving mate. He was with me for fourteen years. He was reliable, good with customers, and kept the boat clean the way I wanted it. Dickie had been a quiet, likeable college kid when he heard I was looking for a mate. He knew nothing about fish or boating. Sometimes this is an advantage over an experienced mate who has his own ideas on how to fish. During his time with me, he was drafted and did one stint in Vietnam as a pay clerk.

It was partly my fault that he got into the booze because I had my bottle under the chart table, down in the cabin, and so did Dickie. But when I climbed out of the bottle in

1976, I couldn't get Dickie out and he kept getting worse. The final crunch was our grueling overnight trips. Dickie had no time to hang out at the bar in the evening so he had to drink fast. One time he was climbing the mast steps going up to the bridge. He got almost all the way up and fell backward onto the motor box, bounced off the motor box, and rolled onto the deck. One of my customers rushed over to him, and I yelled, "Leave him alone! You don't know if he has busted his ribs or anything. Let him get up by himself." After a couple of minutes, he woke up. By this time, I had climbed down from the mast and was standing there, looking at him. Dickie regained consciousness and stood up. I could see he wasn't hurt, so I told him to go down into the cabin and stay there until we got to the fishing grounds. He went to the cabin, stopped in front of our kerosene stove, turned around, and slumped on top of the unlit stove. That was his final trip after fourteen years. I lost the battle of the booze with Dickie and finally had to let him go in the middle 1980s. He didn't last much longer after that. The booze got to him and I heard that he had passed away in the late 1980s.

As the World Turns

A really bad hangover couldn't start to compare with what happened to me one summer, on July 1, 1967, when for some wacky reason I woke up earlier than usual. It was about an hour before daylight, and I got out of bed to find the world was spinning fast, so fast that it pushed me hard against the wall! The only way I could walk to the bathroom was by hanging on to the walls. I grabbed hold of the sink and looked into the mirror. By keeping one eye shut, I could see a little.

I don't know how, but I got dressed. The next job was to stagger out to my truck. That faithful truck was out in the driveway, right where I must have left it last night. This was in my drinking days, so the previous night's events were a little foggy.

Walking was out of the question. I had to crawl to the truck on all fours, but knew that, even in my condition, I could still drive to the dock because at that time of day there wasn't much traffic around. By now, everything was spinning around so much that I drove the five miles to the boat with only one eye open. This helped slow the spinning down somewhat.

When I reached the parking lot just behind the boat, I stopped the truck, and out of one eye, I could see my party was already on the boat, watching me bring the truck to a stop. It must have been a funny sight for them as they saw me get out of the truck and crawl to the boat on my hands and knees. They probably thought, "Here comes our fearless captain." I kept telling them that my condition was *not* a drinking problem!

I knew I couldn't get up on the flying bridge, so I told them we had to search for another captain. Captain Roley Clark and Chip Edwards had the boat *Wahoo* right alongside. They weren't chartered and offered to operate the *Cricket II* for the day, while I lay on the bunk and shouted out orders, where to go and what to do.

All day I was in that bunk, with a bucket handy because I had the dry heaves and couldn't keep anything down. Once I tried to get up on deck but couldn't make it. Something was *definitely* wrong with me.

When we got back to the dock, I asked one of the boys to call up my wife and make sure to tell her I had not been drinking. I knew by then that I could not have driven home by myself. I needed Janet to come and pick me up. When she first saw me, Janet still had that look of suspicion in her eye, but even that faded away as she watched me crawl off the boat. When I stood up, Janet had to help me walk to her car. When the wife called up to speak with the doctors, they said for her to bring me right in.

Dr. Carver Livingstone (no wisecracks, that's his name!) took one look at me, and said, "If I had to guess, I would say it was your inner ear that has let go, but we will have to call in a specialist."

I trusted his advice as Dr. Livingstone was a good surgeon and all-around doctor. If he didn't know what your problem was, he would say so. Three days later, the specialist examined me, and said, "Admit yourself into the hospital right away."

"What for?" I asked.

"A possible brain tumor," he said.

I told this doctor, "First, you ain't putting me between two white sheets in the summer. Second, this is July and I have customers wanting to catch fish. Third, I'm not going into the hospital for a *possible* brain tumor."

Janet was jumping up and down when the doctor said to me, "It's up to you; it's your life." She was afraid that the doctor was right. After the specialist left, Dr. Livingstone told me to let him know when I was finished fishing for the season and he would make arrangements to send me to the "head hospital" (Presbyterian Hospital) in New York.

It was about a week before I could get up and move around. Finding somebody to run the boat at that busy time of year was not exactly the easiest thing to do. And getting myself back on the boat was also not the easiest thing to do, either. I had lost my balance and came home every night full of black-and-blue marks from slamming into things. If the boat rolled to the right, it would start me on a pendulum action. I'd keep on going in that direction until I hit something that brought me to a stop. There was no counter reaction at all.

The worst was bending down to pick something up. It was plain suicide. I knew I was going to keep on going in the direction I was bending in until something (or someone) broke my momentum. So I spent three weeks slamming and banging around, and felt like I was going over Niagara Falls in a barrel.

In the meantime, I kept on fishing. Everyone on the boat thought it was funny to see me slamming my body into something all day. The rest of that season went by crash, bang, boom, until Dr. Livingstone made the arrangements for me at the head hospital. Then, on December 3, 1967, my friend Harry Hoffman volunteered to drive me to the Presbyterian Hospital.

I was in hospital for two weeks, during which time I had my transom reamed out: the specialists put me through a battery of tests that seemed a cross between Chinese torture and astronaut training. One time, they strapped me to what looked like an upturned metal wheel and spun me around. I felt like the girl in a knife-throwing act.

For another test, they strapped me to a table: on my right side, one doctor had a bowl of steaming hot water and a big rubber syringe, while on my left side, there was another doctor with another bowl of water loaded with ice cubes and another syringe. At a given moment, both doctors hit me in the ears, simultaneously, with the hot and cold liquids. They told me that the squares in the ceiling that I was looking at were supposed to change appearance, but they didn't. So another experiment had failed.

Then I had a brain scan: my head was x-rayed by a revolving camera which took twenty-one pictures in half a minute as it moved around my head. I was watched closely by the experts for six days before they turned me loose. It was during this time that Peter Gimbel dropped in to visit me and told me some good news about his fund-raising efforts for *Blue Water, White Death*.

About a week after I got home, Dr. Livingstone called, asking me to come to his office so he could give me the results of my hospital visit. When I got there, he told me the report was two-pages long, "two pages of doctors' gobbledygook," as he put it. Then he asked me if I wanted it in doctors' jargon or in laymen's language.

"Give it to me in my language so I can understand it," I replied.

He held up the papers and said, "These two pages here tell me one thing: whatever you had is gone, but it will leave you with a small scar."

"I think I know what the small scar is," I said. "Because when I'm walking and trying to read somebody's license plate in the distance, I have to stand still to read it." I told him that the motion of the boat did not bother me and that I only had problems when I walked on a hard surface.

"This is what I thought from the beginning: the problem was in your inner ear," Dr. Livingstone said as he laid the report down on his desk.

To this day, I carry that small scar: My sense of balance is still off by 30 or 40 percent.

Harry Hoffman and the Case of the Lost White Shark

My best friend Harry Hoffman, displaying his 1,040-pound white shark that he caught on June 15, 1973.

Harry Hoffman started out as one of my customers and turned into a loyal personal friend. Every time we got together for hunting or fishing, we always got into some kind of crazy mischief. I knew him for more than forty years. For some reason, Harry always reminded me of a cigar-smoking Barney Rubble, complete with the same carrot top of light-red hair. He had a shop, Diesel Injection Service, in Huntington, New York, where he repaired diesel injectors. Harry was one of the best diesel mechanics that I have ever come across. He was not only good with injectors, but was also an excellent all-round mechanic. Harry left this planet on January 22, 2003. One of his sons, Jay, now runs the shop and is doing a very good job.

I worked in Harry's shop for a couple of winters, helping him out when he had bursitis in his arm. This was in the days before Harry's eldest son, Jay, was old enough to take over the injector business. During those winter months, I saw Harry fix many motors over the telephone, free of charge, correctly diagnosing the problem each time with the precision of a surgeon. Harry only made road calls for very important cases such as when the lighting company couldn't get their spare diesel generator running.

Harry Hoffman always guaranteed his work. For example, one time I heard him tell the lighting company over the phone that his time started when he closed his shop door behind him, but if he didn't diagnose the problem completely or get the machinery running, there would be no charge.

Because of Harry's thorough knowledge of machinery, he took on the job of keeping the *Cricket II*'s diesel motor running smoothly. In return, I took him fishing and only charged him for expenses.

Every time Harry Hoffman and I got together, you could be sure that something out of the ordinary would happen.

At one point, Harry was trying hard to quit smoking and thought that going out on a boat for a five-day trip, without cigarettes, might help him kick the habit.

In the winter of 1971, Harry and I rebuilt the spare 6-71 General Motors diesel motor that was in my garage. Harry tore it apart and put in all new pistons and bearings, etc. Then, in the early spring of 1972, before our fishing season started, we took the old motor out of the *Cricket II* and replaced it with the rebuilt one. I was now anticipating a trouble-free motor this up-and-coming season.

We fished three or four local shakedown cruises for shark before Harry's five-day trip, scheduled for June 13, 1973. Our next concern was to have the electronics checked out. I called Sag Harbor Electronics and asked them to check the loran and the radio to make sure they were in good shape before I took Harry out fishing.

Before long, it was time to leave the dock for Harry's five-day trip. My mate Dickie accompanied us, and Harry brought along our mutual friend, Paul DiAngelo, in case we got into action on this trip and needed an extra pair of hands.

We loaded plenty of ice, chum, and food onboard and away we went, with the weather on our side. I steered the *Cricket II* in the direction of our favorite fishing grounds, a place known on the fishing charts as The Dumping Grounds. It was an area located south of Martha's Vineyard and was an eight-hour trip. Everybody thought the steady hum of the rebuilt motor would never stop. Harry and I felt pleased with our work.

Once we arrived at our destination, I shut off the motor and the *Cricket II* began her five-day drift off the Vineyard, almost in sight of Nantucket Island. It didn't take us long to chum up our usual bunch of blue sharks. The blue sharks showed up in large numbers, like the homeless at a free lunch.

At the end of the first day of fishing, I went down below and tried to take a loran reading to see how far and in what direction we had drifted.

"No good," I said to Harry, as I came back up into the cockpit. "Would you believe it, I had Sag Harbor Electronics come out and check everything before we left!" The fact that I was unable to take a reading didn't bother me too much. When we first started shark fishing, for the first nine or ten years I only had two instruments to go by: the clock and the compass.

The second day of our drift, I tried again to take a loran reading: still nothing. We continued to drift and play with our blue sharks, teasing them with a fish on a string with no hook. They would chase the fish and try to catch it as we pulled the fish away from them.

Sometimes, the sharks stuck their heads clear out of the water and slammed their jaws shut, trying to catch our fish-on-a-string. As they opened their jaws and tried to snap at the bait, the sharks would always roll up what looked like their eye lids (the nictitating membrane), just as our eyelids automatically close when we think something gets too close to them.

These sharks ranged in size from 50 pounds to 150 pounds. In the past, I have used thirty-pound blue sharks for bait to catch a three-hundred-pound or four-hundred-pound shark. On this trip, I would probably use one of the one-hundred-pound blue sharks to catch a one-thousand-pound, or bigger, white shark.

After a day or so of standing in the cockpit and looking down into the water, it became physically impossible to count the many blue sharks we had coming and going in and out of the slick, picking up small pieces of ground-up chum. There must have been hundreds of them. Harry and I decided to catch five or six of these blue sharks and hang their corpses in the water for teasers in case a white shark showed up.

When a white shark appears, you know it ahead of time because all the blue sharks scatter. If the white shark is hungry, they disappear. A few seconds later, the white shark shows himself under the boat. At this point, in the middle of the night, it is important to hold his attention until daylight. Nobody in their right mind would try to catch a big fish like that in the dark. Someone could get killed trying to put a tail rope on it.

The best time to catch a white shark is during daylight hours. First, you have to raise one, then you have to make him eat. It's not like in the movies. They all don't come up to the boat with their mouths open and their pearly-white teeth shining in the sunlight. Most of them just appear slowly out of the deep, curious to see what all the blue sharks are doing. At first, you see a discoloration that begins forming into a bigger grayish-brown mass. Eventually, it turns into the familiar torpedo-shaped outline of the great white shark. Now you have to tease him and tease him again, until he gets mad enough to take your bait.

When Harry's white shark first appeared in the middle of the night, we had to use our blue-shark teasers as appetizers. About every half hour, the white shark came up to take a bite. After shaking his head, sometimes half a blue shark would be missing. Then we had to catch another blue to replace what the white shark took.

One time, I was standing in the cockpit, looking down at the blue sharks that were as thick as fleas on a hound dog's back.

All at once, the blue sharks were gone.

"He's gonna come back again!" I hollered. And when he did, he grabbed hold of one of the blue sharks that we had hung by its tail. The white shark rose halfway out of the water, shaking his head, with the blue shark clamped between his jaws, like a dog chewing on a big bone.

I could see that he was not going to be satisfied with just half of the blue shark. He wanted the whole thing. If he wanted half, he could have closed his jaws, bit the blue shark in half and gone on his way. Instead, he shook his head back and forth out of the water furiously until he had flipped off the tail rope that had tied the blue shark to the mast.

We watched the white shark swim away on the surface, with his head out of the water, shaking and thrashing that blue shark, until he was out of range of the deck lights and had disappeared into the darkness. I told Harry I was afraid that, come daylight, the white shark wouldn't be hungry anymore as he was feeding all night.

Before daylight, I fed Harry and my crew their bacon and eggs knowing that after daylight we would be too busy to eat. We always ate good meals. Just like Long John Silver, I was the ship's cook (and captain).

At daylight, on our third day of drifting, I checked my old military-surplus loran once more, but still couldn't get a reading. This unreliability was not unusual for this type of loran, and I thought I knew where we were anyhow.

In the meantime, we had a white shark to catch and had to get everything ready. I put Harry in the fighting chair, attached the bucket harness to him, and adjusted the footrest. It was light enough now to see what we were doing. The next time the white shark showed up, we were ready to give him the bait with a hook in it. We used a foot-long fillet of blue shark for the bait, about six inches wide and a couple inches thick.

To make it more appealing, I cut a slit in the bottom half of the fillet, hoping to create a fish-tail effect as it trailed through the water. I also attached a trailing bait the same size and thickness as the first bait to make it bigger and more attractive.

The blue sharks were still with us. We couldn't throw the bait in the water until the white shark showed up because one of the ever-hungry blue sharks would grab the bait.

"Where the hell is he?" asked Harry anxiously. "We played with this shark all night and almost every half hour he came back up to the boat."

"You'll find out when the blue sharks disappear, just hang on," I told Harry. What seemed like hours was probably only half an hour. Suddenly, all the blue sharks vanished again, just like they did last night every time the white shark appeared.

I hollered to Harry, "Get ready, we're going to be in business very shortly!"

I had no sooner gotten those words out of my mouth than the fish rose out of the depths. I didn't have to tease him at all. He jumped right on the bait and away we went. My job was to hit the starter button. I knew we had to chase this fish around the ocean.

Dickie stood directly behind the fighting chair, turning the chair to the right or to the left, always facing Harry toward the fish.

On his first run, the shark had taken out about thirty yards of line; then he stopped and shook his head and our hook pulled out. In disgust, Harry said a few words that I can't repeat here. Then he asked, "What do we do now?"

"Noise, Harry, noise," I said. "Get the rifle that you brought along out and start shooting straight down into the water. I'll take my .30-caliber carbine and do the same thing."

I shut the motor off and stayed in that spot where we had lost the shark, hoping the sound would attract him. It only took fifteen or twenty minutes of chumming and shooting until the blue sharks showed up. I told Harry this was a good sign. We probably waited another half an hour watching the blue sharks before it happened.

The blue sharks disappeared once more. "I think we're in business, again, Harry." Five minutes passed after I made this statement, and up it came. This time, that big fish had been nicked by the hook and was gun-shy, and didn't appear as hungry as he was the first time. I had to tease him for a while before he took the bait. Away we went again, chasing him across the horizon, gaining and losing line as we went. The Penn 130 International reel was holding up well under this endurance test.

After about three quarters of an hour or so, the fish surfaced about thirty yards off the transom and made a half-circle breach. Dickie turned around and screamed up at the bridge to me, "It's a male! It's a male!" as a pair of foot-long white claspers flopped around while the fish was in the air.

"Right now, I don't care whether it's a male or female! We'll catch him first," I hollered back.

Everybody has a small job to do in order to land a big fish, and if one person goofs up at the last second, we lose the fish. My job was to run the boat and follow the line as it cut through the water. When the shark came to the surface, I had to get the boat going at the same speed, and in the same direction as the fish was moving. Meanwhile, Dickie had to continue making sure that the fighting chair and Harry kept facing the fish, especially at the last few minutes of the fight.

Once the fish had risen to the surface and I got the boat lined up, we were ready to take him. When the end of the twenty-five-foot leader wire showed close to the boat, Paul De Angelo attached a small snap at the end of the swivel. The twenty-five-foot leader was now secured to a line that went up the mast to a single block pulley and back down again to the cockpit.

As soon as Paul put the snap in, Dickie ran over and started pulling on that line. Meanwhile, Harry slacked off on the drag in order for Dickie and Paul to pull down on the rope and raise the leader wire, drawing the fish closer to the boat. When this happened, I turned the *Cricket II* in a slow, hard circle so that the back of the boat stayed away from the fish. I didn't want the shark going under the boat and being chewed up by the propeller. With Dickie and Paul pulling down on the line, we brought the fish closer and closer to the boat. Now it swam very slowly on the surface, at the same speed as the boat.

Once Dickie and Paul had gotten the shark alongside the boat and the *Cricket II* was idling slow ahead, I jumped down off the bridge, took the line from them, and put it on the electric winch. Now we had the fish's head close enough to put a reverse tail rope on him; it was Paul De Angelo's job to help get this tail rope on the white shark.

Paul made an open loop from a quarter-inch stainless-steel cable. He held the main part of the cable in his left hand while holding an opened shackle (instead of a snap hook which might break) in his right. Leaning overboard with his right arm around the leader wire, Paul connected the shackle to the main part of the cable. This formed a complete lasso.

Now it was Dickie's turn. He had to slide the cable over the shark's head and past the dorsal fin before he could start pulling it tight. That's why I call this device a "reverse tail rope," it starts at the head and goes to the tail.

While Dickie worked on tail-roping the shark, Paul headed to the transom where the end of the tail rope was, and kept the rope tightly wrapped around the stern bit. What could possibly go wrong now? Well, if the fish got excited and merely shook his head, he could bust the rope that went up to the mast through the pulley and down to the electric winch. He could also tear out the pulley, or even blow out the top of the mast with all his weight. Either way, it would be a mad scramble to keep somebody from being hurt.

Meanwhile, I held the fish alongside the boat, using the capstan on the winch. When Paul gave me the OK, I slacked down on the cable line, and the fish started heading for the bottom. With the boat going ahead in a hard right-hand circle, it only took seconds for the shark to reappear, sliding across the surface backward, lassoed by his tail. He tried to thrash around, but being pulled in reverse, it was soon over for the fish.

I estimated this shark was in the one-thousand-pound class; small, but a keeper. We pulled him backward like that for a half hour or so. Then I told Harry, "That should be enough to take the kick out of him. Let's hang him on the side of the boat, from the mast."

With her equipment, and if the weather conditions were right, the *Cricket II* could pick a maximum of two thousand pounds out of the water. When we hoisted this fish so that his nose was up out of the water, we found that the weather was just a little too jumpy. He might slam around too much on the way home, tearing something apart. So we decided the safest method was to leave him in the water and tow him home.

My "navi-guessing" and dead reckoning told me we had about six hours or more to go before we got in.

"Where do you think we are?" asked Harry. "We've been drifting for over three days."

"Going by the seat of my pants, Block Island should be about there," I said, pointing a little to the right of our course. "We are running our usual cruising speed of 1,500 rpm, but that white shark isn't going to slow this boat down much. We'll still make our usual ten knots."

Harry sat in the corner of the flying bridge, watching the white shark splashing in and out of the water. "Didn't you say you would call your wife on the ship-to-shore radio if we got one?" he reminded me.

"OK," I said. "Here, take the wheel and I'll try."

Harry slid over and took the wheel, while I tried to make the call. To my surprise, my main radio and my CB radio were out of order.

I turned to Harry. "I hope nothing happens because we are out of communication with the outside world!" The radios must have gone out of commission at the same time the had loran died. "This is nice," I said to Harry in a laughing tone. "Just like the old days: no radio and we don't know where we are."

The wind had swung around to the northwest and cleared up the visibility somewhat. "We should start to see Block Island soon," I told Harry. It was just about then that all hell broke loose under the motor box. There was a horrendous sound, followed by acrid clouds of billowing black smoke. I hit the throttle to slow down the boat and then checked the oil gauge: the needle was dropping fast.

Harry jumped down into the cockpit while Dickie and Paul slid back the motor-box cover. Harry took one look and said, "You've got a blown piston. The oil is going straight through and out the top of the piston. That's what's making all the smoke."

"What are we supposed to do now?" I asked Harry.

"How much spare oil do you have aboard?"

"About six gallons," I said. He told me to fill the motor up to the high mark on the dipstick.

"Now, go!" Harry said, "and keep your eye on the oil-pressure gauge. When it starts to drop, slow the boat down and we'll put in more oil."

"That's another fine mess you've gotten me into!" I joked.

"I don't make the pistons, I only buy them," Harry quipped. "It's not my fault if a brand-new piston has a defect in it."

By this time, slippery black oil was spewing all over the boat. We even found some up on the flying bridge. No matter where we went, the boat was covered in a slick of black oil. It was almost impossible for us to keep our balance on deck. I felt like I was walking on ice. After twenty minutes of running time, I had to stop the boat and put in another gallon of oil. Every twenty minutes of running time was costing us one gallon of oil.

Here we were, on our way home, with not a boat in sight. After our third oil stop, I told Dickie to go up into the top of the mast and find us land. He was only up there five minutes when he hollered, "Block Island—off the right side of the bow!"

"That's right where it's supposed to be," I said. After another ten or fifteen minutes, we could see it from the flying bridge. "Block Island is still a long way off," I said to Harry. "We ain't gonna make Block Island even if we change course and head straight for it. We don't have enough oil. It will take us at least two hours to get there, and after we run out of oil this time, we've only got another half hour before we'll have to stop and drop anchor. We've been through a lot together, Harry, but this is going to be the worst one."

"There's not a boat in sight, anyplace," said Harry. "How come? No commercial beam trawlers here either."

"At this time of the year, they don't fish in this area," I said. All of a sudden, talking about boats made me think about the two open boats (or "head" boats as they are called because they charge people by the head to take them out cod fishing) that should be aiming for Montauk about this time of day: the *Peconic Queen* and the *Viking Star.*

I decided to take a chance and head them off by changing my course more to the north. These boats would be heading almost west. If they had not yet passed by the area, we had a chance of intercepting them.

My oil pressure gauge was dropping dangerously and I stopped to put in our last gallon of oil.

This would be our final twenty-minute run.

"Somebody had better pull a rabbit out of their hat now," said Harry.

No sooner had Harry spit out these words than the *Peconic Queen* appeared out of the east, on her way home. I tried to intercept her, but I was too far away. We lit some day-time flares to get her captain's attention, but for some reason, he didn't see us and kept on going.

"How come he didn't see us?" Harry asked disgustedly.

"Today is Friday. Yesterday was Thursday, and Thursday night is when the Montauk boatmen have their meeting. Last night they had their annual party," I said.

"What does that have to do with it?" Harry asked.

"I'll make a bet that her captain is in the sack because of a hangover from last night's Montauk Boatmen's party, and he has put somebody at the wheel, set it on auto pilot, and told him to look straight ahead for floating logs, etc. He would never have seen us as we are hard to the left of him. (We found out later that this was exactly what had happened.) We still have one last ace up our sleeve. Captain Paul Forsberg on the *Viking Star* was up at Coxe's Ledge, and if he hadn't already gone home, we still have a chance to pick up a ride," I told Harry.

By now, everything was blackened by the oil. Thick black smoke poured out of the motor box and out of every vent hole that let air go down into the motor compartment.

"I think I can see the *Viking Star*! Look, a small white dot, way up to the east'ard," I hollered excitedly, hoping that the appearance of a *Star* in the east was a good omen!

"We might get out of this mess after all," Harry said.

"Get a couple of daylight flares ready," I said to Dickie. "This is our last chance and I'm going to get right in front of him so he'll have to run over us or pick us up."

By now, I was running the motor at idling speed to conserve what little oil we had left in that crank case. That white spot was getting closer and closer. Pretty soon, everybody could see that it *was* the *Viking Star*, captained by Paul Forsberg. Now I steered a little to the right and a little to the left in order to get directly in front of his path.

The *Viking Star* was approaching us—fast. Paul didn't pull back on the throttle until the very last minute. At first, he thought the *Cricket II* was on fire, but when he saw everybody standing around, waving, he realized there was no blaze aboard. Paul pulled the *Viking Star* alongside us and we tossed him a tow line. At the same time, I told Paul what our trouble was and asked him to release us off the tow line, just outside the inlet. From there, we could head in under our own power at idling speed.

The *Viking Star* was three times bigger than my boat and twice as fast. With all her power, she pulled the *Cricket II* and the white shark faster than either of them had ever gone before! When the *Cricket II* got to the inlet, we were all cleaned up. On the way home, I had given everybody a scrub rag and soap. Good thing we had a lot of liquid Ajax with us on that trip!

As promised, Paul dropped us off outside the Montauk inlet; and now, in calmer water, we lifted the white shark up on our mast, with his head hanging over the side, just above of the water. Steaming into the inlet under her own power, the *Cricket II* carried the fish to the scale at the Deep Sea Club Marina.

Harry's great white weighed in at 1,045-pounds. He had the taxidermist make a fiberglass mount made of his white shark's head and Harry hung it in the office area of his diesel-repair shop.

Now we were back to where we had started, in more ways than one: the new spare motor with the blown piston had to be pulled out of the boat and repaired, but the old one we had taken out last winter hadn't been rebuilt yet. A week later, during our autopsy of the engine, Harry discovered that he had been right: there was a defect in the blown piston. It had a hole big enough that you could poke your finger through.

The First and Second Time
I Lost My License

I lost my captain's license three times during my career. The first two times, it was suspended for one month in the winter because I was a bad boy. The final time I lost it was in the spring of 1989, when I forgot to mail the paperwork in and renew it.

The first time the coast guard took my license away was in 1957, for "abandoning ship." Once in a while, we would pick up a last-minute split party where different people shared the total expense of a charter boat for the day. Frank Tuma Sr. organized some of these striped-bass split charters once in a while (and took out a 10 percent commission). The *Cricket II* only got the leftover charters after all of his regular boats were taken care of. His excuse was that the *Cricket II* was "a shaaaark [*sic*] boat" and so he had a hard time sending me customers who wanted other kinds of fish. This excuse was very convenient. This way he didn't have to send me any charters.

One morning, on August 18, 1957, when the *Cricket II* didn't have a charter of its own, I picked up a split charter that Tuma's Charter Service had booked to go tuna fishing: two men and two women. This was a normal August day and the school tuna had been in the fifteen- to twenty-pound class. The ocean was flat calm, but flat-calm water makes for tough fishing. If you were lucky enough to run into a small school of tuna, you would wind up with a few at the end of the day; otherwise, you might only pick up one or two fish here or there. Toward the end of the day, we were on our way home at around two in the afternoon. We had caught a few fish that day—enough for my customers to take home, but not enough to make them happy.

On the way home, we came across the charter boat, *Frances Ann.* Her captain, Doug McCabe, looked like he was into some kind of big fish. Because I knew Doug pretty well, I turned my radio on and gave him a call, asking what was happening. He said he had a big swordfish on and had been fighting it for the past three hours. He had it up alongside his boat twice, but his young mate, Paul Forsberg, had never handled a big fish like this before. So I offered to come aboard his boat and help land the fish. He gladly accepted, and I got ready to jump from the *Cricket II* to the *Frances Ann*.

I didn't hesitate because I had a good mate, Johnny Likey, who could operate my boat well. So I walked out onto the *Cricket II*'s twelve-foot-long harpoon pulpit and Johnny Likey lined up the *Cricket II* so that her pulpit reached over to the *Frances Ann*'s cockpit. This way, when I got in position, all I had to do was slide down off my pulpit and into Doug's cockpit as the *Cricket II* backed away.

Meanwhile, I told Johnny to carry on fishing on the way home and collect the rest of the charter money. It only took us a half hour or so to get the swordfish up alongside the boat and I handled the leader wire, pulling the three-hundred-pound fish close enough for Paul Forsberg to gaff. I always feel good helping somebody catch a big fish, even if it's not from my boat.

When we got back to the dock, Doug's party was very happy and appreciative for the help they got from me. But all this fun was not to last; my mate Johnny came running down the dock and told me that the party we had out wasn't going to pay the rest of the charter money. Their excuse was that I did not give them a full day of fishing because I had switched boats. I told Johnny to catch up with the first couple while I pursued the second couple, who were aiming in the opposite direction.

They saw us coming and started running for their cars. We tore through the gravel on foot, chasing both couples around the parking lot, hoping to catch them before they reached their cars. When we caught up with them, we managed to persuade the quartet to accompany us to Tuma's tackle store as he was responsible for collecting the rest of the money. Under the threat of police intervention, the couples shelled out the money they owed us.

A week went by, and I got a dockside visit from a coast guard officer who enquired if my mate had his captain's papers. I told him, "No, he does not." And I asked why he wanted to know this. The officer told me that the split party we had out last week had put in a formal complaint to the coast guard. Because my mate did not have a license, the officer said, "This is what the marine law considers as *abandoning ship*." I couldn't help bursting out laughing because this accusation sounded funny to me.

"This is no laughing matter," he said sternly, and notified me that I would be receiving a letter in the mail when the court case came up.

The case was called, I lost, and the coast guard suspended my license for January of the following year. The suspension didn't bother me, anyhow, because I don't fish in the winter time. They also told me that if I was brought up on charges of "abandoning ship" one more time, they would take away my license permanently. Once more, it was a case of "If you catch them fish, you're a hero; if you don't, you're a bum."

The second incident happened on July 7, 1964, on a day when the *Cricket II* was chartered by Harry Hoffman and his brother, Fred. A slight southwest wind pushed us along on our drift and visibility was good: you could see all the way to England. This trip took place during the early stages of our shark-tagging program. At that time, many boat captains were not yet familiar with the distance they should stay away from other boats that were drifting and chumming because chumming for sharks was a new technique that I had started. Most captains were more familiar with the standard method of trolling for tuna: dragging feather lures around on the surface.

We had the whole ocean to ourselves that day. My party was tagging blue sharks and had tagged eleven so far, when along came a white shark. He wasn't a very big one, probably a little over 1,000 pounds. The white shark swam into our slick, in fast pursuit of a blue shark, and Harry wanted to catch him. We were concentrating on capturing that white shark when a private boat came over the horizon and plopped down in our chum slick. Harry and I hollered and made hand signals for him to leave us alone. I could see somebody standing on the flying bridge with a rifle in his hand. He was looking right at us and paying no attention despite the fact that he was within earshot of us.

We hoped he just wanted to catch one shark and leave. It was bad enough that he dropped right into our slick, but now he started shooting at the sharks with his high-powered rifle. We had just finished tagging the eleven blue sharks and the thought of him killing them made us mad. Worse yet, was the horrible thought of him firing a salvo at that white shark.

BANG! BANG! BANG! He continued shooting from his flying bridge at the blue sharks on the surface, which were between our two boats. This was dangerous: a stray bullet could go skipping across the top of the water and we were right in its path. So I climbed up on the flying bridge and stood up on my dashboard, as high as I could to be seen, and screamed at him, "GET THE HELL OUT OF HERE!"

As I yelled at him, I took my hat off and waved it in a "go away" gesture, but he just looked at me and kept on firing.

Both Harry and his brother, Fred, were concerned about stray bullets hitting our boat or putting a hole in their hats. There was no sign of the guy moving his vessel and he continued shooting. I decided to drop my marker buoy, which marks the head of our chum line, and chase him with my boat.

As I got close enough to him, I slowed the *Cricket II* to idling speed, and maneuvered her down his starboard side, across his transom, then up his port side.

"What the hell's the matter with you?" I asked him. "Why are you shooting the sharks that we chummed up? Go away and get yourself a bucket of chum and raise your own sharks to the surface to shoot at."

He just stood there on the bridge, with his rifle in his hand, an impassive, athletic-looking, tall dark-haired guy who never said a word. The last thing I said to him was, "If you don't move your boat, I'll drive my pulpit right between your cabin windows!" Then I headed in the direction of my marker buoy and pushed my motor back up to running speed so I could resume shark fishing.

When I looked over my shoulder to see if the private boat was moving, I saw Joe Munchkin[4] emerge from its cabin. He should have known better. Joe Munchkin owned a dock where I had moored my boat a few years earlier.

I watched Joe make hand signals to that tall, impassive guy on the bridge, as if to say, "Don't pay any attention to Mundus; he doesn't own this ocean." This really made the hair on the back of my neck stand up. I spun the *Cricket II* around and headed back at them at half speed. He didn't know how fast I could turn my boat—but I did! I also knew how dangerously close I could come to them and still miss their boat.

He saw my pulpit aiming at them and must have remembered what I said. The tall guy started up both his motors, and was so excited, that he put them in reverse instead of forward. He must have gotten my message. The last I saw of him, he was speeding over the horizon; but because I didn't have my radio on, I didn't know that he had called the coast guard and told them the *Cricket II* had tried to ram his boat—a vessel that he said was "carrying women and children"—in shark-infested waters.

Well, it didn't take long until the U.S. Coast Guard letter arrived, telling me to attend a marine-court hearing in New York City. When I appeared, I took Harry as a witness. I figured I didn't need a lawyer because the case was cut and dried. When it came time for them to testify, Joe Munchkin's bunch denied shooting between the two boats. Soon, it was Harry's turn to be cross-examined by the plaintiffs' attorney. Their coast-guard lawyer turned to Harry and asked, "Did you see the bullets?"

Harry sat in the witness chair in dead silence, and the lawyer asked him the second time, "Did you see the bullets hit the water?"

More silence on Harry's part, until the judge piped up, and said, "You will have to rephrase that question as no human eye can see a speeding bullet." Laughter broke out in court, and the judge banged his gavel down hard on the desk to restore order to the proceedings.

After the coast-guard lawyer thought for a minute, his next question was, "How did you know that he was shooting between the two boats?"

Harry looked back at the lawyer and, with his best deadpan Jack Benny face, said, "Well, I knew it wasn't raining!" Again, this broke up the court with laughter, and the judge had to bang his gavel once more on the desk.

When the judge got the court settled again, he turned to Harry and bellowed, "One more wisecrack like that and you're going to be in contempt of court!"

Then the coast-guard lawyer said to Harry, "Did you see the bullet hit the water?"

Right away, this lawyer got hollered at again by the judge, who said, angrily, "You will have to rephrase that question."

This time, the lawyer asked, "How did you know he was shooting between the two boats?"

Harry's answer to that was, "Because I could see the man with the rifle on the flying bridge shooting between the two boats."

Because the judge was not ready to make a decision yet, the case was postponed. When I returned to Montauk and explained what took place to the Montauk Boatmen's Association, they supplied a real lawyer to represent me at the next hearing. During my second court appearance, we went through almost the same thing. The judge said that I was negligent for trying to run down the private boat and he turned his findings over to the coast guard for them to decide a penalty.

They took away my license for one month to make it look good on the books, suspending it in January because they knew I wouldn't need it at that time of year. When the second hearing was finished, I asked their coast-guard lawyer, outside the court room, how these cases are decided regarding who is at fault. He said that the person who files the complaint first is the one who is believed. As I began walking away, my last words to him were, "If you lawyers need the business, I can send you in a dozen of these complaints a year!"

Close Calls

My old man used to say, "If you're born to hang, you'll never drown," and he should know. During World War I, my father was swept out to sea while on bow watch aboard the USS *Langley*, about fifty miles off the coast of England. In those days, the ships did not have radar, and so a man was stationed on the bow to notify the bridge of any danger.

On this particular evening when my father was standing his watch on the bow, the sea conditions were moderate but the fog was so thick you could cut it with a knife, just like in those old Norse legends where superstitious Viking warriors would use a huge serrated knife to cut the fog so they could see where they were going!

My father probably wished he'd had such a blade, especially after a large wave came from out of the fog and swept him off the bow. Two waves later, he was washed back onto the fantail of the same ship! In the process of being washed back aboard by the wave, my father was smashed against a steel door. Grabbing and groping for something to hang on to, he clutched at the door handle, and as the door opened, the wave washed him into a room that turned out to be the officers' quarters! So I guess he was right when he said, "If you're born to hang, you'll never drown."

I've also had some close calls with the saltwater. It must be a family tradition! When I was fifteen, I bought my first single-barrel .12-gauge shotgun: now I was a hunter! A friend of mine, Phil Chadwick, lived with his grandmother on Barnegat Bay, and he became my duck-hunting partner. I used to leave our house the evening before, spending the night at his place so we could go duck hunting before daylight. Phil got sick and had to stay home for one of these trips, so I decided to go alone in my fourteen-foot canoe. At this time of year, the dead of winter, Barnegat Bay was almost frozen over. For about a city block, from the high tide mark out into the deep water, there was almost solid ice.

I was out there in that deep water, paddling my canoe, with my shotgun across my lap, looking for ducks, when a diving duck popped up hard on my left side and started to fly away. I should have known better, but I picked up my shotgun, aimed it at the duck, and pulled the trigger. This is when it all started. When I pulled that trigger, shooting sideways, the kick from that .12-gauge shotgun turned the canoe over. Luckily for me, the bay was not too deep. The first thing I remember after my canoe turned over was losing my upper set of false teeth. (I'd had a full set of upper false teeth for a while by then, due to accidents and the effects of the osteomyelitis medicine.)

I was gasping for breath from the cold when my teeth fell out. Frantically fishing blind for my teeth, as they began to sink, I managed to catch them when they were at about waist level. Because I was six-feet tall and the water was only six-and-a-half-feet deep, I could touch the bottom when I was at the lower part of a wave. After I got my teeth back, it dawned on me that my shotgun had gone down also. I dove down quickly for a one-and-only try. By chance, my hand hit the barrel and I was able to save the shotgun.

Now the real fun began. There I was in the water, behind a half-sunken canoe, dressed in a long, heavy leather jacket and hip boots. My boots filled with water and became three times as heavy, while my jacket pockets were filled with shotgun shells. All this extra weight made it impossible for me to get back into my overturned canoe. The only thing I could see to do was to push the canoe ahead of me and try to make the beach before I froze to death. When I reached the ice, I had to push the canoe and try to break through the ice at the same time. Don't ask me how I made it ashore, but somehow I did—with help from "the man upstairs."

Now that I was on the frozen beach, in panic, I decided to take off my boots to get the water out of them. After I got one boot off and dumped the water out, I found that I couldn't get it back on again because everything was wet, and my half-frozen sock was sticking to the side of the boot.

The only thing that was left for me to do was to run up the beach, as fast as I could to Phil's house, which was about a mile away. I thumped my way up the frozen beach with one boot on and one boot off while the shotgun shells rattled away in my waterlogged pockets. Believe it or not, I did reach Phil's house and banged on his back door. Phil's grandmother opened the door, took one look at me, and immediately knew what happened. She grabbed me by the shoulder and screamed at me, in her squeaky voice, to get inside and take off all my clothes.

While I was trying to do this with my frozen fingers, she filled a large metal washtub in the middle of the room with water. I climbed into the tub and she started pouring water over my head. To me, this water felt nice and warm and I remarked, "The warm water feels great!"

She replied, "This water I'm pouring over you is ice cold! Let me know when it starts to feel cold."

At the time, I didn't know that this was the way to thaw out a person. Phil's grandmother probably saved my life that day. I never even caught a cold or got frostbite. I guess I wasn't born to drown.

Close Call #2: Miami Incident, 1952

My next close call occurred in 1952, during my fishing days with Capt. Red Stuart down in Miami. Sometimes, we'd fish inside the inlet for tarpon, and other times we'd fish in the ocean for sailfish, tuna, and any other sport fish.

This particular day, Friday, January 4, the wind was blowing hard and the ocean was sloppy. Red's charter party decided to stay inside the inlet and fish the calm waters for tarpon. This was the year that monofilament fishing line came on the market.

According to the experts at that time, by catching tarpon up to one hundred pounds on thirty-pound-test monofilament line, we were doing something almost impossible. Nowadays, they catch one-hundred-pound tarpon on five-pound test and on lighter, ultra-light tackle. We had caught a couple of tarpon in the morning and it looked like the wind had quieted down so the party asked Red if we could go offshore to do some trolling. It was only a stone's throw from tarpon fishing inside the inlet to sport fishing outside.

My job was to put the tarpon tackle away and get the sport-fishing tackle out. I had put away the tarpon tackle by the time we cleared the inlet. When we started out into the deep water, I had taken out some rods with trolling lures, and let out the lines on three of them until they were out about fifty feet behind the boat.

Suddenly, I looked up and realized that I did not have my outriggers down. (The outriggers spread the lines apart, holding them that way so they won't get tangled up). In order to let the outriggers down and out from their stored upright position, I had to climb up on top of the cabin roof. When I went forward from the cockpit, I always made a habit of passing by the boat operator, who happened to be Red at that time; otherwise, if I went up on the other side of the boat and fell overboard, no one would see me go.

Soon, I was on my way forward to let down the outriggers, and passed by Red at the wheel, thinking he had seen me. But he was busy bullshitting with one of the customers and his head was turned the other way.

The *Sandona* danced up and down on the choppy sea and there was only a six- to eight-inch wide walkway from the cockpit to up forward. Hanging on to the handrail, hand over hand, and the ledge, toe over toe, I walked slowly along the narrow ledge until I took one particular step where there was no boat! My foot slipped, pulling me down, but I managed to grab hold of that six-inch walkway. As the boat went up, I hung on. When it came down, the force of a wave almost tore my grip loose. I was frantically waiting for Red to pull back on the throttle any second. There was no sign of this and here came another wave.

I knew I couldn't hang on any longer and survive the force of one more wave, so when another wave thrust the *Sandona*'s bow upward and her stern down, after making sure my body was clear of the water, I brought my feet up as high as I could and pushed myself out and away from the boat, going into a barrel roll. The *Sandona* had two spinning propellers, and I knew that if I had tried to hang on, I would have been sucked right into the one on my side of the boat. This little trick worked. There I was, under the water, listening to the propellers whiz by over my head. When I heard them go past me, I knew it was time for me to surface. "No good," I said to myself. "I can't go up yet because those trolling lures I put out will catch me instead of a fish!" So I stayed down, holding my breath a little longer, and surfaced when I thought the lures had passed.

Now I had a real problem. I could see that nobody knew I had fallen overboard because the boat was heading straight at the same speed, and Red was still bullshitting with the same guy. The customer's wife was down below, probably powdering her nose. As there were only two people in the charter, I knew nobody had seen me go. Now

I waited for a wave to push me up high enough to be seen, and I waved my arm and whistled at the same time.

The man who was talking to Red turned his head and looked back, then jumped as I whistled. He tapped Red on the shoulder to tell him he either had to get another mate or go back and pick this one up! By this time, we were five to six miles offshore and I would have had a long walk home if he hadn't seen me when I whistled. Red turned the boat around in my direction, shutting off both engines when he got close. As he coasted up to me and grabbed my arm, Red had this funny look on his face, as he asked, "Frank, when was the last time you fell overboard?" He knew that, usually, the first time you fall overboard at sea is often your *last*.

Close Call #3: Boston-Whaler Incident

One winter in the late 1970s, I was vacationing with two of my friends in St. Maarten after selling my other boat, the *Cricket III*, there. A girlfriend, Boggsy, and I decided to borrow a Boston Whaler from Jose Speetjens, the lawyer I used for my business, and go out to one of the out islands to fish and get conch (giant clams). And so the three of us loaded the fourteen-foot whaler with all of our gear: fishing tackle, cameras, fish poles, and coolers. That day, the weather was the usual light ten- to fifteen-mile breeze that alternated out of the east-northeast and east-southeast.

The out-island we were headed for was about eight miles or so off St. Maarten, a short jaunt for the fast Boston Whaler. When we reached the island, we decided to do some trolling and explore all around this one-mile-square piece of real estate set in the middle of nowhere. I was running the boat, and the thirty-five-horse-power Evinrude outboard motor purred right along. After a while, I cut the power down to a slow idle and my friends put out their light tackle. In no time they were catching all kinds of small fish as we idled our way around the island.

On the lee side of the island, we noticed two sail boats in the forty-foot class, which were anchored just off a small sandy beach. This sandy beach was the only place anybody could go ashore; the rest of the island consisted of sharp rocks and high cliffs.

We found a place where the water was only fifteen- to twenty feet deep and a good place to load up on the queen conch of the Caribbean. The queen conch is one of the biggest of the conch family. They get as heavy as three to five pounds each in the shell. I was doing the diving while my friend and Boggsy waited in the Whaler. I don't know how many conchs I had picked up, but by now, the bottom of the Whaler was covered with them—more weight in the bottom of the boat to slow us down on the way home—so we went back to trolling for small fish.

The tiny island was egg-shaped, and just around from the sandy beach was a cove on the leeward side. It was cut right out of the rocks and had high cliffs. We trolled back and forth across this cove a few times, catching small fish as we went.

It was getting past noontime when I asked Boggsy how much longer he wanted to fish before going home. He said, "Let's make one more pass across the cove and then go home."

So be it. I turned the Whaler around and started our last pass back across the opening in the cove, making certain that I was far enough off shore. About halfway across, a wave broke out of nowhere, rumbling in toward us. We found ourselves inside the wave, sandwiched between three feet of rolling white water and rocks. There was no place to go, so I decided to push my way through the wave to get to the other side. I turned the bow into the wall of green, rolling water. At a time like this, a lot of things run through your mind. One of them was: should I use power and hit this mess of green water fast, busting though it, or stay at the same speed and let the bow go through easy? Because the Whaler's bow is flat and it does not come to a point, it would not slice through the water, and therefore I was afraid of using power. I had two other people with me—someone could get hurt if I tried to bust through the wave fast, and so I decided to go slow.

With all the weight we had in the boat, we never made it through the wave. The Whaler came to a fast stop. It all happened so suddenly. One second we were going straight through the wave, and the next we were being pushed backward. Worse yet, this Boston Whaler's transom had a "cut down" where the outboard was attached. This cut-down was about four inches lower than the rest of the transom, and was bad because the water came in and over that low cut-out spot as the boat was being pushed backward. I thought this was OK, because the way it looked to me, the worse that could happen was that we could wind up with a bellyful of water; but I was wrong.

As we were thrust backward and water surged over the back of the boat, the Whaler dug into the water and flipped over, end over end. Boggsy and my girlfriend were tossed overboard, but because I had hold of the outboard, I managed to hang on. During the chaos, I caught a quick glimpse of the boat and all the equipment falling down on top of me. Now I was underneath this mess and was disorientated. I did not know which way to swim out from under the debris. It seemed like a long time before I saw daylight and got air in my lungs. By now, the boat was upside down. When I surfaced, I couldn't see anybody, so I hollered, "Where is everybody?"

"Over here," a voice answered.

Both my friend and Boggsy were on the opposite side of the boat. As that freak deepwater wave turned the boat upside down, both anchors that had been lying in the boat, ready to go, were automatically dropped. The boat had been pushed inshore the length of the anchor lines, about a hundred feet or so. Boggsy decided to climb on top of the upturned Whaler and he hollered out for us to join him. I told him that this was the wrong way to go, that we had to swim around to the sandy cove where the sailboats were on the other side of the island. We couldn't go ashore where we were because of the sharp coral and the waves pounding against the high cliffs. The three of us would be cut to pieces or beaten to death.

We had no place to go. Boggsy got knocked off the boat by the next wave and decided to join our wagon train, which was heading to the other side of the island. At this moment, Boggsy decided to do his Tarzan swim, and I hollered at him to slow down because we had a long way to go.

To calm my two friends, I kept telling them that we were just going on a swim around the island to the sandy beach. Slowly, the three of us started the long swim. Because I had some experience with water, a disturbing thought went through me: what's going to happen to us when we reach the point of land that we have to go around? Will there be a strong tide or current to sweep us out and away from the island? I did not share this thought with my companions.

Slowly, ever so slowly, we were reaching the Point. By this time, we had been in the water for an hour or so. As we made our way around the rocky Point, we could see the two sailboats. They were still anchored in the sandy cove so we had a chance. We were so close but still so far from making it. One more time, I remembered the words of my dear old dad, "If you're born to hang, you'll never drown," but Boggsy didn't want to wait for me to test this theory. He tried reaching the sailboats with his vocal chords, "HELP! HELP!" he yelled.

I thought we were too far away to holler yet, but Lady Luck was on our side. A mate out on deck on one of the sailboats heard Boggsy's lovely voice. In short order, we could see the mate jumping into a dinghy that they had trailing behind.

It was only seconds until the dinghy was alongside us. Help had arrived. After we had climbed aboard, I noticed that I had a deep two-inch gash on my right forearm, probably from the outboard or from one of the hundred conchs that had landed on my head! If Boggsy and my girlfriend had known that I had been bleeding throughout our three-mile swim, they might have panicked, thinking about the possibility of a shark attack.

Turning to them, I said, "Now that we have saved our asses, how about going back to see if we can save the boat before it goes up on the rocks?" I didn't have to take a vote on that one. They both said the same words at the same time, "Take us to the sailboat. Now!" So I told the mate to take them to the sailboat, and then he and I would go back to try to save the Boston Whaler.

We put them aboard the sailboat and headed back to the Whaler as fast as we could go. When we reached it, the Whaler had been pushed farther toward the rocky beach, but the anchor line was still holding. I told the mate I would go overboard and get the anchor line, then hand it to him and he could tow the boat off the beach. However, the best laid plans of mice and men can go wrong. I dove overboard and swam in to find that the anchor line was tight from the anchor to the boat: too tight. I could not pick up the anchor because there was too much pressure from the boat pulling on it. Also, the mate couldn't get in any closer with his boat because of the breaking waves. I tried taking hold of the tight anchor line in the middle, somewhere between the anchor and the boat, and attempted to walk out toward the mate's dinghy.

By now, my head was under the water more than it was above. I was hanging on to the anchor line with one arm, with my left arm outstretched, hoping the mate could grab hold of it. He shot in between the breakers and made a couple of passes, trying to reach my left arm. He almost grabbed it one time, but only had seconds to work with because a wave was breathing down his neck; so the mate had to go back out beyond the breakers and wait for another chance. He unsuccessfully tried this three or four times. By now, we both realized it couldn't be done. We needed a long rope, which we did not have. So I motioned for him to stay outside the breakers. I let go of the anchor line and swam out to him. We gave up and returned to the sailboat.

The owner of the sailboat was a doctor and he noticed the cut on my arm. He treated it by putting a couple of clamps on the wound, apologizing that he couldn't stitch it up as he didn't have the necessary equipment. The doctor used his radio to call St. Maarten for help. In about an hour or so, a friend of mine came out in a small boat to take us home. On the way home, we took a look at what was left of the Boston Whaler. The anchor lines had been cut by the sharp coral and rocks, and the boat was smashed to pieces on the rocky beach. There was not a piece left any bigger than your hat.

We were in one piece, but my pocket book had a large hole in it, about four thousand dollars' worth. No, Speetjens had no insurance on the boat, so it had been an awfully expensive boat ride, but thank god I made it home: one more time.

Close Call #4: Ice-Cream Cone Saves Boy

This occurred when a former girlfriend and I made a trip from New York to Mexico. First, we went to San Francisco, where we met up with my daughter, Pat, and she gave us a tour of the town (when Pat was working for Exxon, she was based in San Francisco for a while).

Then my girlfriend and I rented a car and we drove down the coast, along the infamous Highway Number 1. I'd heard about it from truck drivers and everybody else. It's a horrible, twisty-turny road that's up there a couple of hundred feet, with no guard rails. One slip and you're down into the rocks.

Although my girlfriend had wanted to take this road down the coast and stop in at Hearst Castle, she was scared to death much of the time because it was too high, and to tell you the truth, I didn't like looking at the rocks and saltwater because I've seen too much of them.

We spent half a day at Hearst Castle, didn't see Hearst: he wasn't home! Then we dropped in on another friend of mine, Franklin. We stayed over at Franklin's place that night. Next morning, we took an airplane and flew down to Gordon Rynders's condo in Mexico. Gordon had invited us down and we were supposed to stay for two weeks, but needless to say, one week was enough down there, doing nothing.

Gordon's condo was up on top of a mountain along with twenty other condos. They were all in one lump and resembled a small city. It was about a fifteen-minute ride up the road to where the condos were. When I got there, it was nothing, just a few rocks. I sat there and looked down at the ocean and at the town. That's all I did, just sat there and looked down.

I said to Gordon, "Hey, are we going fishing, or what?"

The fishing station had no phone, so Gordon decided, "All right, we'll take a ride down there tomorrow to make arrangements to go fishing the following day."

"OK," I said. "At least it will be something to do."

Gordon told me it was about three-quarters of an hour's drive to the fishing dock, so the next day, my friend, Gordon, and I drove down the monotonous dirt road to the fishing station. We found the so-called captain, and he said it would be OK for tomorrow. All right, we bullshitted with him for a while and then it was time to go back home. By this time, it was late afternoon.

We were driving back home when I said to Gordon, "Hey, ain't there a place around here where you can get an ice-cream cone?"

He said, "Yeah, there's a place up ahead of us, about five or ten minutes away." So we drove down this long dirt road, stopped in at a little tourist trap, and we each got an ice-cream cone, if you can call it an ice-cream cone. I didn't: it was the size of a marble. It didn't take me long to inhale this little thing, so Gordon was ready to go.

I said, "Wait a minute. Hold it. I'm gonna get another one." So I got the second so-called ice-cream cone and said, "Wait a minute. Let me eat it. I don't want to dribble all over the car." So I ate it there and then climbed in the car and away we went.

After we had driven back up to Gordon's condo, we saw everybody standing with their arms out, their chins straight down, and their eyes wide open. They were frozen, and to me, everybody looked like Muppets; something had just happened and the dust still hadn't settled. In fact, it was still in the air! We went running around and found people standing right in front of Gordon's condo. Everything was a mess. It looked like somebody had just dropped an atom bomb.

We discovered that the ceiling of the outside porch had collapsed, the same porch where I usually sat and had my chaw [sic] of tobacco, after coming back from town. When I say "collapsed" I mean fell down! At that time in Mexico, there was no strict building code, so they just built things the way they wanted, with plenty of cement and sand. There was no wire or reinforcing rods holding the cement ceiling together. It was made fast to nothing. The chunks of debris where I would have been sitting were six-inches thick, and some were three-feet round. I tried moving one and it was impossible. All the flower pots were squashed, and if I had been sitting there, I'd have been squashed too, but thanks to the time that it took me to eat my second ice-cream cone, my life had been spared!

CHAPTER 7

PIRATE OF THE CARIBBEAN

From 1968 to 1976, I pioneered sport fishing on the island of St. Maarten in the Caribbean. That part of my life was spent going back and forth like a yo-yo, running two charter boats on two different oceans. I spent summers shark fishing the *Cricket II* off Montauk, and winters taking out tourists on the *Cricket III* off St. Maarten. The *Cricket III* was formerly a Montauk open boat by the name of the *Sea Queen*. I converted her, with a chainsaw, to make her look like the *Cricket II*. My St. Maarten Caribbean connection all began with a simple phone call.

My pirate days.

St. Maarten, Ready or Not

Back in 1968, when Claude Philippe, the one-time general manager for the Waldorf Astoria, was building his El Creole Village in St. Maarten on the French side of the island, he needed a sport-fishing boat to take care of his guests. A message was relayed to me that he wanted to interview me in New York. So I made an appointment, and it wasn't long before I was standing in front of Claude Philippe's big mahogany desk. While he began interviewing me in English, Mr. Philippe was simultaneously talking in French on the telephone and signing different papers as his secretary neatly dropped them on the desk in front of him. Our conversation wasn't very long. He simply asked me if I wanted to take a charter boat to St. Maarten in the near future for his hotel project. He said he would guarantee me x-amount of fishing trips, whether I sailed them or not. Right then and there, a new venture (and adventure) began unfolding.

I returned to Montauk that day and immediately began looking for a business partner; money wise, I could not handle this by myself. Jimmy, a new friend of mine in Montauk, seemed interested and took his wife down to St. Maarten to look the situation over and do some research on Mr. Philippe's project. After Jim and his wife had walked on the white sandy beaches and swum in the blue Caribbean, he was happy with what he saw and decided to go in with me on this project. We immediately started looking around for a boat. This involved checking all the newspaper ads and visiting boatyards. Jim and I had also spread the word around Montauk that we were looking for a boat. Word came back to us that Stanley Blados's son owned a boat, the *Sea Queen*, over in Shelter Island.

Stanley's father had operated this boat out of Montauk for many years and I had fished alongside him, so I knew how seaworthy his vessel was. The price was right, but the conversion would be costly. The *Sea Queen* had been an open boat. We would have to cut the cabin in half and make a charter boat out of her.

That fall, Jim brought the *Sea Queen* to Montauk and we began work on her. The two of us worked in extreme weather conditions, where the temperature seldom rose above freezing. The two hardest jobs were installing the new windows and painting the bottom. When we were putting the windows in, the wind was blowing twenty-five to thirty miles an hour out of the northwest, coming across the frozen Long Island Sound. And when we painted the bottom, the temperature was eight degrees Fahrenheit.

The boat had been hauled out for conversion at Sag Harbor, and when everything was complete, the travel lift picked the *Sea Queen* up to put her in the water. As she was lowered, the *Sea Queen* first had to break through six inches of ice in the travel lift's slip. This was only the beginning. Then we had to break through a lot of ice on our way back to Montauk. It was only a short run, but it took us all day. The weather was so cold, that the incoming water which cooled the motor was freezing long before it reached the saltwater pump. Because Long Island Sound was just about frozen over, for most of the trip I had to lie in the bilge with a propane torch, holding it on the pipe to melt the ice.

Before we could move the boat to St. Maarten, first Jim and I had to make a cradle that could be assembled when we reached Staten Island, where we would be meeting the Sea Train Shipping Company. They shipped all their freight out of here. Sea Train would transport the *Sea Queen* (soon to be renamed the *Cricket III*) as deck cargo to San Juan, Puerto Rico.

To complicate matters, there was a longshoremen's strike on at the time and nothing moved at the waterfront. This was the longest dock strike in history and we had become caught up in it. However, Jim and I were lucky enough to have a good connection who knew somebody at

Sea Train, and so the *Cricket III* was one of the first boats shipped out after the labor dispute ended.

Jim and I were notified to meet the ship in San Juan. Then we ran the *Cricket III* over to St. Maarten, with an overnight stop at St. Thomas.

When we reached St. Maarten and went ashore on the French side, the two of us got a nasty shock. Claude Philippe had gone bankrupt—for the third time—and abandoned his project. El Creole was only half-finished and many of the locals on the island were looting it. With no welcoming committee to tell us where to go, or what to do, everything was beyond the pioneering stage. Here we were in a foreign country with nowhere to go, so we decided to take the boat around and anchor it on the Dutch side.

Our equipment included a small dinghy, so we were able to row ashore after anchoring up. Jim was not used to this pioneering business, which included living on the boat and jumping overboard when we wanted a shower. So he went back to New York, saying that his father was sick. A week after he left, I got a phone call from Jim, telling me he was not coming back and I could repay the money that I owed him a little at a time.

Now I was all by myself and the fun started. After I got friendly with the hotel beach attendants, they stole towels for me to use as bed blankets. Finding charters was hard. After I got wheels, it made the job a little easier: I bought a small second-hand mini moke for a hundred dollars. Because the St. Maarten telephone service back then was very bad, I had no way of contacting the hotels to find out if they had charters for me. So every day, I had to drive to each hotel to make and confirm charter arrangements. Then I had to chase down people who had booked a trip and wanted to go fishing. Finding them was not easy. They could be any place: at the beach or in town.

So things fell into place very slowly. There were so many complications; for instance, I had to find some place to store all the extra equipment we had brought down. I also had to find a local mate, find out where to buy bait, and rent a freezer to store bait in. Eventually, I bought my own freezer with a $1,000 tip that Casey, one of my Chinese customers, gave me!

Casey was a fellow boatman who felt sorry for me and the mess I was in. Because I had no place to keep my bait, he bought me a brand-new freezer, telling me I could pay him back later. Every time I saw Casey, I asked him, "Hey, Casey, how about the money I owe you for the freezer?"

And he would always say, "Pay me back later."

This went on for the whole of that winter. As Casey would never take the money for the freezer, I considered this a $1,000 tip.

With all the complications that I had, getting the freezer was a bonus. Down in St. Maarten, it seemed that just when I had sorted out one frustrating situation, a new unexpected problem popped up in its place.

A trip to the post office and the bank would take all day. I went to the post office to rent a PO box, and they laughed at me, using their famous phrase, "It's finish!" meaning, "No more; it's all sold out; kaput!" So I had to take my place in the long line of lost souls who could not get a box. Sometimes, I would have to stand in line for up to two hours. So I gave one of the local kids twenty-five cents to go to the post office for me, but the lines were just as bad in the bank.

It also took all day just to fuel up the boat: I had to go to the gas station to tell the man that I would like to have the fuel truck down on the dock in the morning. And every time, he would show up late, around 10:30 or 11:00 a.m. So by the time I helped the driver drag the fuel hose all the way from the truck and out on the short pier to the *Cricket III*, the day would be about shot. One day, I was standing around, waiting for the fuel truck to arrive, when I mumbled out loud in frustration, "Why does everybody take so long to do anything down here?"

I forgot that my dark-skinned mate was standing alongside me, and he answered, in storylike style, with an emphasis on certain words like many of the locals did when they were answering me. "Frank, if a *man* comes to *this* island and *expects* people to be on time, he will be *very* disliked."

It took me a long time to get used to this slow lifestyle. After a while, I figured out what to do and how to do it to save a little time, and my sanity. For instance, one of the charter parties invited me over for breakfast and insisted on having it at their hotel before we left for a day's fishing. I tried talking them out of this because we were going to be late getting started.

"Well, they open the restaurant at 7:00 a.m. How late could we be?" one of them asked.

"You'll find out," I said.

We met in the dining room at 7:00 a.m. All the tables were set and nobody was there but us. The boys picked a table against the far wall, one farthest away from the kitchen. The party and I sat there, waiting, with our cups neatly turned upside down on the saucers. A hundred feet across that large dining room stood a dark-skinned waitress, leaning against the wall with her arms folded, watching us. After a while, one of the boys decided to get her attention by beckoning her. She walked all the way across the dining room, empty-handed, and said, "Good morning," in a cheerful singsong voice.

One of the party replied, "Good morning. Could I have a cup of coffee?"

"Yes," she said, and turned around to walk all the way back across the dining room to the big coffee pots. She returned and poured him his cup of coffee. Then she walked all the way back and put the coffee pot down.

The party was dumbfounded. They couldn't believe what they had just seen. Another one of the boys beckoned her to come over. She walked all the way across the dining room floor, empty-handed, and said, "Good morning."

Charlie said, "Could I have a cup of coffee too?"

"Yes," she said, and walked all the way back across the dining room floor, picked up the coffee pot, brought it back to our table, poured Charlie's coffee, turned around, and began walking back again.

One of the other guys yelled, "HEY! Can we ALL have coffee?"

"Yes," she said calmly, returning to pour all the coffees.

It was then that one of the other guys could not help himself. He asked the question, "Why didn't you give all of us coffee from the beginning?"

She smiled and replied, in her Caribbean lilt, "*You didn't arsk me, mon* [sic]." So the boys had discovered something I already knew, that it would take us a couple of hours just to have a cup of coffee with our breakfast!

Marlin Branded

Back in January 1973, Dick Bebon, one of my Long Island customers, came down to St. Maarten to fish with me, and we decided to do an overnight trip on the twenty-seventh. Normally, Captain Abel and his son ran the *Cricket III* for me, but when I had one of my good customers book a trip, I always rode along too. The first day, we trolled around the island of Saba, catching an occasional barracuda or two. Then we anchored up for the night close to the island so that we could catch some small bottom fish.

Then came daylight. At this time of day, there was plenty of trolling action, and it didn't take long before we were catching small tuna. After about half an hour, a blue marlin appeared behind the boat, chasing one of the small tuna that we were winding in. I hooked a small tuna on for bait and threw it overboard. The marlin picked it up right away and started heading for the horizon. I handed the rod to Dick and told him to strike the fish. When the line came tight, the marlin shot to the surface, waving his two-and-a-half-foot bill out of the water slowly to the right and to the left. This is a good indication of a gut-hooked fish. A gut-hooked fish will not run, fight, or jump. Most of the time, all you have to do is wind them right up to the boat, but you had better be prepared because that fish is going to do a lot of fighting at the boat when you get ready to take him. And that's exactly what happened.

I underestimated the size of the marlin (thinking it to be a little over one hundred pounds) and said to the mate, "I'm going to bill this fish," meaning, I was going to reach down and grab hold of its bill, then slide the marlin into the boat; I have done this plenty of times before to fish around a hundred pounds.

As I grabbed hold of the bill, the fish jumped straight up in the air—with me holding on. And when it came down, the fish's weight slammed my chest across the *Cricket*

III's gunnel. By this time, I couldn't let go because I was all tangled up in fifteen feet of leader wire. Then the marlin started to wipe the side of the boat with my body, slamming me back and forth, as he shook his head right and left. I desperately hung on, yelling for help, and the mate reached down and grabbed the bill with me.

Now we were both being smashed to the right and to the left. I hollered for Captain Abel to hurry down from the bridge to help us. It seemed like hours before he reached me. Now the three of us had hold of the marlin's bill. We pulled the fish up and slid him across the side of the boat and into the cockpit. There was one more thing I forgot to tell the boys: Don't let go!

It was too late: as soon as the fish dropped onto the deck, the boys let go and ran for safety. It was then that I saw how big this fish was, close to two hundred pounds, and over seven feet long. I immediately fell to the deck, hoping to use my weight to anchor the marlin's head down. I couldn't let go, otherwise he'd have killed me with that powerful, spikelike bill. "Hit the sonofabitch in the head with the club before it sticks me in the gut!" I screamed to the mate, who was in such shock that his stutter kicked back in, so bad that he couldn't hit the fish. Now the fish started to jump up and down repeatedly, thrashing his tail and slamming it flat on the deck with each downward thrust. This went on for about five minutes until the fish finally died.

By this time, my face and chest were covered with blood. Someone asked if I was hurt. I didn't even know it myself, and so I said: "I'll find out in a minute." Taking a bucket of water, I splashed it all over my body. Fortunately, the blood turned out to be the fish's—this time.

This had been yet another close call. The only thing I got out of it was an eight-inch chafe mark on my skin where I had I tucked the fish's coarse bill under my right arm to hold him down when he was thrashing up and down on deck. And so that was the time I got marlin branded.

My St. Maarten Rain Dance

In the pile of homemade audio cassette tapes that I took down to St. Maarten with me were some from Gordon Rynders. He had duped them from the *Daily News'* soundtrack files and they were the authentic sounds of cows, chickens, ducks, thunder, lightening, and Indians. Yes, Gordon sent me a real North-American-Indian rain dance to add to my collection.

During the winter months, I rented a house in St. Maarten for a few years, from Arnez, a dark-skinned widow, who was raising her two young grandsons: one was about six, and the other, eight. They lived in the small tin shack that had no water or electricity, directly behind the house that I was renting. Arnez's slow-moving aged father lived in another tin shack, about fifty feet away from her hut. Every morning, he emerged, carrying his piss pot. Instead of saying "Good Morning" to him, Arnez always asked disappointedly, "You still with us?"

Because she didn't have any running water, Arnez had to use the hand pump that was under my kitchen window. One morning, she was pumping water with her two grandsons standing alongside her watching, while I was at the kitchen sink washing some dishes.

"Good morning, Arnez," I said. In St. Maarten, you always have to start your conversation out slow, and usually with a greeting.

"Good morning, Frank. How are you?" she asked.

"Fine. How are you?" I replied.

Because she saw me washing dishes, her next statement was, "We haven't had rain in a while." (meaning, "Take it easy on the water.")

I told Arnez that I knew we depended on rain for our fresh water. "I am going as easy on the water as I can. How low are we?"

She said, "Very low. We need rain."

Jokingly, I said, "I can make it rain. I have a North-American-Indian rain-dance tape."

Arnez looked at me surprised, and said, "Could you make it rain?"

"Sure," I said, forgetting to tell her that this was a joke. "How much rain do you want?" I asked.

"Plenty," she said.

"OK," I said, "Hang on."

I turned on my tape recorder and started jumping and dancing around the kitchen floor, while the Indians sang, "HY-OH-HY-OH-ITCHIN-HY-OH."

I did this for about five minutes and figured that was enough. When I stopped jumping and dancing, I looked out of the window and Arnez was still standing there, with her eyes as big as the bucket she was carrying, while her two boys were stepping on their chins, their mouths wide open in amazement.

That night it rained. And it rained. And it didn't stop raining until four days later. The rainstorm washed half of the island away. In the middle of all this, Arnez came to me and asked me to make it stop. I told her, "You said that you wanted plenty, so I can't make it stop. Once you've put your order in, that's it."

Then we had two months of dry weather. Arnez came to me again and asked for more rain. Kidding her once more, I asked, "How much rain do you want this time?"

"A little," she said cautiously, thinking about her last order.

Still joking, I suggested, "How about one hour of hard rain?"

"That's fine," she said, satisfied. So I turned on my tape recorder for ten to fifteen seconds, did a short dance, and then shut it off.

The next day, we got a couple of hours of hard rain. I had forgotten that the locals were very superstitious and my joke backfired because they *knew*, they didn't think, that

I had done some kind of black magic. From then on, every time that Arnez pumped her water, she looked at me as if I was some kind of god, and the two boys would not let me get anywhere near them. They were scared half to death.

Soon after, I was getting ready to go home to New York, and once more, Arnez was outside my kitchen window, pumping her water. After saying, "Good morning," she asked, "Could we have some more water before you go home?"

About now, I realized I was stuck. I could not afford to gamble on the Indians paying off again, so I told her that my tape was broken and I couldn't do the rain dance anymore.

In Dutch Trouble

In my drinking days, wherever I went, the police were not far behind. This included the island of St. Maarten in the Caribbean, where I owned and operated my other charter boat, the *Cricket III*, for six or seven winters from the late sixties to 1976. The availability of cheap booze in St. Maarten didn't help matters at all: Mount Gay Rum was $10.00 a case; and Johnny Walker Red, $3.50 for a big bottle.

In March 1975, I was building a dock in the lagoon in front of my waterfront property, and had just finished a few drinks of bourbon, when Ralph, the dark-skinned mate I recently fired, pulled up close to the house in a borrowed black Toyota sedan. Many mates down there (or help of any kind) are changed like dirty socks because their philosophy is: "Why collect two days' pay when you can survive a whole week on one day's pay?"

I watched this ex-mate of mine drive his car right up in front of my house, jump out, and run inside.

I hollered to him, "HEY, WHAT DO YOU WANT? WHAT'S GOING ON?" as I walked up to the house from the beach, still carrying the hatchet I was working with. Before I reached the house, he had emerged, carrying a huge armful of clothes. I knew he had left clothes at my house and I had washed them for him; but what else did he have in that bundle? I didn't know if he had taken any of my valuable junk. Anyhow, the mate rushed out of my house, threw the clothes in his car, and put it in full reverse, spraying sand and gravel in all directions as he sped backward, heading toward the middle of the big parking lot that was next to my house.

I knew that there was only one road he could take, and that was around the other side of my house. So I ran around to cut him off, still carrying the hatchet. I stood in the middle of the road, waving my hatchet for him to stop, when he came out with his car. There was no sign of him stopping. The man was bent over the steering wheel with a smirk on his face, like "what are you going to do about it?" He was foolish enough to think I wouldn't throw the hatchet through his windshield. That hatchet bounced once off the top of the hood and crashed through the glass on the passenger side. He didn't even stop for this and kept on going.

Heading into town that afternoon was not a good move because I was picked up by the Dutch detectives. They emptied my pockets and immediately put me in jail. I figured it would be a short stay and my lawyer friend, Jose Speetjens, would get me out on bail. Little did I know that in a Dutch jail there is no bail and the magistrate visited the island only once a month. He was the man who had the power to let you out of jail while you waited for your day in court. Luckily, I only had to spend four days in jail, one of them in solitary, until this magistrate visited the island. When a person is jailed on St. Maarten, he or she is placed in solitary confinement for the first twenty-four hours to see if they are well-behaved; if so, they are then put in with the rest of the prisoners.

My daughter, Pat, who was eighteen at that time, had come to St. Maarten on vacation. When Pat discovered I was in jail, she brought me candies whenever she could, sneaking them in between the cracks of the big steel doors that led to the side street. This only lasted a short time until she was caught. I was told by a policeman, "The next time Patti gets caught, she will spend time in here with you."

Over the next few days, the mate and I were each told to make out a written statement for the magistrate. When the magistrate arrived, he read them both and asked me to come into the room where he was. Holding both pieces of paper in his hand he said, with certainty, "I know you're lying, and I know the mate is lying, but I think you are lying less."

Then he let me go home after making me give him my word that I would not leave the island until my court case came up the following month.

On May 7, I had to appear in court. My lawyer, Jose, told me to get all dressed up, wear a tie, and "be very apologetic."

It was a good thing that I knew how to keep a poker face, because when I walked in, the first thing I noticed was that everybody wore a long white wig, everyone except me! Court proceedings are very different in St. Maarten from how they are in the States. There was a judge, his assistant, and a bunch of other people wearing wigs. I half expected to see George Washington in there somewhere! How it all worked, I don't know.

The judge asked me questions about what happened. I told him I was sorry about the incident. I knew it looked very bad that I had thrown a hatchet at the mate and I wanted to pay for the damages.

The judge said, "It doesn't make any difference what you threw at him, whether it was a hatchet, a hammer, or a rock: it would have done the same damage." I stood there and waited as his assistant told me what my penalty was. I had to replace the automobile windshield, or "windscreen" as he called it. He gave me a time limit to do this. I had to bring the receipt to him as proof, and then I would be free to go.

My second run-in with the St. Maarten police occurred when I was accused of helping a criminal escape off the island. During normal fishing days, every customer has to have his or her name registered with the police before the boat leaves the dock. This is the same system that the airlines use: a passenger manifest.

One morning at nine o'clock, a casually-dressed guy walked down the dock with no sunglasses and no hat to hide himself. He asked me if I would take him to St. Barts, the next island, and leave him there. I told him, "Yes," and said I would charge him for half a day's fishing trip. I asked him for his full name to send up to the police station for the passenger list. This was done and away we went in broad daylight.

When I got back to St. Maarten, everybody was jumping up and down, accusing me of smuggling a criminal off the island. Apparently, this American guy who had chartered my boat worked in one of the casinos. He had been accused of embezzlement and had been told by the police not to leave St. Maarten. Legally, the police could not force him to stay on the island unless they arrested him, but at the time they didn't have enough evidence to hold him. Although the Dutch police had just spread the word, I had not been notified of the situation. I was taken up to the governor's house, where the governor verbally wiped the floor with me. The local newspaper even ran a headline story:

"Mundus Smuggles Criminal Off Island."

Whoever looked at the passenger manifest with the so-called criminal's name on it that I turned into the police station did not report it to the detectives: they needed a scapegoat, and I was it. For a while, I couldn't walk down Main Street without people calling me names. The authorities had nothing to legally charge me with; therefore, that made them madder. Eventually, the fuss died down, but in the eyes of the St. Maarten police, I was still a criminal when I left the island for good in 1981.

A St. Maarten Rescue Mission

Any where you have boats, there will be boating accidents, and sometimes, a vacation that turns into a tragedy. The trade winds out of the east were nice and cool for the people on the beach as they slopped sun-tan lotion on themselves, but for the fishermen those nice, cool ocean breezes often made for a rough ride: up one wave and down the side of another.

After a day of fishing, a few drinks and some food, I settled down for a good night's sleep, but at 2:30 a.m. (on Sunday, April 30, 1972) a Dutch cop came banging on my door, telling me of a boat rescue and asked if I could participate along with two other boats. There were only three boats on the island including the *Cricket III* that the Dutch police could muster for a search party, so I could hardly refuse to go.

The cop told me, briefly, that a small sailboat was missing. A man was bringing a sixteen-foot sailboat around from Simpson Bay Lagoon, near the French side of the island, to Great Bay, but had not been heard from since. The man had intended to bring the boat around while his wife headed over by car to meet him. His sailboat ride should have only taken a few hours at the most. When the boat did not arrive at its destination four hours later, the wife got nervous and went to the police because there was no coast guard on the island.

I only took time for a fast cup of coffee then off I went. Our team of three boats—*Windy II,* the *Bon Homme,* and the *Cricket III*—spent all day searching along with two coast-guard planes from St. Thomas. The search party made the ten- to fifteen-mile run from the Dutch side back to Simpson Bay, patrolling close to the beach, then farther off, zigzagging back and forth, covering the territory where we thought he might be. We even tried to take his drift factor into consideration, assuming the boat may have turned over; but our search failed to come up with anything.

Early the next day, someone found a boat turned over up on the beach. The man's body was never found, but he did leave us some kind of clue as to his fate. Scratched into the side of the fiberglass sailboat were the words, "Can't hang on any longer—4/30/72."

As far as we could figure out, he must have broken an arm or a leg when the boat turned over because he did not swim to the beach, yet his wife said he had been in good physical shape. Her husband's body was never found and I felt bad because we did not reach him in time.

Marie Celeste, **Caribbean-Style**

The light easterly breeze pushed its way across our outside table at Pierre's restaurant, while a large umbrella kept the hot Caribbean sun off my mate, Guy, and me as we sat eating our lunch. Guy was one of the "local" boys (the dark-skinned islanders of St. Maarten).

This restaurant was on the French side of the island, but it was only a fifteen-minute drive away in our little mini moke. A mini moke is nothing more than a slightly over-sized golf cart, with a small motor and a license plate; but it got us back and forth, sometimes only forth: it broke down a lot!

Pierre and his wife owned the *Holly,* a nice wooden sailboat, somewhere in the forty- to fifty-foot class, and people chartered her to cruise the islands. Food and liquor were supplied on these trips, where Pierre acted as head chef and his wife took care of the customers. But over time, as more and more boats arrived on the island, Pierre's sailboat business dropped off, and so he decided to open a restaurant and sell his sailboat, which remained anchored close to the *Cricket III* in the harbor on the Dutch side.

Meanwhile, Pierre concentrated on developing his restaurant, which had no fancy French name; it was just known as "Pierre's."

When a cruise ship was anchored outside the harbor, large tenders carried sixty to eighty people from the ship to the small landing, and harbor traffic would be at its peak. On one of these days, April 30, 1969, I was rowing my way out in a small dinghy to the *Cricket III,* which was anchored out on a mooring, when I saw one of these tenders returning to a ship. The tender operator made the mistake of ducking down to light a cigarette, and as he did, his tender plowed into Pierre's anchored sailboat.

I had seen the whole thing and was the only eyewitness. In disbelief, I watched the tender back off and continue on its way to the cruise ship without checking for damage. I realized that this was a hit-and-run and decided to take my boat out to the cruise ship and report the accident to one of the officers in charge. After that, there was nothing I could do except tell Pierre about it.

Pierre sued the cruise-ship company and I testified as a witness. As a result, Pierre collected damages and he told me that lunch would be on him anytime I was visiting on the French side.

On one such day, Guy and I were enjoying our food and a bottle of white wine, when a policeman from the Dutch side of the island came to our table. He had to find us because the *Cricket III* doubled as a volunteer coast guard vessel for the Dutch governor as there was no coast guard on the island. The policeman told me that there was a mayday and he asked me if I would like to go out on a search.

A small sailboat had put out a mayday over the air. This had been picked up by the coast guard on St. Thomas, an island about one hundred miles away from St. Maarten. The message was relayed to St. Maarten because the vessel in distress was somewhere off the other side of St. Maarten, past the island of Saba.

A mayday signal is no joke. Only a vessel in danger would put one out. Leaving half of our lunch, Guy and I hurried to the Dutch side for more details. We were told to head out in the direction of the vessel and rendezvous with a coast-guard amphibious plane dispatched from St. Thomas. We estimated that it would take four or five hours to find this missing sailboat. Our main concern was finding the distressed vessel before darkness set in.

By now, it was noontime, and we were still loading provisions on the *Cricket III* for this trip: food, water, and fuel were our priorities. Three hours later, at 3:00 p.m., the *Cricket III* was doing her ten knots, still searching for the disabled vessel. We saw nothing except ten- to fifteen-foot waves created by the constant easterly trade winds. At around 4:00 p.m., a "duck," the coast-guard amphibious plane, showed up overhead. This plane dropped a note in a jar, telling me to turn on my radio.

At that time, my radio was in the shop being fixed, so I took a bottle of red nail polish and painted "NO RADIO" on the white cabin top. The plane left us, almost disappearing over the horizon, before it returned.

This time it showed us the direction in which we should head. The pilot did this twice. Then he dropped us another note, telling me to alter my course ten degrees to the west, and he said he'd drop off an emergency gasoline-powered water pump for us to use on the sinking boat. I was told to remove the people and take them to the closest port. After a while, the pilot dropped us one last note, reporting that the "duck" was running low on fuel and so he had to head in. He didn't say anything about returning to finish the search. This is where some of our troubles started.

We picked up the gasoline pump that had been dropped off by a cute little parachute. This pump had a small tank of gas, but how could I keep it running when I had a diesel-powered boat? By now, it was five o'clock; the day was ticking away—fast. With this clear visibility, I could see a long way to the horizon. If we did see something, it would take us an hour to reach it with our ten-knot boat.

Aboard the *Cricket III* was a policeman, my mate Guy, some of his friends, and myself. Each of us scanned the horizon in different directions. My job was to look straight ahead where the sailboat should come into view, according to the coast-guard coordinates. By now it was 6:00 p.m., with nothing sighted.

The other boys were looking to the right and to the left. I didn't know how many people were on that sailboat; if we didn't find them before dark, the search would have to start again at daylight. As we fought to beat the clock, a lot of things were going through my mind: how fast was that boat sinking? And did it have a life raft?

About this time, one of the boys, who was looking hard to the left said, "I think I can see something!" On the horizon was a small white object.

But the strange part of it was that the white spot only lasted for a couple of seconds. Then it would disappear for a short time, as if it had never existed. Suddenly, there it was again, only to disappear once more!

My guess was that it had to be our missing sailboat, but it was way off course from the coast-guard coordinates. If I changed course and headed hard to the left toward the object, we may never reach our original destination before dark. But straight ahead, there was nothing on the horizon. So I decided to turn hard left and hoped I was making the right decision.

The white thing was a long way off, and now it was 6:00 p.m. I couldn't go any faster and it was a hell of a feeling, hoping that I'd made the right choice. About a half-hour later, we solved the mystery of the disappearing white spot. At just about the same time, everybody yelled: "It's a sailboat going in tight circles!" That's why we had only seen the white spot for a couple of seconds at a time.

As we approached it, we saw that all the sails on the boat were down, except for the one up forward. The closer we got, the more we could see that there was no life raft or dinghy and no one on deck. We came within twenty-five feet of the boat, yelling for any survivors to show themselves, but no one appeared.

Because of those ten- to fifteen-foot seas, it would have been a slam-bang attempt to get alongside the sailboat, especially with the sailboat going in tight circles and up and down at the same time; somebody was sure to get hurt. Besides, there was the possibility of damage to both boats.

As we drifted and watched the boat going around and around, I noticed that there was a short line hanging overboard, about midships on the starboard side. I also noticed that there was a lull in the circle that the boat was making, just as the boat came straight into the wind, before it fell off and went around again. I asked one of the boys if he could jump overboard and grab hold of the line that was hanging in the water as I got close to the sailboat at the time of the lull. This way, he could pull himself up and onto the boat.

He said he would give it a try. Everything went perfectly and he climbed on board. The first thing he had to do was drop the sail to stop the sailboat from circling. He did this, and now we could make a closer inspection. It wasn't hard to see that this forty-foot fiberglass sailboat was half-full of water but was in no hurry to sink: it must have been like this for quite a while. My guess was that it had a slow leak. Otherwise, the sailboat would have gone down by now. But where were the people?

I told the boy who climbed aboard to look for people. He was only down below a short time before he stuck his head back up and shouted: "Nobody to be found!"

This seemed strange to me, so I asked another of the boys to go over and help him make a thorough search. "There should be *someone* on board," I told them. Getting the second boy aboard was easy because I could get right up alongside. It was just a matter of him diving off my boat, grabbing at the sailboat rope, and pulling himself aboard.

Both boys went below to continue searching. They were down there about ten minutes before they came back up to report. The boys said that there was nobody down there, and with three feet of water sloshing around, they felt like they were in a washing machine full of furniture: everything was slamming and banging around. A loose galley table had almost broken one of the boys' legs.

The coast-guard plane had ordered us to take the people to the nearest port, but there were no people to be found! So I told the boys to look around in the debris and see if they could find a can of gasoline to run the pump. There must be gasoline on the boat somewhere because a small outboard motor was still strapped to the aft railing.

My job was to start looking for any survivors in the water. The best way to do this is to square off your search. Starting close to the sailboat, I began by heading in a two-minute square around the sailboat. First, east two minutes. Next, south two minutes. Then, west two minutes; and finally, north, which brought me back to the boat again. Now for another square, this time of three minutes' running time. My next square was four minutes, and so on, until we got to the point of almost complete darkness, when we had to give up the search.

It is a hell of a feeling to think that we missed someone in the water; they could have been on the other side of a wave as our boat went by. I know that horrible feeling because the same thing happened to me off Miami in 1952, when I was a mate on the *Sandona*, working with Captain Red Stuart, one of the topnotch sport-fishing guides at that time. Will the boat see me on the next wave as I come up out of the trough, is the thought that goes through your mind. Were there any survivors out there asking the same question? By now, it was starting to get dark and we had to abandon our search for survivors.

We returned to the sailboat and saw that the boys were holding their own with the gasoline pump. However, they kept running into trouble with the suction line on the pump.

They could only run the pump a short time before the strainer got plugged up from all kinds of paper and loose debris floating around in the cabin: paper towels, labels off food cans, and toilet paper.

We threw them a tow line and told them it was going to be a long slow tow as we headed back for St. Maarten because the sailboat was half-full of water. If we pulled too hard, something would break. On the way back, we took turns watching for any signs of trouble. At all times, there was always one person on the *Cricket III* looking back at the sailboat.

By now, it felt like I had cotton balls in my mouth. In our hurry to start the search, I had forgotten to bring along some ice. I tried drinking hot sodas and hot water to quench my thirst; worse yet, I thought of those poor people floating around out there with nothing to drink, not even hot water.

Hour after hour, we slowly made our way home through the high seas with one eye on the sailboat. I expected something to break or pull apart at any minute. Normally, it would be a light, fast tow job hauling this sailboat if it wasn't half full of water. All night we plugged through the darkness. It was just about daylight when we arrived at the cove where our mooring was. Now it was time to put the sailboat at anchor and pump her out.

More pumps were brought out, one at a time, till we had four pumps working. Finally, we started to make headway, pumping out more water than was coming in. Soon, we got down to the source of the leak.

The boat leak was way up in the bow, on the starboard side. When the sailboat was being built, they had put in a short step-over bulkhead leading into the chain locker (bow storage locker). This bulkhead had pulled six to eight inches away from the hull, leaving a crack that would open and close as the boat moved from side to side.

Any other seaman would have fixed this crack in a jiffy. Just by jamming a small rag into it, the sailboat's owners could have temporarily stopped the water until they got into the closest port. But for some reason, they must have panicked and abandoned ship.

In the process of climbing on and off the sailboat, I noticed an eight-inch by eighteen-inch framed photograph that was hanging in the cabin, on the port bulkhead. It was a picture of a man and a woman and their two teenaged children: a boy and a girl. We must have left them all out there some place. My crew, the Dutch policeman, and I had done our best to find them, but that hadn't been good enough. As I had headed the rescue attempt, I felt the weight of guilt on my shoulders, and it wasn't a very nice feeling.

I was below, looking at the mess, with the noisy gasoline pumps working in the background, when somebody tapped me on the shoulder, wanting to talk. When I turned around, I was face to face with the man in the photograph. I thought I had seen a ghost! After a couple of seconds went by, I pointed for us to go outside and talk.

He explained, "The coast-guard chopper picked me and the wife up in their rescue basket."

I asked him what time they were rescued.

"Around two in the afternoon."

Now you could see steam coming out of my ears. I was pissed. They had been picked up at two! The coast-guard plane that dropped us the pump and two notes in a jar had told us to pick up the people. That was two to three hours *after* the couple had been brought in. Now I wanted to hear the rest of the story.

"Hold it—slow down. Let's start from the beginning, when you were sailing around in your boat."

He said, "Everything was going fine until I sent my wife down below to get my sunglasses. She came up and told me there was about six inches of water over the floorboard, down in the cabin. I immediately told her to go down and turn on the emergency electric pump. After a half hour or so went by, I could see we were sinking and had to do something about it. I thought about the dinghy we were towing, but I had to drop the main sail and put that away so we could have room to work.

I pulled the dinghy up alongside and told the wife to climb in while I made the line fast to the midship cleat. After she climbed in, I started running back and forth, throwing her all kinds of survival gear and supplies: food, water, canvas, etc. In the process, the line slipped off the cleat and the dinghy started drifting away from the sailboat because the sail in the bow was still up. I had to make a decision—fast. Should I stay with the big boat, or join my wife in the dinghy. I dove overboard and swam to my wife. We drifted around for about an hour before the chopper rescued us."

"What about the kids?" I asked.

"The kids stayed home for this trip. We wanted to sail around and see the Caribbean by ourselves on our second honeymoon."

I found out the next day that his insurance company had paid him in full for a complete loss. Thanks to the efforts of my crew and me, he had managed to retrieve all his things off the boat—all the linens, silverware, even a .30-30 rifle. I tried to claim salvage rights, but my lawyer, Mr. Speetjens, told me that the Dutch government claims almost all of the Caribbean waters as theirs. This put the sailboat in inland waters. I could only claim salvage if the boat had been found in international waters. The only thing that I could do was bill the man's insurance company for the cost of a tow job.

Meanwhile, we cleaned up the sailboat, fixed the leak with a fiberglass patch, and hoped for the best while the case remained in the lawyer's hands. I hung on to the boat for about a year and a half before a decision was made. During this time, I had to pay a watchman to stay on the boat and make sure that the rain water wouldn't sink it if the electric pumps failed.

The insurance company gave me a choice: I could take $1,500 for the tow job, or I could keep the boat for all the work I had done on it. I decided to keep the boat and sell it. It soon became a money pit: the longer I kept it, the more it cost me to keep. When I did sell it a year later, for $3,500 and took out what I had put in, it wasn't a very profitable deal.

Nun but the Brave

After spending a lot of time drinking and running around the concrete sidewalks of St. Maarten in my bare feet, I woke up one morning in April 1971, and discovered a steady pain under the big toenail of my right foot. Apparently, I must have stubbed my toenail on something the night before. The pain continued day after day, until I decided to do something about it. Because I was fishing every day, I got the bright idea of soaking my foot in a bucket of saltwater. This helped, and each day, my toe was getting better, but just about the time when my toenail had healed up, another incident happened . . .

We got to the dock one day with a load of grouper fish, and after my mate had thrown them all up onto the concrete pier, I jumped off the boat; but when I landed, my right foot slipped and one of the large grouper fins jammed right up underneath my sore toenail. That did it, because the next day my toenail was *really* talking to me—*THUMP, THUMP, THUMP, THUMP* it went. I knew I had to break down and see the doctor at the clinic, and that this was going to be a day-long operation because there were always fifteen or twenty people standing in line outside.

When I eventually got in to see the doctor, he took one look at my toenail, gave me a shot in the ass, and told me to come back tomorrow, saying, "I might *only* have to take off the nail." He also suggested I bring some clothes because I might have to stay in hospital for a while. I didn't sleep very well that night because the doctor's words kept ringing in my ear, "I *might* only have to take the nail." But might he also take my toe off?

The next day, I arrived at the clinic, and when the doctor finally got around to seeing me, he took one quick look again, and said, "You're lucky that I'm only going to take your nail. How do you want it? Do you want to be knocked out or shall I freeze it?"

"Go ahead, freeze it," I said boldly.

"This is going to hurt," the doctor said. "I'm going to get in there, and the first pop that you'll feel is me splitting the nail down the middle and pulling one side off. The second pop will be the other side; and the last pop you'll feel will be me pulling out the back section."

Next, he told me to lie down on a stretcher. Then two nuns entered the room. This is when I found out that the nurses in this hospital were nuns. As I lay there, flat on my back, and the doctor started to freeze my toe, the nuns leapt into action: one held down my left arm, while the other clutched my right arm in a tight grasp to keep me from jumping up. It was evident that these sisters had some wrestling experience!

"Here we go," said the doctor cheerfully.

I glanced at the nuns. They each had a fixed, very businesslike expression, so I closed my eyes and prepared for the worst. And then came the sharp pain of the "first pop." Next came the second pop, which also didn't feel very good. It was quickly followed by the third and final pop. Although it was daylight, by now, I was seeing stars.

When the nuns saw that the doctor had finished, they let go of my arms. Immediately, I sat up, grabbed hold of my ankle, and began squeezing it as hard as I could, when one of the nuns asked me the $60,000 question: "Does it hurt very much?"

Grinding my teeth and still clutching my ankle, yet knowing I shouldn't say any bad words, the first thing that came to mind was, "It only hurts when I laugh!"

So the nuns gave me the medal of honor for being a good boy and I returned home with a big bandage on my toe.

My only other scary encounter with nuns goes way back to the 1940s, when I had my little boat, the *Cricket*. I was mackerel fishing out of Brielle, New Jersey, in the spring of the year and had an all-nun charter, six of them to be exact.

We caught mackerel all day and the nuns were covered from head to toe in mackerel scales that flew off the mackerel as they raised them out of the water. In spite of how neat they tried to be, by the end of the day, those nuns had dirty habits!

Soon, it was time to go home, and I couldn't get that little gasoline engine started. As I worked on the motor, the thought went through my head that I would be stuck out here with no radio and a boatload of nuns until somebody found us the next day. Luckily, the Good Lord intervened and helped me get the motor started. I guess he didn't want to see those nuns stranded out there all night with me either!

The Caribbean Out-wives' Club

After wintering in St. Maarten for a while to establish my charter business, I started learning about the island's local customs and laws. One of the laws that struck me as the funniest was the one that allowed the local men to have multiple wives in addition to their one "in-wife." The surplus spouses were known as "out-wives," and as far as I understood, the law said that you could have as many out-wives as you could afford to keep. So, many of the island men had out-wives.

When Charlie, a friend from the States, was staying with me for a short time, we heard a ruckus late one night. I got up and went out on the front porch to see what was causing all the racket. Dietrich, a local friend of mine who owned a liquor store down town, was visiting Out-wife Number One, who happened to be my next-door neighbor. I knew her visitor had to be Dietrich because his brand-new brown and white station wagon was parked in the driveway of her house.

Meanwhile, Out-wife Number Two was standing on the road, picking up rocks and throwing them at Dietrich's shiny new station wagon. Every time she threw a rock, she screamed something in Papiamento (a Caribbean dialect), punctuating the end of each sentence in English, with the word "nastiness."

Her green Volkswagen Bug was parked on the road, right where she got out of it, and the driver's-side door was still open. I stayed on my front porch and watched as Out-wife Number Two continued her ritual of throwing rocks at Dietrich's station wagon and shouting in Papiamento.

"Hey, Charlie, you've got to come out here and see this!" I hollered to my buddy, who had been sound asleep. I knew he wouldn't want to miss the excitement.

It wasn't very long before all the local neighbors came out of their houses to watch this scene. Before it was finished, there must have been twenty to twenty-five people gathered around Out-wife Number Two's Volkswagen, just watching, saying nothing. There were no lights on in Out-wife Number One's house for a few rocks. I wondered how long Dietrich was going to take this abuse because some of the heavy rocks did make their mark in the side of his new station wagon—*THUMP-THUMP*.

When it happened, it happened fast. Dietrich came flying out of the house, wearing nothing but a pair of white briefs and running at top speed toward Out-wife Number Two. Out-wife Number Two saw him burst out of the house and ran for her car. Now it was Dietrich's turn. He picked up a rock the size of a baseball and made a home run, throwing that rock as hard as he could, hitting her in the ribs, just as she was getting into her car. She fell to the ground for a second, got up, crawled into her car, and drove off as Dietrich stood there and watched.

The neighbors who were watching never said one word. Then Dietrich calmly walked back into the house, the neighbors dispersed, and I went back to bed.

Next day, I stopped in at Dietrich's liquor store to buy some booze. I didn't want to say anything to him about what had happened last night; but then, as he handed me my change, Dietrich smiled, and asked, "How did you like the show last night?"

I didn't want to be nosy, but I was curious as to what had been going on, so I ad-libbed, "My only complaint is that it was in black and white. The next time, make it in color!"

Dietrich gave a short laugh, then explained, "She was wrong, and everybody knew it. She was just jealous because I only gave her one kid and the wife I was with last night has two."

Every Sunday and every holiday, Dietrich would drive around, picking up all his out-wives and their kids, and took them on a group outing. His main wife, an American, must have been a very understanding person.

I was glad that I didn't get tangled up with anybody's out-wife. There was one close call when a neighbor's out-wife, dressed in a very light see-through nightgown, knocked on my door one evening and asked me if I would like to come over and fix her TV. I politely declined her offer, using the excuse that I didn't know anything about television sets.

Another custom I heard about was that of the "sweet man." A sweet man was a local dark-skinned man who was kept by a local dark-skinned woman. She would go out and work, while he sat around the house all day and drank beer, waiting for her to come home.

The locals divided their own people into two categories: light-skinned and dark-skinned. I also found out there were three words they didn't like: "native," "clown," and "black." According to them, nobody was really black.

One day, I was sitting at a table in a local bar with Bill, an American charter-boat captain. We were busy taking inventory of the paraphernalia with which we designed our advertising posters for the hotels: pencils, pens, and cans of spray paint, when in walked a light-skinned local. Bill tapped me on the shoulder, and said in a low voice, "That guy doesn't like dark-skinned people. Watch this," he said, as the light-skinned man approached us.

Bill turned, and said to this fellah, "I want you to meet a friend of mine, Frank. He's light-skinned and I know you'll like him."

As I reached out and began shaking the light-skinned man's hand, Bill took a can of black spray paint and sprayed my arm, saying, "Now Frank is black, so you don't like him anymore." And before I could let go of the light-skinned man's hand, Bill sprayed his arm, and said, "Now you don't even like yourself."

The man's mouth dropped open in amazement, trying to figure out what was really going on. He never said a word, just shook his head and walked away.

In fact, the only time I heard the word "black" from the lips of a St. Maarten local was when my dark-skinned mate, Guy, emerged from the bilge of the *Cricket III* after cleaning her plugged-up scupper holes, and announced jokingly, "Look at me, I'm blacker than my grandmother!"

A Ringed Ear and a Ring Dare

Back in my drinking days, when I had the *Cricket III* in the Caribbean and was going back and forth from Montauk to St. Maarten each winter, I put an earring in my left ear; or rather, I was browbeaten into having my ear pierced. As a result, the earring became part of my trademark, and it still is.

One day, I was sitting on my favorite bar stool at the West Lake Fishing Lodge in Montauk, having a bit of grog with the other charter-boat captains, when the subject of me leaving for the Caribbean came up. One of our local characters asked me, "When are you going to go down there with the rest of the pirates?"

Before I could answer, another bar rat butted in, "He ain't no pirate. If he was, he would be wearing an earring."

Then another added, "He wouldn't dare."

So to save face, I had to say, "Just wait and see."

My daughter Pat had just walked in at that moment (she knew I was there—I couldn't hide my Chevy truck with all the printing on it). At this point in the conversation, Pat piped up, and said teasingly, "Dad, I know of a lady here in Montauk, Mrs. Joyce, who will pierce your ear for nothing."

Well, this was like pouring fuel on the fire: the boys at the bar really got going now. As I left with Pat, some of the louder comments came through, like, "Chicken," "You wouldn't dare," and so on.

Now, I really hadn't figured on this happening in the way it did, but I guess I was stuck, and so I told Pat to make an appointment with Mrs. Joyce. Her husband, Alex, was the contractor who used his bulldozer to pull the 4,500-pound white shark that I caught in 1964, up on the beach, just inside the inlet by Gosman's bar.

A week later, I was back in the bar, sitting on the same stool, having a bit of grog with the same guys, and telling the same fish stories, when in walked Pat again. This time she said out loud to me so everybody could hear it, "Let's go. It's time for your appointment!"

Of course I asked, "*What* appointment?"

She replied, "With Mrs. Joyce, to have your ear pierced."

That really made the bar rats explode and jump up and down, screaming with laughter so loudly that I couldn't hear myself think. Away we went. When we arrived at Mrs. Joyce's house, Mrs. Joyce was shaking with excitement: she said she had never pierced a man's ear before.

I was laughing to myself when we left the bar because I knew that an earring had to be soaked in alcohol for twenty-four hours before it can be put in, but so did Pat. She had known, and she had a small earring all ready to go, soaking in a bottle of alcohol in her pocket.

Mrs. Joyce figured I needed something to steady my nerves, so she offered me a drink of scotch. Of course I said yes, for medicinal purposes only! The ear-piercing operation was over and done with before my scotch had settled. Mrs. Joyce was happy, Pat was happy, and I was bewildered as I headed back for the bar.

That first earring was a small thin gold thing. It could hardly be seen and I said to myself, if I'm going to wear an earring, it will be big so that everybody can see it. This was the year of my divorce (1976), and one day, while I was in New York City, I dropped in to see the boys at the Diamond Center. Franklin, the boss man, had taken a special liking to me for some reason. He and his workers had fished with me for half a dozen trips by then. By this time, we were all getting along well.

On this visit to the Diamond Center, Franklin saw the earring, and as always, he spoke out, "Where did you get that puny little earring?" He had heard of my divorce and saw the wedding band on my left hand. "Let's make you a decent earring from your wedding band," Franklin suggested.

The price was right, so I said, "Go to it." Because I had worn the wedding ring for so long—over thirty years—they had to cut it off with a little gadget that looked like a small can opener. The ring was off in seconds and in Franklin's hands for only a moment, as he tossed it to his goldsmith in the next booth, and said, "Make a decent earring out of this for Frank and put in some diamond chips to make it look classy."

The goldsmith put in two diamond chips and threw it back to Franklin, who immediately put it in my ear so he could see what it would look like. "No good," Franklin said, "got to put two more in," as he took it out of my ear and threw it back to the goldsmith. It seemed like only a few minutes later that the goldsmith threw it back to Franklin, and said, "Try this."

Franklin stuck the earring back in my ear and we both looked at it, but Franklin wasn't satisfied. He wanted to put four more diamonds on the inside of the ring. I said, "Whoa, no, stop! Enough is enough!" Now I had a classy, four-chip diamond earring. This caused a commotion in Montauk, a place where I could not even spray-paint my window shutters on the front lawn without inviting biting comments from the locals.

The men hated my earring, but all the ladies thought it was nice. A lot of the men who spoke out against it the loudest were the ones who wanted to put one in but were too chicken to do it. Our local hardware-store owner was my worst critic. Every time I entered his store, he announced my arrival with some kind of insult to draw everybody's attention to the earring, but it bothered him more than it bothered me. At that time, the only men who wore earrings were pirates in the movies.

That little round gold ring dangling from my left ear drew a lot of attention in public places. If you had been there, you would have seen heads going together, where one person saw the earring, told the other person, and then both heads turned around and looked at me. Then they would laugh and turn away. There was no doubt that they were talking about it.

Only once in public did a man voice his opposition and hostility about the earring to my face. This happened in an elevator at the New York Boat Show. He was a young man in his midtwenties, and was under the influence of alcohol.

"That earring doesn't do a bit of good for you," he sneered.

I spun around and stood face to face with him, "You know something? It doesn't do a bit of good for you, either!" I shot back. He was silent for the rest of our elevator ride.

Caribbean time was getting close and I knew that the St. Maarten locals would be intensely curious about my pierced ear. They are very straightforward with their questions and would expect a straight answer about my earring, so I had to have my answer ready. I wasn't on the island but ten minutes, walking down one of the dirt streets, past a local store that had one light bulb hanging from the ceiling, when the owner invited me in for a drink. This was a custom in St. Maarten. If the store owners knew you, they always invited you in for a drink.

Before our first drink was finished, here came the question, "Frank, can I ask you a personal question?"

"Sure," I said. "Go ahead."

With both elbows on the table and one hand clutching his drink, he peered over the top of his bottle of Scotch and asked, "Why does a man of your color and faith wear an earring?"

"You know I have a boat in New York and you know I have a boat in the Caribbean, don't you?" I said.

As he nodded "Yes," I put my right hand to my face, with the thumb facing in and the pinky out to divide it, and said, "This half of me belongs to New York, and this half with the earring belongs to the Caribbean."

The store owner was happy with this answer, and for as long as I was on that island, I never did get another question about the earring.

I've been through a few earrings since those days. I'm still holding on to the fourth. The first little thin one got thrown into the deep six when the diamond studded one came into the picture. Then the diamond earring got lost in the gravel at Cove Marina boatyard in Montauk when I was painting the bottom of the boat. So I made another trip into the Diamond Center to have a bigger, heavier gold earring made up.

I had an embarrassing close call with this one while out fishing. We were in the process of catching a white marlin and I was showing a new mate how to handle this billfish. After the fish had been brought up alongside the boat by the angler, I reached out and took hold of the fifteen-foot leader wire with my right hand, taking a twist (or turn) with my hand so that the wire didn't slide back out.

"This is how it's done," I said to the mate as he stood by, watching me pull the fish in closer to the boat; but a little birdy told me something was wrong. The wire had slid alongside my ear and dropped into the earring! Now it was inside the loop.

I could not let go of that wire no matter what happened. I had to go through the whole procedure with the wire around my neck. I hung on in an attempt to save my ear, as the fish thrashed and pulled. Three minutes went by, and it seemed like hours until I was able to reach down and get a firm grip on the white marlin's bill in order to lift him up and slide him over the gunnel and drop him into the cockpit. Only then could I take the time to slide the wire out of the earring.

If I had lost my grip on the wire and the fish had gone back out, he would have taken the ring and a piece of my ear with him. It would have been like they say: ear today, gone tomorrow!

A couple of weeks later, this ring and I parted company the easy way because the catch on the back slipped off and the earring fell out, adding some more gold to Davy Jones's locker. The one I have in now is quite secure because it has a threaded bolt that goes through the ear, and it uses a nut that winds up tight against the inside of my ear, holding the ring on.

Another of my trademarks is the harpoon-dart belt buckle which I wear constantly. It is four and a half inches long, an inch and a half wide, and is shaped like an arrowhead. A lot of people, when they first see it, think it is an arrowhead. I got the idea for the harpoon belt buckle after seeing someone wearing one some place in my travels.

Tap-Tap

On one of my trips into the busy town of Philipsburg, St. Maarten, I had to pick up a few things for the boat. In a normal town, a hardware list for the boat would be easy to fill, but here in Philipsburg, everything was in a different place from where you expected it to be. For instance, if you went into town to buy some turpentine, you would go to a hardware store that sells paint, turpentine, etc. Not so here in Philipsburg. To buy turpentine, you had to go into a drug store.

I went from store to store, pushing my way through tourists on one of the busiest streets on the island, where Front Street met a side street leading to the pier; here the cruise ship dumped off herds of people. As I was crossing the street, I saw a girl standing on the road, in the path of a taxi that was waiting to back out of a taxi stand. She was a young-looking woman, a little on the thin side, and was wearing a scarf and a large pair of sunglasses.

As I approached her, I could see that the taxi wanted to back out and she was standing in the way. In St. Maarten, the taxi drivers are very polite. They just wait until somebody gets out of their way. The direction I was heading in took me right past the woman.

As I approached her, I could see that she was not going to move, so I tapped her on the shoulder, with one finger, and said, "Get the hell out of the way before you get run over!" and I pointed toward the taxi that wanted to back out.

She immediately stepped aside, and I kept on heading toward the sidewalk. At this time, I noticed two or three local guys standing in the doorway of the liquor store, making all kinds of funny hand gestures toward me. Naturally, I couldn't figure out what was going on until they told me, "Do you know who you just tapped on the shoulder? You just tapped Jackie Onassis on the shoulder!" and they pointed out to sea. "There's Onassis's yacht."

"So what," I replied, "you wanna buy this finger? What's the big deal?"

I'm not the type of person to worry about who I tap on the shoulder. I would have done the same thing to Nixon if he had been standing in the way of the taxi, wearing a scarf and sunglasses!

St. Maarten Shark Scare

I was trolling around one of the outer islands one day, trying to catch a couple of barracuda for the tourists that we had on board. Every day, I made a habit of heading around a huge rock that was a tourist attraction. This rock had a hole in the middle, big enough to drive a truck through. As the waves rolled into this hole, they sprayed out of a small hole at the top of the rock. The effect resembled a spouting whale.

One day, as I trolled past this huge rock, Mother Nature was performing nicely and so I stopped the *Cricket III*. I noticed one of my customers had an underwater camera similar to mine, and I asked him, "Do you want to go snorkeling with me?"

"Sure," he said, "but I don't have any flippers or a mask with me."

"No problem, we always carry extra," I told him, reaching under the bunk and pulling out what he needed. So, the two of us went overboard while my mate Guy stayed on the boat with the rest of the customers. There was no tide, current, or wind, so I could just let the boat drift for the short amount of time that we would be in the water. Besides, the mate knew how to run the boat.

We swam in as close as we dared go, staying away from the rocks and the rolling swell. It didn't take each of us long to shoot up a roll of film and then start back to the boat. When we reached the *Cricket III*, Guy had put out the boat ladder for us to use, and as usual, I always let my customer climb up first. I told him to take off his flippers and hand them to me, then climb up the ladder. After I had handed his flippers to the mate, I got ready to take off mine.

I was lying flat in the water, my left hand on the lower rung of the ladder, while reaching back with my right hand to take off a flipper. When I looked up, I saw Guy standing there, waiting for me to hand him my flippers.

All of a sudden, he pointed over my shoulder, and shouted, "SHARK!" His face was grim and straight. And for a split second, the only thought that flashed into my mind was, "It's *all* over." I knew that I would not have time enough to get up the ladder.

Everything went deathly quiet . . .

It took about four seconds for the mate to laugh. Then, and only then, did I know he was joking. After I climbed up the ladder, I told him, "If you *EVER* do that to *ANYBODY* again, it will be the last time that you do *ANYTHING!*"

The St. Maarten Sting:
or How I Sold the *Cricket III*

Nineteen seventy-six was a year full of surprises: I had badly dislocated my shoulder, the first wife left me, and against all odds, I sold my boat, the *Cricket III*, in St. Maarten.

I dislocated my shoulder on January 6 and was unable to get the medical treatment I needed in St. Maarten. For a couple of weeks, I suffered with my shoulder problem, hoping that it would straighten out by itself; but after a while I decided to return home to New York to see my regular doctor on Long Island. Charlie, a friend of Harry's, picked me up at JFK airport and handed me a pain pill that he had gotten from his doctor. I immediately took the pain pill without thinking, and when that pill hit my booze-soaked body, it exploded. I was like a telephone—busy at both ends for the next twenty-four hours, and felt as sick as a dog. Charlie dropped me off at Harry's place and I stayed the night. The next day, Harry took me to my doctor, who said that there was nothing he could do for me. He advised me to keep my right arm in a sling and rest it, but the doctor down in St. Maarten had advised me to exercise it, and that was what had torn it all up. I had traveled all the way from St. Maarten to Long Island just to find this out!

Harry drove me back home to Montauk because I was still feeling the effects of the pill-and-booze cocktail. When I got home, nobody was there. The house was empty. My wife had left me and taken almost everything, except for our refrigerator and a couple of chairs. I was standing in the middle of the empty room, scratching my head, when the neighbor tapped on the door. I let her in. She nervously handed me a folded piece of paper and said sheepishly, "I was told to give this to you," and left. I opened it slowly, one handed, and read the first word: "Summons." Janet was divorcing me and I was ordered to appear in court the next week. Worse yet, the house we were renting had been sold by the landlord while I had been down in the Caribbean and no one had told me. I scrambled around to find a new place and a charter-boat captain friend of mine offered to let me use one of his spare rooms until I found something.

I showed my summons to Charlie, and he said, "Don't worry. I'll get it postponed. You go back to St. Maarten and finish up your business there."

On my first day back, I walked down the beach with my arm in a sling, and headed for the *Cricket III*, which was out on her mooring. When I stopped to shake the sand out of my sandals, I saw my friend Robert Boggs "Boggsy Old Boy" on board, lifting hatches, and he had a guy with him. When they came ashore the man left, so I asked Boggsy, "What's going on?"

"Well," he says, "that was a Frenchman and he wants to buy the *Cricket III*. I was just showing him the boat."

"OK, that's fine. Did you tell him $15,000?"

"Yes."

"Does he speak any English?"

"No."

"Do you speak any French?"

"I speak enough to get by with."

"Good. You can be my interpreter, Boggsy. By the way, what did you tell him?"

"I told him to stop by the house tomorrow when you're there and we'll talk business."

Sure enough, the next day, this Frenchman came around and Boggsy had to tell me what he was saying. After some negotiation, we agreed on a final sale price of $13,500: as is, where is, with nothing on the boat. OK, he was happy with the deal, and Boggsy told him, "You're going to have to give us a deposit." So this guy whipped out a check for $500 and away he went. I figured I would put the check in the bank and see what happens. Sure enough, it cleared.

The Frenchman came back the next weekend, but Boggsy wasn't there; he was off swim-diving or something. I finally found Boggsy and dragged him home, where he and the Frenchman went though this back-and-forth business, until I asked, "What's up?"

And Boggsy said, "Well, this guy wants to give us a check for the rest of the money and he wants to take the boat."

"No good. It's Friday afternoon. I can't find out if the check is any good; the banks are closed. Tell him to come back next weekend, but bring cash," I said to Boggsy.

Boggsy told him this and the Frenchman went away, mad at us because we wouldn't trust him with the boat.

The next Friday, March 12, the Frenchman returned while Boggsy was shopping in town. The guy gestured to me, trying to tell me that he had the money on him in cash, but I didn't know what he was talking about until I saw him slap his hand on his pants' pocket. Now I had to chase Boggsy down again, so I put this French guy in my little mini moke (I didn't want to lose him) and we rode all over town, looking for Boggsy.

When we got home, Boggsy was there, so I said, "OK, Boggsy, here we go. Let's make this deal." Boggsy and I were sitting at a table, close to the door that lead to the front apartment, as the Frenchman began laying the money out on the table in $100 bills. Then who walked in the open front door, but one of the biggest pirates on St. Maarten: "Bobby Hogan[4]." He saw all this money, came over, and asked, "What's going on?"

I said, "We're selling the boat. Now go away and leave us alone. It's private business. What do you want?"

"I stopped by to see if I could buy these rods and reels that you had on the boat," he said.

"No. I sold them all to the marina next door," I said. "Go away." Bobby hung around, and hung around, and watched what we were doing, while making believe he was looking at all the tackle and hardware on the shelves. Boggsy counted out $13,000 in one-hundred-dollar bills, handed it to me, and I put it into my pocket. Now Bobby Hogan came over to me, and asked, "What are you going to do with all the money?"

I said, "What money?"

He said, "The thirteen thousand you've got in your pocket."

I replied, "Bobby Hogan, it's none of your damn business what I'm gonna do with it."

Then he said, "Well, it's Friday night and the banks are closed. You'll have to carry that money around until Monday."

I said, "Bobby Hogan, you let me worry about what I'm gonna do with the money and how I'm gonna protect myself." While talking to him, I thought, well, how *am* I gonna get rid of this money? Then I said to myself: *The Sting*.

I hoped Boggsy had seen the movie and I also hoped "Dog," the guy who was living in the front apartment, had seen the movie too. Maybe with the three of us we could pull a sting on Bobby Hogan before he pulled one on us. We could switch the money around. Here goes, let me try. I hollered to Dog, "Hey, Dog, you got any beer in there for me?"

Well, Dog knew damn well that I don't drink beer, only booze. So he knew there was something wrong, but said, "Yeah, come on in."

I left the table and went into Dog's place. I looked around and saw that Dog was watching me, wondering what was going on. I picked up a rag that was lying on a counter, took the money out of my pocket, and put it in my left hand. With my right hand, I pushed the rag back into my pocket to make the same-sized lump. Then I hollered, "Hey, Boggsy Ol' Boy, there's one more beer in here for you. You'd better come and get it quick." Now, Boggsy didn't drink beer, and he knew that I didn't drink beer, so he probably asked himself, what the hell was going on?

As he came through the doorway, I stuck my head out, watching what Bobby Hogan was doing on the other side; at the same time, I reached behind my back and handed somebody (and I hoped it was Boggsy) the $13,000. He took it out of my hand; then I walked in. When I entered the room, everyone could see the lump in my pocket (but now it was a rag). What Boggsy did with the money, I didn't know yet. I found out later that Boggsy had stuffed it down into his under shorts, just like Robert Redford had done in the movie *The Sting*.

Now I told Bobby Hogan to go away and leave us alone. Boggsy came back out and we finished up with our business. The deal was that I had to move the boat from the Dutch side of the island to the French side, a three-quarter-of-an-hour's boat ride away. When I had done this and stepped off the *Cricket III*, I could wipe my hands clean. Done. Finished. I asked Boggsy to tell this to the Frenchman.

Before we left the dock, I had ordered my mate to start stripping the boat. The *Cricket III* was tied up at my homemade dock, in a lagoon right in front of my house. He took the wheelbarrow and went back and forth to the *Cricket III*, removing everything that was loose. I told him to leave a couple of life jackets, a few old fishing rods, and the old spare anchor and short anchor line.

To move the boat out of the lagoon, we had to open the bridge. Boggsy went down to help the bridge tender operate the crank handle.

This bridge needed to be opened by hand because half of the time the electricity didn't work. I started up the *Cricket III*'s motor, we threw the lines off and out we went: me, my local dark-skinned mate, and the Frenchman. It was just starting to get dark as we went through the bridge when I saw Boggsy hanging from a high beam on the bridge, shaking his fist at me as he spun the crank handle on this old, dilapidated bridge, so I waved, and said, "Hi, Boggsy. Bring the car around to the French side of the island and pick us up later." I asked myself why was Boggsy mad at me when he was the one who had jammed the money down his shorts, but knowing Boggsy, he was probably thinking, "Another fine mess you've gotten me into."

Out the inlet we went, into the Caribbean, making a hard right and heading for the French side of the island. Thank god the weather was on our side—the wind was not blowing and the water was not rough. The sun was setting and we didn't have much time before it got dark. We had enough complications without adding blackness to it.

The thirteen thousand dollars I had in my pocket had to be bothering a lot of people: Bobby Hogan, the Frenchman, and my mate. The Frenchman or the mate might bop me over the head, or perhaps Bobby Hogan could catch up to us in a fast boat, with a rough crew! I couldn't outrun him, as the *Cricket III* was only a ten-knot boat.

It was just getting dark. From the flying bridge, I could see the mate's shadow, cast on the water by the cabin light, as he sat on a side bunk in the wheelhouse below. This is when I got the bright idea of pulling the sting *again*.

I signaled to the Frenchman to come over and take the wheel of his new boat, motioning for him to head straight. It was just about light enough for me to pick out a landmark for him to aim at, while I made an excuse to go below.

Then I climbed down the ladder from the flying bridge and headed over to my mate. I already knew what I was going to do. I asked the mate if he knew about the $13,000 I had wrapped in a rag in my pocket. He answered quietly, half-scared to death, "Yes, *mon* [sic]."

I had my back to the mate while I was talking to him, and it was then that I made the switch. In my other pocket I kept a small change purse that I used for separating my French and Dutch coins. I quickly pulled the rag out of my right pocket and put it on the table. At the same time, I pulled the coin purse out of my left pocket, quickly wrapped it in the center of the rag, and jammed it back in my right pocket. Turning to the mate, as I put my hand in my pocket, I said, "Here, take this money and put it in your pocket because the Frenchman knows I have it." Then in front of the mate, I took another rag, rolled it up, and pushed it in my pocket to make the famous $13,000-bulge look.

I climbed back up on the flying bridge and signaled to the Frenchman that I would take the wheel. We only had a half hour to go, but it seemed a lot longer.

As the French harbor came into view, I was still looking over my shoulder for Bobby Hogan to show up in his fast zodiac. So far, so good, as we slid into the harbor. When my mate stripped the boat, he had been smart enough to leave two old lines for us to tie up with. As I jumped onto the dock, I gave the Frenchman my "washing of hands" signal: the boat was now his.

My chauffeur, Boggsy, was there, waiting to pick us up in my Toyota station wagon. The Frenchman asked Boggsy something. He wanted to be dropped off some place. Boggsy agreed and the four of us climbed into the car. For a while, no one spoke. I was thinking how to ask Boggsy what he had done with the money. Finally, I said, in a loud singsong voice, "Boggsy Ol' Boy, how's things in Glockamorra?"

He thought for an instant before replying mysteriously, "I almost tore the ass-end . . . out of this car . . . going up that steep hill . . . with the heavy load."

I had to think a minute on this one before I decoded it. I thought to myself, the only heavy load I can think of is the money. The steep hill is where lawyer Speetjens lives. It's almost the steepest road on the island. I turned to Boggsy, and said, "I gotcha, Boggsy Ol' Boy."

A short distance down the road, we dropped the Frenchman off and then we went home. Boggsy, the mate, and I went into my house to celebrate. As I poured drinks for us, I turned to the mate, and asked, "Where's the money?"

The look I got from Boggsy could not be put into words, as he said, "Mundus, you're bad!"

"Put the money on the table," I said to the mate. The poor confused mate was scared out of his skin as he reached into his pocket and put the rag onto the table. Then he slowly backed away. "Count it," I ordered, in a loud voice. "I want to see if it's all there."

Again, Boggsy muttered, "Mundus, you sonofabitch."

Again, I shouted my order to the mate, "Count it!"

Very slowly, the mate started to unwrap the rag on the table. When he got to the small change purse that was in the center, the mate froze, looking like he had seen a ghost. This is when I had better tell him, I thought, before he has a heart attack. So I told him the whole story and he finally laughed, while Boggsy just shook his head in disbelief. At the end of that day, I was real glad that Dog, Boggsy, and I had all seen *The Sting* and could reenact the movie.

We waited until Monday morning to go to Speetjens's office. Boggsy drove because my dislocated shoulder was giving me lots of trouble. I walked into Speetjens's office on Front Street and knocked on the frosted sliding-glass window. His secretary slid back the window, and said, "Good morning, Mr. Mundus. I have something here for you," and pushed a brown paper bag through the window. I hoped that there was $13,000 in that bag.

Back out to the car I went, with my little brown bag in my hand. Boggsy asked, "What bank do you want to go to?"

I said, "No bank. To the police station."

"The police station?" he asked, surprised.

"Yes, you'll see," I told him. "To the police station, Boggsy!"

Being the good chauffeur that he was, Boggsy drove me to the nearest police station. This police station was fifty feet across the street from the bank. I walked into the police station, sat the brown paper bag on the counter, and immediately had a welcoming committee of Dutch police and detectives, because everybody knew that if Mundus was here, trouble wasn't very far behind. The desk sergeant asked me what I wanted. As they all listened closely, I said, "I *demand* police protection!"

The sergeant got up off his chair, and asked indignantly, "Protection for what?" In a dramatic tone, I replied, "In this brown paper bag, I have $13,000 in cash and I *demand* police protection to the bank."

There was nothing they could do but grant me the protection I wanted, because international law states that a foreigner asking for police protection has to get it. The sergeant grunted something over his shoulder in Dutch. The only thing I could understand was the last word: Mundus, or "Mundoos" as he called me. Then out of the woodwork came a policeman in full uniform. I figured that this was my escort. He led the way and we walked the fifty feet across the street to the bank.

In the bank, we were greeted by one of the tellers. I told her I wanted to see the president or vice president because we had a large deposit to make. As I was escorted into a room, I glanced over my shoulder and saw the uniformed policeman leaving the bank. I seated myself on the opposite side of the large mahogany desk as the vice president of the bank asked me, "What can I do for you?"

I picked up the brown paper bag and turned it upside down. His desk was immediately filled with $100 bills. "There should be $13,000 there," I said. He called in the teller to count it and put it in my account. I asked her if she could give me two receipts instead of one, which she did.

Then I went back out to my faithful chauffeur, Boggsy, who was patiently waiting for me. "Where to now?" he asked.

"To Speetjens's office," I replied.

By this time, Boggsy was through asking questions, and

shaking his head, he drove me to Speetjens. I walked into Speetjens's front office and tapped on the glass. His secretary opened the window and I handed her the second receipt, asking her to give it to Speetjens, knowing that when he got it, he'd realize that the money was safely in the bank and that was the end of the story. Bobby Hogan never found out what I did with the money and, stranger yet, didn't ask.

CHAPTER 8

JAWS AND ITS AFTERMATH

A lot of things happened to me over the three decades following the movie *Jaws*. I caught a world-record mako shark, followed by the largest white shark caught on rod and reel (1986), remarried (1988), fished with a prince in Saudi Arabia (1985), sold my boat four times (1988, 1989, 1991, 1995), moved from Montauk to Hawaii (1991), had two heart operations (1998 and 2000), and went on a South-African white-shark safari with the Discovery Channel in 2004!

Jaws, the Man-eating Shark

While the movie *Jaws* was being filmed on Martha's Vineyard, my customers gave me a blow-by-blow description of what was going on day by day. To give the movie extra publicity before its release in 1975, Universal sent Peter Benchley and his friends back out on my boat in October 1974 to make a TV special for ABC's *American Sportsman* show. The program was about sharks and included some behind-the-scenes footage of the *Jaws* movie, which was still in production at that time. It was ironic that they chose to charter my boat to film a publicity plug for *Jaws*. This program took five days to complete. It was the time that I thought Peter Benchley was going to say that one word I'd been waiting for: Thanks. Benchley was shoulder to shoulder with me on the boat for all these days, yet he never said it. I never would have been able to figure out why if I hadn't talked to some of my customers who were lawyers. They said he was probably told by his lawyers not to say thanks because it would be an acknowledgment of the fact that he had based Quint on me and had used a lot of my fishing background in his novel and movie screenplay. If Peter Benchley had publicly given me the credit that was due at that time, it would have helped my charter business. Almost a decade later, when it became common knowledge that I was the inspiration for Quint, it was too late because I had already built up my business by then.

When it was released in 1975, I thought *Jaws* was the funniest comedy I had ever seen. The first time I saw it at our local movie house in East Hampton, it was a wonder I didn't get thrown out because I rolled around in and out of my seat, with tears running down my cheeks. Whenever I wiped them away and could see again, there was another funny or stupid thing getting ready to happen.

I've been out at sea a lot of nights and have never had a shark follow me around the ocean, banging on my boat like the one in the movie did.

Near the movie's end, the angry shark eats Quint out of vengeance, intentionally jumping in the boat to seek him out. What kind of fish thinks this way? If sharks could think like "Bruce" in *Jaws*, I wouldn't be here writing this book.

Finally, the character Hooper would have been killed from concussion after Chief Brody blew up the air cylinder in the shark's mouth. I don't think that any scuba diver could have survived the force generated by that explosion because one of my ex-mates, "Davy Crockett," who had been one of the original navy frogmen during World War II, told me that the concussion from one stick of dynamite under the water would kill any submerged diver who was within a half-mile radius of the explosion.

David Letterman asked me what I thought of the movie when I made my first appearance on his show in 1986. He thought *Jaws* was "entertaining." I said, "So was *King Kong* but it was stupid. A real white shark wouldn't act that way, neither could a giant-sized monkey climb the Empire State Building."

I also made a guest appearance on the *Larry King Live* show in 1986. I enjoyed being on Larry's show because he asked me a lot of good, sensible questions, knowing that many of his viewers were interested in sharks.

Whenever people ask if I was the role model for Quint and if all those things in the movie ever happened to me, I give them a blow-by-blow account of how "Jaws" was put together and how it borrowed ideas from every large shark that I caught. Although Peter Benchley added fifteen pounds of fiction to his novel and screenplay, *Jaws* did borrow my shark-catching techniques and personality for the gruff and surly shark hunter, Quint. All this fishing information was in *Sportfishing For Sharks*, a book written by me and Bill Wisner, published in 1971.

For instance, every large shark I caught over a thousand pounds was caught in a different way. All that Benchley had to do was keep track of all the different newspaper articles. For instance, where was his opening scene? It was a bathing beach set off a fictitious summer resort by the name of Amity. The first white shark I caught in the three-thousand-pound class was captured in seventy-five feet of water, right off the bathing beach of Amagansett, Long Island, on June 5, 1960. Then, exactly one month later, on July 5, we brought in a 3,500-pound white shark. The first fish made headlines in the *Daily News* and created a lot of disturbance, but the second fish was hushed up by the press.

The night scene in *Jaws*, where Brody and Hooper come across Ben Gardner's half-sunk boat and find a huge hole in the hull made by the shark's bite was inspired by an incident that happened to me on June 28, 1962, when we brought in a white shark that weighed around two-thousand pounds. As I was getting ready to put a tail rope on him, the shark had bitten into the side of my boat and had driven five of its teeth into the planking. I later dug out these teeth from the *Cricket II's* hull. They were embedded three-quarters of an inch into the wood.

I went on to tell the press that if the *Cricket II* had been the average-sized boat with only three-quarter-inch planking, the shark would have bitten a large hole in it, and the boat would have sunk immediately. Even if the planking was thicker than three-quarters of an inch, if the boat had been built out of a soft wood like cedar, the shark would still have torn a hole in the hull. Thank god the *Cricket II* had two-inch planking made of long-leaf yellow pine, a tougher wood compared to most.

In the scene where Brody is thumbing through a book about sharks and trying to figure out what kind of monster he was doing business with, the camera goes over his shoulder to look into the book. It shows half a dozen photos, some of which were shot right off the *Cricket II* by my friend Peter Gimbel. One was of a blue shark eating a dead porpoise.

Another photo, taken off Durban, South Africa, of a man posing with a few dead white sharks, was given to Bill Wisner and me when we were writing *Sportfishing For Sharks*. This photo appears on page 177 of our book. We sold the rights for it to Universal Studios for use in their movie *Jaws*. I got $45 for it, which I have since spent!

Another example of my indirect involvement with the movie *Jaws* is when Brody, still thumbing through the books, sees a painting of two men in a white double-ended dory being attacked by a shark. *National Geographic* had approached me in 1967 to help critique their artist's sketches of how the white shark would have attacked the dory. The painting eventually appeared in the February 1968 edition of *National Geographic*.

Another piece of evidence is from 1964 when we brought in the biggest white shark ever caught at that time, a 4,500-pound fish. The story of how I caught this shark was widely reported. It was even listed in the 1977 edition of *The Guinness Book of World Records*. More proof of where Benchley got his information from came in the form of a letter, dated June 9, 1974, that he wrote to my customer Peter Brandenberg (Brandenberg had been aboard the *Cricket II* when I caught the 4,500-pound white shark in 1964). It read:

June 9, 1974

Dear Mr. Brandenberg:

Thank you for your letter. I'm surprised that I had the date wrong. I thought I remembered the incident more clearly.

I'm not particularly surprised, however, that I was misled about the fish attacking the boat. Since I didn't have your immediate perspective, I had to rely on

hearsay, which, as you know, grows more and more
dramatic with the passage of time.

I'm glad to have these two facts, and if I have another
opportunity to mention the episode on television or in
print, I'll make sure I mention it correctly.

Yrs.

Peter Benchley

The similarities between Quint's fishing techniques and mine are, for some reason, very close; for instance, I tried to bait this big shark first on rod and reel, and so did Quint. In the movie, the shark-scientist Hooper uses a metal snap with a rope on it that he puts in the leader wire when they were getting ready to wire up the fish. I described this technique in detail four years earlier on page 272 of *Sportfishing For Sharks*, in the section "Wiring Up A White."

Then we had motor trouble as we were chasing down the barrels; so did Quint, but his motor trouble was self-inflicted. We put five harpoons in our shark and he dragged four metal beer kegs all over the ocean. (After we put the fifth harpoon into the fish, we held on to him, and did not let him run any more.)

Then there were the two mysterious men, a year or so before the movie, who came to my house, armed with professional four-by-five graphic-flash cameras (used almost exclusively by the press). These men only took pictures of the inside of my old garage where I had shark jaws hanging all over. When I saw the movie *Jaws*, I was surprised to find myself looking at an almost exact replica of my garage! The only difference between my garage and Quint's boathouse was that I had no upstairs area and no pot of boiling shark jaws.

Me, in my garage, circa 1973. It's possible that they got the idea for the layout of Quint's boathouse from this. Mine is full of shark jaws, so was his two years later in the movie. Photo credit: Gene Spatz.

Over the years, I was on most of the national programs: *Larry King, David Letterman,* and many more, including a bunch of smaller ones all over the country. Each time, the same question kept coming up: "Did you receive any money from the movie *Jaws*?" My answer was that I did not expect a green Cadillac convertible and I didn't expect a free case of beer. All I wanted from Peter Benchley was one word: Thanks, and to this day, I never got it.

Interestingly enough, back in the early 1990s, I received a letter from Universal Studios' (Orlando, Florida) vice president of publicity and public relations, Jim Canfield, in which he invited me to become a paid spokesman, publicizing their new "Jaws" ride.

August 26, 1992

Dear Mr. Mundus:

It is my understanding that your background is strikingly similar to the character "Quint" in the film "Jaws."

Universal Studios Florida will be opening "Jaws," an incredibly exciting new ride, during the Summer of 1993. We are currently planning promotions and publicity activities around the "Jaws" opening. Your background is obviously of great interest to us. We wonder if you would be interested in participating in our publicity efforts and serving as a paid "spokesman" in conjunction with the opening of this new attraction.

If you are interested, we certainly visualize a prominent role for you in the promotion of this major addition to Universal Studios Florida. Universal will be very active in pre-opening publicity activities around the country.

People are very interested in you and would be fascinated to have the opportunity to learn more about your exploits.

Please let us hear from you. We hope your interest
will suggest further discussions.

Sincerely,
Jim Canfield
Vice President
Publicity and Public Relations

This deal fell through because he wanted Benchley and me to appear together at the promotions. I told Mr. Canfield point blank that if Benchley heard that I was going to be there, he would not show up. That was the last I heard from Universal Studios, Florida.

In 1996, one of the *Jaws* actors, Roy Scheider, best known for his role as the shark's nemesis, Chief Brody, acknowledged my contribution to the movie when he was interviewed by reporter Debbie Tuma for a Long Island TV show, *Interview in the Hamptons.* In it, Mr. Scheider observed [about me], "He's the inspirational character for Quint in *Jaws.*"

Over the years, people have asked me what I thought of Shaw's portrayal of me in the movie. Well, I thought he did a pretty good job of impersonating me, but his attitude wasn't ugly enough. However, there were some big differences between me and Shaw's Quint: I always had everything orderly and in good running shape aboard my boat, but Quint's boat, the *Orca*, looked sloppy and run down; everything was misplaced and it looked like the city dumps compared to the *Cricket II*. And regardless of a situation, I always listened to suggestions from my customers and crew, weighing them out, but Quint was hardheaded and stubborn, which led to his downfall.

Many people have made the statement, "The movie *Jaws* made you." My answer was, "No, I made the movie *Jaws.* The movie *Jaws* didn't make me." And so there was no applause from *Jaws*, although I helped inspire the movie.

The only thing that *Jaws* did was to shake the trees and the nuts rolled in my direction. The movie also made everybody else a shark-fishing expert. After *Jaws*, everyone that had a boat was an instant shark fisherman in their own opinion.

Before the movie, I had trouble finding a boat that would take our overflow customers out shark fishing. People told me that when they fished on my boat, they also used to fish two or three times a year on another boat and sometimes asked their regular captain to go shark fishing on one of their annual trips. "If you want to go out and catch that garbage, go out with that nut, Mundus," these captains told them. And so, they sent these customers to me, and then turned around and accused me of stealing their customers because after these people fished with me, they never went back to their original boat.

When the other boats did start to take out shark charters, some didn't give the customers their money's worth. For instance, sometimes, when the customer arrived at the boat in the morning, a captain would make the excuse that the weather was too bad and they weren't going offshore. Instead, some of them took their customers inshore blue-fishing around the lighthouse. Or if they did go shark fishing, some captains cut the day short and didn't bring home any blue sharks[5] for food, telling the customer that the blue sharks were no good to eat because they urinate through their skin. This is a stupid excuse, and a lie. Most of the so-called shark-fishing experts are glad that I am pushing pineapples here in Hawaii. I was not very well-liked by the other Montauk boat captains. If you speak the truth and give your customers value for money, instead of a boat ride, your fellow businessmen will despise you.

I was constantly ribbed and teased by the other charter-boat captains. If this wasn't bad enough, their wives would sometimes get in on the act. When I used to pick up my mail at the Montauk Post Office, one skipper's wife would often taunt me with the words, "Did you go *shaaarkin'* today?" meaning, "My husband doesn't go out for that sh——," and the local chamber of commerce thought that I was chasing tourists away by bringing in the big sharks. But the last big white shark we brought to the dock (in 1986), a 3,427-pound rod-and-reel fish, lured in more than a million dollars' worth of business to Montauk and the Hamptons.

Overnight Trips

We started the overnight trips around 1975. I wanted to prove to my customers that by doing the overnight trips, they not only got more time on the fishing grounds, but they also wound up with prime fishing time, which is daylight. An overnight trip is really a double-day trip and more, because you're on the fishing grounds for twelve hours, whereas on a daytime trip you're only on the fishing grounds for about four hours. Five hours on the fishing grounds would be a lot on a day trip.

By the last part of the '70s I did overnight trips exclusively. On an overnight trip, the boat left the dock around 7:00 p.m. the night before. My customers fished through the night and daylight and we would return to the dock the following afternoon, at around 3:00 p.m.

By the time we got there, it was around midnight. I stopped the boat, we started to drift, and the mate began chumming. My job was to run the boat out there, and when we reached the fishing grounds, I grabbed a few hours' sleep. We had enough bunks on the boat for everybody: myself, two mates, and five passengers. When somebody got out of one bunk, another person took their place. There was always somebody up on deck, either fishing or watching. I slept for about five hours until daylight. Daylight is the best fishing because everything moves at that time. This is the main reason we did these overnight trips. It is the only way you can be on the fishing grounds at the best time, by going there the night before. By the time daylight rolls around, you have established a sizeable chum slick, and if there's a decent fish roaming around, he's going to find you. Almost all of our big fish arrived at daylight or shortly after. Then at around eight or nine o'clock, we'd pick up our gear and start for home, but we would throw some feathers in the water and do some trolling for tuna fish or whatever we could find as we zigzagged our way back.

When the *Cricket II* got close to the lighthouse, I told my customers that once we hit the dock, I'm gonna kiss 'em goodbye: I'm gone! I'm not gonna hang around because I had a lot of things to do: take care of the answering box on the telephone, pick up the mail, and answer inquiries. Once in a while, if I made enough money, I'd go to the bank. But anyhow, I had those jobs to do, as well as taking care of the shopping list for the next trip. The mate handed me the list before I got off the boat and I'd bring the stuff back with me.

I generally had supper at the house and just enough time to shave and shower. No time to lie down before I had to be back on the boat again at 7:00 p.m. And away we'd go again around the clock. As I climbed aboard and headed for the flying bridge, the customers were all waiting for an introduction, but because time is always scarce and there is no sense in wasting it at the dock, I'd mumble over my shoulder, "I'll bullshit with you guys on the way out, no time now." Then I jumped up on the flying bridge and sang my song: "Over the river and through the woods to grandmother's house we go."

I ran the boat for the first half hour or so, while the mates took care of the fishing tackle and stored the gear. When this was done, one of the mates would jump up on the flying bridge to take the wheel. Then I could go down and bullshit with the customers, welcoming them aboard.

Lots of times, we would fish a bunch of these overnight trips back-to-back during our busy season. You get punchy after a while and don't know whether you're coming or going. As a matter of fact, I told all my mates that when they wake up and hear the motor slow down, before they open their eyes they'll ask themselves: "Are we getting to the fishing grounds or are we getting back to the dock?" After a while, they came up to me and said: "Hey, do you remember telling me I was gonna wake up and not know where I was? Well, it happened to me just now!"

The 1,080-pound Mako

On August 25, 1979, a Mr. James Melanson and his friends chartered the *Cricket II* in search of a mako shark. They had caught a lot of blue sharks back home, off Massachusetts, but had never boated a decent-sized mako.

This was a typical overnight trip where I ran the boat out for its four-hour ride and finally got into the sack at around midnight or so. The usual few blue sharks were caught during the night, but at daylight, on August 26, all hell broke loose. My mate, Tommy Hoffman, noticed the absence of blue sharks and thought there must be something big out there in the slick, chasing the blue sharks away. To find out what was lurking out there, my other mate, Dickie, put a whole Boston mackerel out for bait and sent it deep into the chum slick.

I was just having my cup of coffee when a big mako picked up that bait. "HOLY SHIT, LOOK AT THE SIZE OF THAT MAKO!" somebody screamed.

"He jumped over here!" another one said.

I frantically tried to get dressed while the party and crew watched the jumping mako. Suddenly, Tommy stuck his head around the cabin door, and shouted, "WE'VE GOT A BIG MAKO ON AND WE'VE GOT TO CHASE HIM DOWN!"

Before Tommy got his thumb on the starter button, I shouted back to him, "GO AHEAD, GET STARTED. I'M ON MY WAY UP!"

In the short time it took me to get up onto the bridge, that big mako had jumped ten-feet clear of the water five times, and was making his sixth and last jump. Most big fish will come up and jump, then spend the rest of the time fighting deep. Later, they return to the surface, and that's when we're able to get close enough to gaff them.

But this fish was entirely different.

After his last jump, he stayed hard on the surface for the rest of the fight. My job was to outsmart the fish and bring the boat alongside him, heading in the same direction and at the same speed in order for the mate to grab hold of the leader wire and pull the fish in close enough to be gaffed.

The customers were losing it, going nuts looking at the shark swimming on the surface, with his dorsal and tail rising high out of the water. Time and time again, Dickie almost got close enough to grab hold of the fifteen-foot steel leader wire, but every time I maneuvered the boat within inches of the leader wire, the fish made a turn and headed in a different direction.

"Either he is very smart or very lucky, but sooner or later he has to make the wrong move," I told the party. From its size, I knew this was a world-record fish and I told my two mates right from the start, "Don't make any mistakes with this fish because he looks like one for the record books."

An hour passed. Our angler Jim Melanson started to show signs of fatigue. His arms were getting tired from fighting the fish, and we could not change anglers because it would disqualify our potential world record. I knew I had to get up on the fish with the *Cricket II* as fast as I could. As luck would have it, the mako was tiring too. He made his final bad move after heading in a straight direction on my port side.

I was trying to line the boat up with his direction and speed, like I have done plenty of times before; but instead of him turning away, the fish made a U-turn toward us, aiming for the *Cricket II*'s transom. That was when I decided, "It's now or never."

I took a hell of a gamble, putting the boat in reverse, trying to match his speed: I could have accidentally backed into the fish, chopping him up in the propeller.

I told Tommy to jump up on the bridge and take the controls because I still had the boat in reverse, and once

Dickie had taken hold of the leader wire, I jumped into the cockpit and got ready to gaff the fish. When I saw that Dickie had the fish up close, I signaled for Tommy to take the boat out of gear. Dickie pulled the fish up for me to get a shot at it with the flying gaff. This was our only chance. If Dickie pulled too hard on the wire and broke the fish off, we would lose him; and if I didn't get a good purchase on the mako with the flying gaff, he'd be gone. As luck would have it, everything went smoothly. Our teamwork paid off: Tommy stopped the boat in time, Dickie pulled the fish up, and I gaffed it.

About then, all hell broke loose once more. The mako didn't like being restricted by the flying gaff. He thrashed around furiously, churning up white water all over us, but we were lucky: my modified flying-gaff head held fast. I had invented a new type of point for the flying-gaff head, which I called the "plough gaff" because once it was inserted into a fish, it would plough all the way in.

In order to put an end to the fight, we had to put a tail rope on this fish. It took another fifteen minutes or so to do because every time we pulled the fish up close to the boat and attempted to lasso his tail, everyone got a thrashing from the mako's tail and the flailing flying-gaff rope, which gave us all rope burn.

We could hardly see anything because the mako buried us in the saltwater that he was churning up. Finally, we got the tail rope on and this mako was ours. It had taken an hour and fifteen minutes to outsmart this shark. At that time, this fish held a double record: the largest mako taken on rod and reel, and the largest mako taken on fifty-pound test line.

Recently, an angler caught one a few pounds heavier on bigger tackle. But as of now, our fish is still the largest mako taken on fifty-pound test line. However, records are only made to be broken . . .

Snowbird, or How I Discovered Hawaii

If you didn't have to go outside and work for a living, Montauk was a nice place to live in the winter. Looking through my picture window at those birds ass deep in the snow on my front lawn was nice, as long as I could throw another log on the fire and didn't have to go out there with them. Looking back at the early days in Montauk, and thinking of all those cold days working outside to put food on the table gives me a cold chill.

In the fifties, sixties, and early seventies, I had to take any kind of outdoor manual labor I could get. One winter, in order to make some double-overtime bucks on a construction site, I had to climb inside the drum of a cement truck and use an air hammer to chip away at the encrusted, hardened cement. The sound was deafening and I wasn't given any ear or breathing protection. No human being could have endured more than two hours in that drum, and I did this twice a week for one whole winter! I always spent most of the next day spitting up cement dust.

My roofing job was also a classic, putting shingles on people's roofs, with my one-eyed boss who never felt the cold. Some of those days it was below freezing, so cold that when I reached into my carpenter's apron for a nail, my fingers were so numb that I couldn't feel the roofing nails. Then there was dock building, splashing around in cold saltwater and mud. One winter I spent as a steel worker down at Montauk Point, putting up a government radar tower. We worked sixty-five feet in the air with no safety protection. On some of those days, it was so cold that when we showed up for work, the boss would say, "We can't work up there today, too cold!" Another winter, I worked as a deck hand on the Catherine McAlistair tugboat lines, handling frozen lines. Some of them were so frozen to the towed barge's cleats that I had to chop them off with an ax!

By the seventies and eighties, there were a few winters when I got paid for doing sport shows around the country. My job was talking to people at the shows about how good the Penn fishing reels were, how good the Stren fishing line and the Berkley swivels were, and answering any and all questions about big-game fishing.

Some of the far-out places where I was sent to talk saltwater and big-game fishing were unbelievable. I found myself in places like Upstate New York and the hills of Pennsylvania, where the people never did any saltwater fishing and didn't know what a heavy-fishing rod was. I could tell by the way they were dressed that these were farm people. I saw them coming and knew exactly what was going to happen, because it had happened to me plenty of times before.

As they approached my booth and looked down at the heavy-fishing rods I had on display, one guy, who was their spokesman, would always point at the rods, then put both his thumbs in the straps of his overall suspenders, rock back and forth from toe to heel, and say, "Looka dere, Zeke. You could yank stumps right out da the ground wid dem." I had to turn my head to keep from laughing. If I heard this once, I must have heard it a hundred times on the sports-show circuit.

I made appearances at about four or five of these sport shows each winter. Each show lasted four to seven days. By the time you helped set up the show and took it down, you were looking at about a week. The rest of the month, I watched the birds hopping through the snow, and threw another log on the fire.

I was between shows one winter in 1983, when the phone rang. It was one of my customers, Louie. Louie was a good con man and could talk the pope out of his cross at high mass! He had moved to the Big Island of Hawaii a few years earlier and was running a sports desk there (Louie, that is, not His Holiness, the Pope). Louie wanted me to visit him, but I told him that I had seen Florida, the Bahamas, and then St. Maarten in the Caribbean. "What's so different about Hawaii?" I asked.

"I've rented a nice condo, and there's plenty of room," he said. "Come down for a couple of weeks to see this place." That was when I made my first trip to Hawaii, on St. Valentine's Day, 1984. It didn't take me very long to see the big difference.

The first thing that caught my eye, and that turned out to be the most important thing, was that here on the Big Island of Hawaii, you can pick the elevation at which you'd like to live above sea level. For instance, I wound up at the one-thousand-feet level. Kailua-Kona, the main town, is at sea level and it's hot there. By going up to the one thousand five hundred to two thousand feet level, it will be five to ten degrees cooler. At three thousand to four thousand feet, it is another ten to twenty degrees cooler. There are people living up there at three thousand to four thousand feet who say that in the summer, it is often forty degrees Fahrenheit at daylight, and an average of thirty-five degrees in the winter. If you go up any higher, you'll find snow up on the top of the mountains in winter. Providing you use a four-wheel drive, you can travel from eighty degrees at sea level up to below zero at the mountain summit of Mauna Kea.

The first two winters I was here, I started shark fishing and began building up a clientele once the word got around. In the summertime, I fished in Montauk. Then, in the winter of 1985, a prince from Saudi Arabia requested my services: I was to teach his crew how to catch sharks in the Red Sea . . .

Mundus of Arabia (1985-86)

One day, in October 1985, the telephone rang. On the other end was an executive from the Bertram boat company, wanting to know if I was interested in going to Saudi Arabia. He was the personal friend and ex-college buddy of a Saudi prince, Khalid bin Sultan. Prince Khalid, the nephew of King Fahd, was a boating and fishing enthusiast, and he wanted me to teach his crew how to catch sharks in the Red Sea. I didn't think the executive was serious, so I said "Yes."

I still didn't realize the seriousness of the situation until, two weeks later, Federal Express pulled into my driveway with a package that contained my airplane ticket. I must have made circles on every rug in my house that afternoon! Once it had sunk in, the job of figuring out what to take with me began.

I was told that when I got there, my telephone would already be hooked up internationally, and any fishing tackle I wanted from any place in the world would be delivered immediately to me in Saudi Arabia. But I still wanted to take some of my own hooks, leader wire, and fishing line to begin with, and so the packing process began.

It seemed like no time at all went by before I found myself on a Saudi Airlines flight. I had barnacles on my back pocket before we reached Saudi Arabia: an eleven to twelve-hour direct flight is a long ride, no matter how you look at it, or sit on it! (I later found out that Prince Khalid owned Saudi Airlines!) When my flight landed, it was not yet daylight. Looking down at all the street lights below me, it seemed like there was a lot of activity on the ground, but the next day, I was told that because the cost of electricity was next to nothing there, all the empty side streets were lit up as well as the main roads. I should have expected it, I suppose, since the Arabs are experts in this field. In the tenth century, they had street lighting in Muslim-run Cordoba, Spain.

Because I was a tourist who couldn't speak any Arabic, the aftermath of my arrival at Saudi Arabia International Airport was an educational experience. Just about everybody and his brother were dressed in long white robes (*thobes*) and were standing in four long lines. The place was covered in people, some of whom were lying on the floor near an airport wall. Some were sitting and others were eating while they were lying there. You might think that there would be an aroma with so many people huddled in one place, but there wasn't. I was impressed that it wasn't like the airport in New York: nobody was pushing, shoving, or arguing about their luggage. The Saudi passengers were very quiet and orderly.

My main problem was that I couldn't read any of the airport information signs, which were all written in Arabic, so I didn't know which line to stand in. A half hour later, an airport worker noticed the stupid, confused look on my face and he asked, in broken English, to see my papers. It was then that I discovered I was in the wrong line and had to start queuing up all over again!

The prince's dock master, Collins, a British national, had been sent to pick me up at the airport. He was standing on the other side of the custom inspectors, but I didn't know this or what he even looked like. However, the dock master didn't have any trouble recognizing me: I was the only person not dressed in white! Before long, Collins walked up to me and shook my hand. He was in his midforties, a soft-spoken, short wiry Englishman.

During the drive back to my apartment at the compound in Jiddah, I was surprised to see so many walled pieces of land. Collins explained that when an Arab obtains a piece of property, the first thing he has to do by law is put up a four-sided wall "high enough that a man on a camel cannot see over it." Then he builds his house.

There were plenty of nice big stores and supermarkets in Jiddah. Most of the automobiles on the road were

Japanese—and American-made cars. During my four-month stay in Saudi, I only saw one camel on the side of the road (without a driver!). The Saudi main roads were like our superhighways. Most of them had two or three lanes on each side, separated by wide grass dividers which contained palm trees that were cared for daily by water trucks. When it came to manual labor, the Saudis brought in outside help, mostly from Pakistan. For me, it was funny to see a truck driver clad in a flowing white robe jump out of his vehicle.

Collins told me that because the Saudis got their fuel almost for nothing, they built large generators, producing all the electricity they wanted and then set up large desalinization plants to make all the fresh water that they needed. Those men who drove the water trucks had a lifetime job. They never had a day off on account of rain or from a lack of rain either!

On my travels, I noticed that the Saudis had traffic circles which were very unusual and fancy. Situated about three to five miles apart, each had a highly-polished tiled deck with a statue in the center, and there was a story or moral behind each image. One was a giant hand and wrist made of bronze, about eight feet high and about fifteen feet in diameter. This was supposed to represent the penalty for theft: amputation. Another contained a thirty-foot-high, fifteen-foot square cement block. Each side had a couple of automobiles sticking out of it. I was told this monument warned people to drive safely! There were many others, but I never found out what they represented. For instance, one had two giant sunflowers made of bronze. Each was about eight feet in diameter.

The one I found the most amusing was a giant bicycle, twenty-five to thirty feet high; it was so big that you could park your car on the bicycle seat. And set on one side was a giant-sized spare bicycle wheel. Another eye-catcher was a thirty-foot-round monument: a detailed glass globe of the world, which was lit up from the inside at night.

And then there were the boats. One traffic circle had a cement boat, sixty to eighty feet foot long, plopped in the middle of it. Another circle was decorated with an old eighty-three-foot U.S. Coast Guard cutter; it seemed like they had just picked the vessel up out of the water and set it up there.

It was about a half-hour's ride from the airport in Jiddah to my apartment. My living quarters were inside an American compound that contained about one hundred apartments. The compound was divided into sections for married couples, families with children, and the bachelors' quarters, where I would be living. I was very happy to discover that my apartment had a color TV, a full kitchen, and air-conditioning. The Saudi television broadcasting company selected three American channels that we could watch and these shut down between 10:00 p.m. and 10:30 p.m. each evening.

I was joined at the compound by two other Americans, Butch and Ajax, who had been hired as the prince's official crew for his boat, a fifty-four-foot Bertram. Prince Khalid had put both men through an intensive training course at the Bertram boat factory.

The first day we were taken to our apartments, Butch quickly made friends with another American, who gave him a couple of shots of homemade booze. Due to the strict Islamic prohibition on alcohol consumption, some people were making their own booze inside the American compound. The Saudis knew about this and let them get away with it as long as they did their drinking at home; but if the security guard heard any unusually loud noises, he would report it. Then a Saudi security team would break into the apartment and confiscate all the booze (and they knew all the hiding places), and that was the end of your party. The offenders received a warning, but get too many warnings and you're out. Also, you would be taking a chance, trying to smuggle booze or women into the compound because there was always a gate master on duty who inspected the cars of the returning compound occupants. And a Saudi security guard patrolled the compound every hour or so on his little motor scooter.

Butch didn't have his phone hooked up yet, so when he needed to place long distance calls, he had to use the public phone booth in the compound. The Saudi switchboard operator, who manned the phone booth, smelled booze on Butch's breath and called the cops immediately. That little caper could get you a fast free ride to the airport and instant deportation. No, you are not allowed to go back to your apartment to pick up your belongings before you're on your way. Butch was lucky. He was given the warning, "Next time, it's goodbye."

Butch and another American, "Ajax," had been hired as the prince's permanent captain and mate respectively, on a year-long renewable contract. "Ajax" only lasted a couple of weeks in Saudi because he found the rules too tough: no booze, no broads, no freedom to travel. When a foreigner asks to go home shortly after he gets there, it is a slap in the face to the Saudis, who think their hospitality has been rebuffed. I found them to be very courteous people, from storekeepers on the street to the prince in the palace.

One morning, the dock master drove me into town to pick up some items for the dock and the boat. Just before we entered the hardware store, I noticed a Saudi standing on the corner, waiting for somebody. The man had something in his mouth, about the size of a small cigar and he was methodically moving it around, using a scrubbing action. The object resembled a four- to five-inch stick and was about a half-inch round. I was going to ask Collins what this guy was doing, when we entered the hardware store, but my attention now focused on the many shelves that were well-stocked with heaters of all kinds: electric, gas, and kerosene, of all makes and sizes.

"What are all those heaters doing here in Saudi Arabia?" I asked the dock master.

"When you got here, it was around seventy degrees at night, and to you it was cool, but the locals felt so cold they had to turn on their heaters," He replied.

Out of curiosity, I wanted to find out how hot it was in the direct sun, so I brought down a thermometer that could read over the normal 125-degree limit and took a reading in the sun, down in the cockpit of the boat. At 10:30 a.m., the temperature was 160 degrees. I was so amazed, I took a photograph of this thermometer reading and decided to take more. Moving along fast in a cool breeze aboard the prince's fifty-four-foot Bertram, I got a reading of 130 degrees on the floor of the cabin doorway.

In the cabin, two air-conditioners were running constantly, so it felt cool when I stepped inside, but it was still a sweltering eighty degrees in the cabin.

When Collins and I emerged from the hardware store, the Saudi man was still standing on the corner, pushing and shoving that thing around his mouth. I asked Collins, who had lived in Saudi for the last fourteen years, "What do you suppose he has in his mouth?"

Collins was amused by my question. "That's his toothbrush," he laughed.

Apparently, the Saudis use a fibrous stick which, once moistened, breaks down into thousands of fibers, like sugar cane or bamboo. By this time, the end would resemble a small mop. I bought a pack of these sticks from a street peddler. I even tried one of them and it worked, but kept me very busy spitting out the small broken ends.

After we got back from the hardware store, Butch decided to make a trip to the bank, and asked if I felt like going with him. He wanted to set up a savings account. I decided to ride along because I was interested in finding out how different Saudi banks were from our banking institutions. So we drove the short distance to the bank.

I noticed all the tellers were male and they were dressed in long white robes, but the vice president, who sat behind a large fancy desk, wore a suit. As we approached, he asked in very good English, "Can I help you?"

Butch replied, "Yes, I would like to open up a savings account," and asked in the same breath, "how much interest do you pay?"

The vice president raised an eyebrow, and asked, "Do you want interest?"

"Is it against the law?" Butch asked cautiously.

I sat there, absorbing this conversation, trying to keep a straight face, but it was hard: what vice president of a Western bank would ask, "Do you want interest?"

"If you were a Saudi, it would be against your religion," the vice president told Butch.

Again, Butch asked, "Can I get interest, and if so, what does this bank pay?"

The man behind the fancy desk finally said, "If you open a savings account over $1,000 reals [about $300.00], the bank will pay you 2 percent interest."

So Butch opened up his account. I didn't bother because I was only staying for a short time in Saudi.

One payday, I went to the bank with my salary to buy a cashier's check to send home. In the middle of my transaction, they closed all the doors because prayer time had begun. I took a seat and watched the bank tellers walk back and forth past me with large armfuls of money, handling it as if they were carrying firewood. A half hour later, they reopened the doors and resumed business.

Most of the time, Butch and I had a strict daily routine, with time out for grocery shopping or to visit the bank. But most mornings, at 8:00 a.m., Butch picked me up in his company car, a brown Ford Blazer, and we began our half-hour ride to the prince's four-hundred-foot long tiled dock, where Prince Khalid kept his fleet of boats, including a speed boat, an eighty-foot sailboat, a pontoon boat with two outboards, sixty-foot Italian-built Riva (his luxurious home away from home), and the fifty-four-foot Bertram (the prince's fishing boat). There was even a gas pump at the end of the dock.

During the drive, we would be stopped once or twice by military roadblocks on the way to and from the boat. Soldiers armed with rifles demanded to see our work permits ("Papers, papers!") and searched the car.

Judging from the serious looks on their faces, these guys did not have a sense of humor. And as the only English words they knew were "Papers, papers!" we had no idea what else they were looking for and we didn't ask. Each day, these roadblocks were stationed at different intervals along the road.

Eventually, we arrived at the ten-foot wall which surrounded the prince's beach house. The wall was guarded by a gate man who screened visitors before opening the large electric gate that led to the parking area behind the beach house. This setup reminded me of the gatekeeper who guarded the palace of the Wizard of Oz. All we could see were his head and shoulders as he peeped though a small sliding-glass window.

The prince had a small air-conditioned cottage on the end of the dock, which acted as a waiting room. Butch or I had to pick up Prince Khalid's guests from the shaded parking area close to His Highness's beach house. We used an electric golf cart to drive them to the waiting area and then to the boat once we were ready to roll.

Most days were spent cleaning and working on the boat, keeping it in 100 percent tip-top shape. It was like working for the fire department; we never knew when we had to roll. Actual fishing trips were few and far between, depending on the prince's schedule. Out of the four months I spent in Saudi Arabia, the prince only fished with me four times.

We were told by the dock master that when we fished with the prince and he wanted to go home suddenly, Butch or I had to run up in the bow and *immediately* cut off our one-inch nylon anchor line so that we would not waste time lifting the anchor; but I just couldn't see wasting all that anchor line and anchor when it would only take us five minutes to raise it with the electric winch. So I always picked the anchor up with the winch, and nobody ever said anything about it.

The rest of the time, when Butch and I wanted to do some experimental shark fishing in the Red Sea, we had to get permission from Collins, the prince's personal dock master. In fact, all our orders came down through Collins, who was very protective of the prince's new toy, the fifty-four-foot Bertram. We often had to convince him that the sea conditions were OK, and that the boat and crew could handle it.

Back home, off the east coast, when the wind blew hard, I often got salt spray in my eyes, ears, and face; and my hair became stiff and straight. But out on the Red Sea, I got sand spray in my eyes, ears, and face; and my hair became stiff and gritty! When the wind blew here, it whipped up sandstorms—on water and on land. I witnessed two of them: one on land and one at sea.

On our way to the boat one morning, Butch and I got hit by a sandstorm. Driving was hazardous because the truck ahead of us disappeared in a cloud of sand if it got any farther than fifty feet away. When Butch and I reached the boat, we had to secure the boat with extra lines because of the fifty- to sixty-mile-per-hour winds.

It wasn't the wind that bothered me. It was the sand.

As far as I was concerned, the sand that was being moved around looked and felt like heavy dust. Face protection was a must. During the sandstorm, Butch and I wore handkerchiefs around our mouths. When it was all over, it was *all over* the prince's fancy fishing boat that we had kept spotless, but was now a mess. As soon as I hit the dust with the dock's wash-down hose, it turned into mud because it was more dirt than sand, lacking the gritty texture of the sand I was familiar with.

And the funniest part was yet to come. When I got back to my apartment, I found that, even with all the doors and windows closed, everything was covered in a layer of that light sand. When I had finished cleaning up, I had two wastepaper-basketfuls of this stuff.

We were out fishing when I experienced my second sandstorm. It was a sandstorm without the wind. Butch and I were on the prince's Bertram, anchored fifteen miles off land, on a two-day fishing trip. And Prince Khalid and Collins were nearby on the prince's luxury cruiser, anchored on the same reef. When we got up in the morning, everything was covered by the same thick layer of sand. It was so heavy that I left behind sandy footprints when I walked up into the bow. Around 8:30 a.m., Collins brought the prince over to fish for the day. At the first chance I got, I asked Collins, "Where the hell did a sand storm come from without the wind?"

He just laughed and pointed up toward the sky. I couldn't figure out what Collins was telling me, so I asked him once more, "What the hell do you mean?"

He laughed, and said, "It came from the sky. It always comes from the sky as fallout when there's no wind at all."

And so, we had yet another week's cleanup ahead of us. If the wind blew, we had sand, and if the wind didn't blow and it was flat-calm, we had sand.

When the time came for me to go shark fishing, I asked the dock master if he knew any fishermen in the area who could show us where the sharks were. Finally, he said, "Oh, yes, I know a couple of *expert* shark fishermen. We'll have them come around and they can go out with you one day. *They'll* show you where the sharks are."

So I waited, and finally, a few days went by then the dock master said, "OK, they're coming. You guys can go out tomorrow and catch some sharks."

I called these two shark experts "Barney" and "Fred." That's who they reminded of: the two main characters in

The Flintstones. Both men dressed in traditional Arab clothing: long white gowns and sandals, with headdresses of black-checkered cloth. The next day, they came marching down the dock; each equipped with a plastic shopping bag. This was their fishing tackle! And they didn't have much in them, either: a spool of one-hundred-pound test monofilament hand lines, some rocks for their sinkers, and hooks.

When they climbed on the boat, naturally, they didn't speak any English, and naturally, we didn't speak any Arabic; so everything was, "Uggghuhuhooohhuh."

And if Fred and Barney were arguing among themselves about where the fish were, it was, "Weeeuggooohuhhgg," and they would each point to different directions. So Butch and I went to where they said, "Weeuggooohuhhgg," and when we got there, one of them would point to the water, meaning, "OK, this is the spot." So we stopped and we'd drift, while they fished with their hand lines.

I was afraid that with their one-hundred-pound mono hand lines, one of them might hook a 150-pound fish and get pulled overboard! So when I saw Barney hook a decent-sized fish, I instinctively backed away: I wasn't going to be anywhere near him if he got tangled up in his hand line! Every time he pulled it in, hand over hand, checking his bait, Barney dropped the hand line loose on the deck, and it lay there, in somewhat of a coil, next to where he stood.

At one point, Barney had some kind of fish on for a short time. I don't know what it was, but he had him coming in our direction, and then the hook broke. That was the only thing we hooked that seriously resembled a shark, with our two shark experts, Barney and Fred.

Butch and I did catch a few reef sharks (around 150 pounds each) on our own experimental trips. And we eventually caught the prince a short-fin mako of about two-hundred-pounds. According to Jack Casey of the National Marine Fisheries Service, we were the first ones to record the capture of short-fin mako in the Red Sea. Hassan told me that the prince wanted his fish mounted. I explained that meant my making a double-insulated crate in order to keep the fish in good shape for the taxidermist on Long Island, New York.

"Will the shark fit in that new twenty-one-cubic-foot freezer you just bought for the dock?" Hassan asked me. I told him it would, and he said, "Well, use the freezer as your crate." And so I did. I also made a point of calling the taxidermist, and told him, "Save that crate for me, I'll pick it up when I get home!"

Back on land, I kept my explorations to a minimum, refusing to drive around Jiddah because of the stiff penalties metered out for traffic violations. Collins briefed me on Saudi Rules of the Road 101: if you are caught driving over the white line at a crosswalk during a red light, you automatically get five days in jail.

But it's far worse if you (a non-Saudi) come to a stop at a red light and some Saudi motorist ploughs into the back of your car and is killed—this is *your* fault: by some strange quirk of fate, you were the cause of his death and you must go to jail, no questions asked.

Now you languish in jail until the dead driver's family takes a vote on whether you should receive a life sentence or pay them a huge fine. The snag is, if one of the family members is not yet sixteen years old (their voting age), you stay in jail until that child reaches emancipation. Better yet, the Saudi jails have no air-conditioning and if you like to eat, you had better have friends on the outside bringing you food—the jailers only provide a room, but no board!

Of course, there are other ways to become an inmate— if you get caught taking a photograph of any government building, then it's a one-year prison sentence: no exceptions. I was told the true story of a Dutch contractor who had been hired by the Saudis to build a jail house. When his project was finished, the Dutchman stepped back to admire it and took a photograph.

Moments later, he was arrested and became the first inmate of his new jail—for a year!

I came close to visiting a Saudi jail after riding around with Butch. One day, Butch and I were on our way to do some work on Prince Khalid's boat, when he got the urge to take a photo of those big white tents that the pilgrims stand under to keep from frying in the sun as they wait for buses to take them up to Mecca.

Butch stopped our vehicle on the side of the road and poked his zoom-lens camera out of the window. He was in the process of focusing the lens, when a cop car pulled up next to us. They had seen the whole thing. As they approached the car, I quickly hid my own camera in the Blazer's armrest. The policemen took Butch's camera and muttered their disapproval in Arabic. Then they gestured for us to wait. Soon, a police sergeant arrived on the scene. He told us that if the film in Butch's camera had a photo of those tents on it, we were going to jail whether we were the prince's employees or not. Lucky for us, Butch hadn't snapped the shutter yet.

There had been a public beheading of a policeman in Saudi Arabia just one week before I arrived. The dock master told me all about it: a kid had just gotten his driver's license and had stopped over the white line at a red light. A cop came along and told the kid he would let the youth off if he allowed the cop to molest him. The kid, terrified of spending five days in jail, did as the policeman asked, but afterward he reported the cop for rape. In Saudi Arabia, sex crimes are punishable by death.

A public beheading is performed in the town square at high noon, when the sun is at its hottest. The convicted man is put on his knees, with his hands tied behind his back. Two executioners are present. One stands in front of the condemned man, holding a wide machete-type sword; the other man is positioned behind the prisoner, and wields a long pointed blade. The man in the rear waits for the prisoner to start wilting in the hot sun. When his head starts to drop, the guy behind, with the pointed sword, pokes the prisoner between the shoulder blades.

In a reflex action, the condemned man throws his head up and back in surprise and pain. Now, the man in front has a good shot and lops off the prisoner's head with a machete.

Time flies when you're having fun, and soon it came time for me to go home. Butch had signed on for a one-year contract, but I had requested only a two-month stay as a temporary shark-fishing instructor from December 1985 through January 1986 because I had made prior arrangements with Penn Reels to make guest appearances in their booth at the New York Boat Show from January 11-19, 1986.

One morning, Hassan, the prince's number-two man, walked down the dock, with his head dress and white robe flapping in the breeze. He said he knew it was time for me to go home, but wanted to know if I could stay on for another month or so.

"No," I told him, "I have to go home."

Then he invited me up to his office in the palace to talk about this. Hassan spoke very good English and knew how to bargain. He said the prince would let me return to New York for the show, cover all my expenses, and even keep me on the payroll for the four weeks that I would be away. Hassan was a smart man: he knew that if I wanted to collect my pay, I had to come back to Saudi. So I agreed to return and extend my stay from the end of February through the end of April 1986. On January 11, I went to the New York Boat Show and returned to Saudi Arabia almost four weeks later. The prince kept his word and my next paycheck included four weeks back pay, covering the time I spent in New York.

To complicate matters, early in April, I got some bad news during one of my weekly calls to Teddy Feurer, my mate in Montauk. Ted mentioned that the dock on East Lake Drive, where I had the *Cricket II* berthed, had been sold and we had to move the two walk-in freezers that I had on the dock before the Montauk fishing season started in June. Teddy was hoping I could cut my stay short and return home at the beginning of April to help sort out the mess.

Now I had to ask the prince if he would let me go home three weeks ahead of schedule. I had given him my word that I would stay until the end of April, but if the prince really needed me, I would stay; if not, I said I would like to go home early.

To get word to Prince Khalid, I had to observe protocol and go through his chain of command, starting with the dock master. I told Collins what I wanted and asked him to pass on my request. The dock master then asked Hassan, and Hassan passed it on to Agill, Prince Khalid's right-hand man. And so the word was passed back down to me, telling me that the prince would fish on his boat next week and I had permission to approach him directly with my request.

A week later, we were fishing in the Red Sea and I was standing alone in the cockpit, searching for the right opportunity to approach His Highness, when all of a sudden, he came out of the cabin, and said, "Frank, I hear you want to go home early?"

"Yes, sir, if it's possible," I answered. "But if you really need me, I will stay because I gave you my word that I would stay until the last of April."

The prince stood there pensively for a moment, and then said, "If you want, you can figure on going home around the ninth."

"Thank you, sir," I said appreciatively as he walked back into the cabin. Then I made arrangements to go home right after my next payday. We never knew what day it was on, but when payday came around, the dock master would visit our apartment, after work, telling us to dress up for a visit to Hassan's office in the palace to collect our pay.

Each payday, Hassan brought us into his office one at a time, and gave each of us a brown envelope full of cash, which we had to sign for. Then we would go back to our apartments and count it out. Because of the three-to-one exchange rate for Arabian currency, it always looked like I had a pile of money. On my final payday, I was counting the money out, back at my apartment, and found I had been overpaid. Luckily, I still had Hassan's telephone number at the palace and I called him right away to report the error. He said the figure was right because they had paid me for the original time that I said I would stay for, until the end of April: they had paid me three more weeks' worth of salary just because I had said I would stay until the last of April. I was paid for my word.

During my last few days in Saudi Arabia, I picked up a few trinkets to take back to New York: one was a Persian rug, about six feet by eight feet. It had cost me $600.00 and that was a bargain. Now, I always pack everything well when I travel, so I rolled the rug up tightly and packaged it securely in wrapping paper and twine. I was so proud of my wrapping job that I forgot about one small thing: the Saudi Customs Inspectors. By the time I had finished tying up my bundle, it was about one foot around and six feet tall!

When the time came for me to vacate my apartment, on April 13, 1986, I mentioned to the dock master that, now I had moved out, someone else could have this nice apartment. (My apartment in the American compound had been the last one in the row on the ground floor and was closest to the main road.)

"They won't use your apartment anymore," Collins said.

"Why not?" I asked.

"It's too close to the road and somebody could throw a bomb in it!"

"Oh well, that's nice to know," I said. Nobody had given me this valuable facet of information until I was ready to move out.

The day I checked out of the compound, Collins drove me to the airport and showed me which line to stand in to have my luggage checked. Soon, it was my turn. Two customs inspectors (who spoke no English) immediately flew into my suitcases and packages. When one of them found the rug, he started tearing the wrapping off. Alarmed, I went over to him and tried explaining what the object was in one word, "Rug!"

But the inspector continued to rummage and remove all the wrapping, so I screamed at him: "RUG! RUG!"

He was paying absolutely no attention to me.

The only thing I could do was stand there and watch. When the inspector had removed the final layer of paper, with a flourish, he rolled the rug out flat on the floor, turned to me with a smile of triumph on his face, and announced, "Caaarpet. Caaarpet."

After he had finished tearing everything apart, I had less than half an hour to put it all back together again before my flight departed. Meanwhile, Collins had been standing behind the line of ticketed passengers, watching the entire scene with amusement. I looked back over at him and saw he was enjoying the sideshow: this was probably why he had not told me ahead of time what to expect at the customs area.

Overall, my trip to Saudi Arabia had been a success. Although there had not been too many sharks (or fish of any kind) in the area where we were fishing—out of the inlet by Jiddah—we had caught Prince Khalid bin Sultan a shark: a short-fin mako (on rod and reel) in the Red Sea.

The 3,427-pound White Shark

Once in a while I had a hole in my overnight bookings and knew that when I got back to the dock I would have the next day off. Well, this is what happened on August 4, 1986. We were on the way out and I told the Jerry Rounds party from Advantage Food Company that because we didn't have a trip following this one, I was in absolutely no rush.

"During the day we can zigzag around, look for tuna fish, and get back to the dock late because we don't have a booking for the evening of the fifth," I told them. So they were happy and we caught a few sharks that night. The next day, the *Cricket II* zigzagged around on her way home at around three o'clock in the afternoon. We should have been home by this time, but were still an hour and a half offshore.

One of the other boats, the *Fish On*, run by Donnie Braddick, had a mate on board, Mike Skarimbas, who had fished with me before. Donnie and Mike knew that I didn't have my radio on because I hate that cussed bullshit box. The *Fish On* saw me in the distance and buzzed up alongside the *Cricket II* to give me some valuable information. One of her crew hollered, "Hey, we just came across a dead whale."

"A dead whale?" I asked. "Where?" Donnie gave me the directions. It was only about fifteen minutes from here. So, we pulled up our lines. "Damn the torpedoes and full steam ahead!" I said to my mates.

Sure enough, there it was, sticking out of the ocean like a sore thumb, four or five feet out of the water. The ocean was flat-calm, not a breath of air, not a wave, not a ripple. Nothing around but a bunch of stormy petrel seabirds— and the *Fish On*. Donnie Braddick had arrived there first with his faster boat.

We watched him as he pulled up alongside the whale. Suddenly, I saw his mate, Mike, run out on the pulpit and pick up the harpoon. We all held our breath as it happened. Mike threw the harpoon and the pole stopped as it struck something. They had stuck a white shark, but lost it before the *Cricket II* got to them. Their white shark had rolled around and bit the harpoon line off. The fish either died or left the area, as we never saw it again. He would have been easy to spot, as this shark must have had a three- to five-foot piece of white harpoon line hanging off him from the harpoon dart embedded in his back.

Teddy and I hoped this was not the only fish in the area. If so, we had lost our chance of trying to catch a white shark on rod and reel. In the past, I had harpooned white sharks, but swore that the next one would be taken on rod and reel, just like the last two we caught. Because everybody is sports-minded these days, it would be taboo to bring home a harpooned white shark.

We came up alongside the whale and tied up to him, putting a line on his tail section and one on his head. Then we pulled the boat in so it was right tight to the fish. This is when one of our collapsible side pulpits came in very handy. The fourteen-foot-long right-side pulpit slid across the whale's belly, suspended five feet above it, and extended to the other side where, hopefully, the white sharks would eventually surface, gliding back and forth, picking their next spot to bite out a bushel-basket-sized hunk of meat from the whale carcass.

It was seven o'clock in the evening when Jerry Rounds came to me, and asked, "Hey, Frank, what's going on? When are we going home?"

I replied, "We're *not* going home. I told you I didn't have a charter tomorrow, so we're just gonna sit right here and hang on, because later on one of these white sharks is going to show up. So far, we haven't seen anything, but I know they are there because there's big chunks missing from the side of this whale. They *will* come up again to feed."

Jerry wasn't so sure about this. "Well," he said, "we wanna go home."

"You wanna go *home*?" I asked, thinking he was crazy to miss out on all the action that was to come.

He answered, "Yeah, we've all got things we've got to do."

I offered them the next overnight trip for free, telling him, "We've got plenty of food and we always carry lots of ice for a condition like this. All that you guys have to do is sit back and wait. You're gonna see something that you've never seen in your life!" I told him.

He went away and came back again, and said, "No, I've talked to the boys and we wanna go home."

"OK, all right. I'll call you a taxi."

There were all kinds of boats out there, popping up over the horizon. When a decent-sized private boat, the *First Light*, showed up, I flagged her captain down. He came over and I asked if he was going back to the dock. He said, "Yes."

"All right, do you mind carrying my customers home?" I asked. "They wanna go back, but I'm camping here for tonight."

The *First Light* pulled up alongside us without any trouble because the water was flat-calm. Her crew picked up the people, we kissed 'em goodbye and away they went. As my customers left, I told them, "You idiots are really gonna be sorry you did *this*. We're gonna see a *lot* of action."

At this time, Donnie Braddick had returned to the area with his charter party. He asked, "Do you mind if I put a bait down deep under your boat and the whale? I'd like to see if I can catch something."

I said, "No, go ahead." So he tied up to me, put a bait out, and it slid under my boat and beneath the whale. I held my breath, hoping he wouldn't mess things up for us by hooking a decent-sized white shark. As luck would have it, Donnie hooked some unidentified fish and chased it down. It seemed like the fish pulled him all around the ocean. When Donnie returned, he said that they had lost the fish.

As my party had already left, I asked Donnie's party if they wanted to stay and try to help catch a white shark because I needed a customer in the chair to fight the fish on rod and reel. It would have been a tough job for me to catch a fish of that size with only two mates in the cockpit and me running the boat. Donnie's party refused to stay: they wanted to go home too.

So then I asked Donnie, "Why don't you guys go home, drop off your party, pick up a pizza, and come back out because we need the help?" I told Donnie, "You won't have any trouble finding us because it's flat-calm out here and you can see us from a long way away, especially with your radar."

"Yeah, OK," he agreed. "We'll come back and give you a hand."

Teddy, my first mate, asked me when the sharks were going to show. I said, "Well, they already had their noon feeding. I'm gonna go to bed because I don't think anything is going to happen until around midnight."

He said, "Well, we'll wake you up."

"You won't have to," I said. "I'll know when the action starts."

So Donnie went home, dropped off his party, picked up a pizza, and came back around 10:00 p.m. I was in the sack when I heard him jump on board the *Cricket II* after he had tied his boat up to us. At one o'clock all hell broke loose: *CRASH! BANG! BOOM!*

Two white sharks surfaced and hit the whale so hard that they pushed it against my boat, giving the *Cricket II* a heavy thump. I knew exactly what had happened. Then everybody started hollering, "THE WHITE SHARKS ARE HERE. THE WHITE SHARKS ARE HERE!" This I knew, so I got up and looked at them swimming around. When you've seen one white shark swim around a whale, you've seen 'em all. The boys were all excited, but I said, "The only thing you can do is look at them. I'm going back to bed because we've got a lot of work to do tomorrow."

Nobody in their right mind would try and catch a fish like that in the dark. I hit the sack again, but most of the crew stayed up watching the two white sharks swim around. This was not the first time that I had seen more than one white shark around a whale at the same time. These fish were small and roughly the same size, somewhere in the 1,500-pound class. We called them "the Twins."

When daylight came, I was up and the Twins were back, swimming around the whale. Then one of them disappeared. Now we had to figure out who was going to catch his brother. The crew flipped coins to see who would be in the fighting chair. John DiLeonardo won and took his place. I walked out on the side pulpit, over the whale, carrying John's bait, and presented it to the shark as he swam by. After teasing this fish over and over again, I finally got him so mad that he jumped on it. Then I dropped the twenty-five-foot leader cable in the water and yelled to John, "You're in! You are now the proud papa of a white shark. Hang on!"

We quickly took off the lines that secured Donnie's boat to mine and tied it to the whale, while I backed the *Cricket II* clear and started chasing the fish down. If you sit still, the fish will strip all the line off the reel.

So far, it was a routine fight: the fish zigzagged around the ocean as we chased him. John did a good job as our angler, gaining line on him when he could. After about an hour of this, the fish got the heavy one-eighth inch, seven-strand stainless-steel leader cable in the corner of his mouth and bit it off. We tried everything as a white shark leader, but we could not find anything that a white shark couldn't bite through. All of a white shark's teeth mesh tightly together, but the back teeth mesh *very* tightly together, so exact that there's no room at all. If the cable gets into the back teeth, these teeth act like a pair of cutting pliers and will cut it off like this fish did.

On our way back to the whale, we saw the largest white shark of the bunch. This fish was roughly one thousand pounds heavier than the one we eventually caught. He had come to the whale, sliding up on it so that his dorsal fin was almost out of the water. When he was at his full height, the shark bit into the whale, taking out a huge chunk of flesh as he slid back into the water. Everybody saw him only that once, but we all agreed on his large size.

We tied up to the whale again. Every hour or so, a different shark would show up. I counted a total of seven different white sharks, ranging from one thousand pounds and up. There were reports of two others having been harpooned and lost by private boats, but none of the ones we saw had harpoon lines hanging from them. There's no way of knowing exactly how many white sharks were around that whale, but we had seen seven. Donnie had stuck another and the two private boats had each harpooned a white shark. That made ten so far.

Each of the fish we saw had different markings. One of them had all kinds of scratch marks that ran from his nose to his gill plates: we called him "Scarface." Another, "Big Boy," had a piece missing from the top edge of his dorsal fin. It almost looked like he had nicked it going under a low bridge.

We spent fifteen minutes to an hour teasing each fish that came up. Some of them came closer to taking the bait than others because they were more curious. White sharks are very playful. They remind me of how a kitten reacts when you drag a little fuzz ball tied to a string across the rug in front of it. The first time you drag it past the cat, he looks at it and looks at you, and kind of says, "Go away, leave me alone." He doesn't want it. Now, you drag it in front of him a second time and he's getting more curious, but doesn't do anything. The third time you drag it past the kitten, he tightens up his muscles, scrunches his back, and gets ready to jump, but he doesn't move because he still doesn't really want it. The fourth or fifth time that you pull it past him, he sees it coming, scrunches down, and when this fuzz ball gets right in front of him, he jumps at it. You pull it away from him and he can't get it, so now he's really mad.

Then he goes back and sits down, waiting for this thing to come by, etc., and so every time he gets close to it, you pull it away from him. Now, he just *has* to have it, so you hesitate and let him get it. Well, it's the exact same way when you're baiting most kinds of fish, especially sharks. You tease them to the point where they have to have it, and they'll jump on it.

There was a pecking order among the white sharks. We could see them on the fathometer, one hundred feet below the surface, in two hundred feet of water. They were swimming in circles, stacked up like airplanes getting ready to land. One at a time, they came up to feed. It looked like each was given a certain amount of time on the surface. Scarface convinced us of this because, apparently, he stayed up there too long and another white shark came up, physically pushing him away from the whale, and sending him back down. This went on all day. The mates and I would have never seen all of this white-shark behavior if we didn't have plenty of time to spend watching them.

While I was out on the side pulpit, the white sharks approached the dead whale, one at a time, sliding back and forth against it, looking for a tidbit. I stood on the overhanging pulpit on and off all day, trying to bait all of them that went gliding past. They were so close that I could almost stand on their backs.

As soon as a white shark shows up, it's my job to swing the big bait of mixed-up fish (that I had sewn together) back and forth, pendulum style, throwing it ahead of the shark so that the bait settles down to the same depth as the fish, getting it as close to the fish's mouth as I can. They're often not hungry at all. It's like trying to offer a lollipop to a kid who works in a candy store.

As was the case, I couldn't get this white shark interested, even though my bait was a smorgasbord of mixed-up fish. Here, these white sharks have a fifty-foot dead whale—all this nice red meat with the blood still oozing out of it. Why should they mess with another piece of bait?

One rumor that later went around was of me feeding melon and cookies to the white sharks as I stood on the whale. This is not true. Here's what really happened:

For a joke, I hollered down to Donnie, who was walking around in the cockpit, "I can't get him to take my bait, see if the white shark wants a chocolate-chip cookie." Donnie grabbed a cookie and jumped onto the whale, holding out his hand, making believe he was offering a cookie to the shark. Teddy had my camera, so he took a picture of Donnie on the whale, and my cookie joke turned into a rumor, which turned into a "fact."

During the course of that day, everybody went whale-walking, but I was the first one to walk out on the bloated whale carcass as soon as the *Cricket II* got tied up to the whale. David Letterman once asked me, "Why did you walk on that whale?"

"Well, I didn't have no other place to walk, and it's nice to go whale-walking once in a while!" I joked.

Maybe I did it for the same reason that Sir Edmund Hilary climbed Everest, "Because it was there." I remember crawling gingerly out onto the whale carcass, on my hands and knees at first, until I found out that the footing was firmer than I had thought. It felt like I was standing on the sole of a giant topsider shoe because the finback whale's textured underbelly was deeply-ridged and firm. I stood up slowly to get my balance and noticed that I had sand on my hands and knees. This puzzled me at first until I figured out where that sand had come from. When a whale dies, it goes straight to the bottom, rolling and bouncing around in the sand and currents. After about a day or so, gases start to expand in its stomach and the whale pops to the surface, floating belly up. Even after the sharks have slammed their jaws into the dead whale, shaking their heads like dogs, and seizing pieces of meat the size of peach baskets from its back, the whale still floats belly up.

As the days and nights go by, and all of the big hungry sharks have eaten their fill and stepped away from the dinner table, now is when a big bunch of small sharks, mostly blues, feast. They arrive by the dozen, like piranhas, and hit the whale all over: head, tail, and midsection, wherever they can get a bite.

After the blue sharks have bitten through the whale's stomach and the gases have escaped, that whale will still float because the remaining meat and blubber continue to generate gases that keep the carcass buoyant. In the past, I came across some dead whales that had been floating on the surface for quite a while. They were so badly decomposed that there was hardly any meat left, but the blubber, being six inches thick in spots, kept them afloat. Even the sharks abandon a whale when it reaches this stage. Eventually, these putrefying carcasses disintegrate and sink to the bottom for the crabs and lobsters to eat. The whale we found was fresh. If I had to guess, I would say it had only been dead for twenty-four hours or so. Blood was still running from some of the bite marks.

Because those big white sharks weren't hungry doesn't mean to say that they weren't curious and playful. I was out on the side pulpit every time one came up to play and teased them with my elusive good-looking bait. After a while, it got so that the first thing these sharks looked for when they came up out of the deep was THAT THING: the bait under my side pulpit that I was teasing them with, the same thing that kept getting away from them. It was late in the day when finally, Big Boy, the one that we wanted and eventually caught, got mad and jumped on the bait, pouncing on it so fast that I didn't have time to drop it. By the time I opened my fingers to let go of the leader wire, he had the bait and was on his way.

Now it was Donnie's turn in the chair. I came off the pulpit, jumped onto the flying bridge, mashed on the starter button, and away we went, chasing the fish down.

I was the first to go whale-walking on the floating dead whale.

The fish's first run almost spooled us; that is, his first run was so long and so fast that he almost took all the line off the reel as I chased him down. During the rest of the fight, the fish made short runs, and we could keep up to him fairly easily without the danger of running out of line. An hour and forty minutes went by. Time is very important when you're fighting a big fish. Anything over an hour into the fight, things start to weaken and reach their breaking point: the angler, the rod, the line, leader cable, and the hook, which could be on the edge of pulling out. Any or all of these things could happen.

Donnie was a good angler. He kept the line tight all the time, gaining line when I gave it to him as I ran the boat toward the fish. At this point, the fish made shorter and shorter runs.

Then it happened.

All of a sudden, at about thirty or forty yards off the transom, up he came, straight for the surface, and didn't stop! His head and body rose out of the water. He emerged almost to his dorsal fin. The shark was snapping his jaws as his head jerked from side to side, trying to bite the line.

There was only about five feet of leader cable left. All the cable was wrapped around Big Boy's head and gill plates, and he had trouble breathing—that's why he was fighting so hard. All this happened in seconds, and I had to make a snap decision. I don't like taking a fish directly off the transom because I have to put the boat in reverse fast and risk backing over the shark. You can lose a fish very easily this way; if I don't stop the boat in time, the fish could be chopped up in the propeller.

It was worth the risk. I threw the boat into reverse and hit the throttle. She began moving backward fast, while Donnie wound in the slack. Now I put the *Cricket II* in forward gear and hit the throttle again, slamming on the breaks so I could bring her to a complete stop, close enough to the white shark that the mates could grab hold of the leader cable and put the first flying gaff into the fish.

The best place to insert the flying gaff is between the dorsal fin and the tail, but Teddy and John couldn't reach that deep, so they aimed the flying gaff at an area between the shark's dorsal and head.

When a fish feels restriction, he goes wild, but our luck held because when the mates planted the first flying gaff in its back, that fish rolled into the flying-gaff rope (made of half-inch nylon), wrapping himself up in it and taking all the strain off the gaff. If you gaff a shark that's over three thousand pounds, they go berserk—rolling, pulling, and thrashing; and if you don't have a sturdy boat underneath you, forget about it!

While all this was going on, I stayed up on the flying bridge, running from one side to the other, screaming orders: "Look out, he's coming up on this side! Get another flying gaff ready! Hit him on *this* side. Look out, he's coming up on the other side!" After the large shark thrashed around for what seemed like a half hour or so, the boys were able to get the second flying gaff into him. This is not an easy task because, in a split second, the mates could have their heads squashed between the transom and the big fish's flapping tail as he thrashes around in a frenzy: a slip-up could cost one of my mates a broken arm—at the least.

After this, the shark stayed on the surface, pulling, because he found out he couldn't get away by thrashing and rolling; now he started to pull our heavy boat in circles, spinning the *Cricket II* around like it was a button on a outhouse door.

I hollered down to Teddy, "See if you can get a head choker on him. Now's the time because the fish has stopped rolling."

First Mate Ted Feurer Jr. puts a head choker lasso on the
3,427-pound white shark.

Teddy took a piece of three-eighth-inch steel cable, formed it into a lasso, and slid it as far as he could go, down past the fish's nose and gill plates to where the flying gaffs were embedded in its back. At this point, Teddy pulled the lasso tight and we connected it to the mast's lifting tackle. Even with this head choker pulled around its neck like a necktie and the two flying gaffs in him, the fish continued dragging us around.

Now came the final job of putting on a tail rope, but this was no easy job. It took everybody we had in the cockpit to do it: Teddy, John, Mike, and Donnie and his friend. They all struggled with the shark for another fifteen minutes or so before they got the tail rope on. I never went down into the cockpit to help because I didn't have to. There was enough good help there. I was more useful up on the flying bridge. Looking down, I could see in advance what had to be done and shouted directions, when and where they were needed. I could never have gotten that fish without my good crew.

By around 6:00 p.m., we were on our way home, but towing this monster behind us slowed the *Cricket II* down to eight knots. It took me an hour of running time and of watching the chart to figure out our speed and determine how long it would take us to reach the dock.

I hate pushing the button on that radio, but I had to call Montauk Marine Basin to report this big fish because it was a possible world-record white shark. This marina had the facilities to handle a very large fish. I also knew that, in order to weigh this shark, they had to send a runner halfway down Long Island to bring back a very large scale for the official weigh-in. I told them my estimated time of arrival, guessing it to be around 11:00 p.m. or so.

At 10:00 p.m., Paul Stern brought out the photographer Joe DiMaggio on his boat, the *Tuna Tangler*, and met us ten miles offshore. Joe took flash pictures of us towing home the big shark. This was not an easy thing to do on a dark night, with both boats bouncing around in wind-chopped waters, but Joe's photos came out great. Joe is considered one of the best still photographers in this country.

The *Cricket II* eventually hit the dock at 11:30 p.m. and we were greeted by well over a thousand excited people waiting on the dock, along with half a dozen reporters. The word must have traveled like wildfire. This is one reason that I never use my radio to call in a big fish unless I have to; otherwise it is impossible for me, or anybody else, to move around on the dock.

We had extra problems lifting and weighing this fish because of his huge size. Montauk Marine Basin had a large fork lift that could pick up the weight, but it was the fish's length that we had the most trouble with. At first, the fork lift operator, Carl Darenburg Jr., picked up the fish by its tail, only to find that when the travel lift was fully raised, the fish was still in the water. Then we tried bending the shark head to tail. This didn't work either, so my mate John DiLeonardo and someone else jumped overboard and wrapped a cargo net around the fish, and then it was successfully lifted and weighed in at 3,500 pounds. Next, we deducted the weight of the ropes and gaffs. This gave us the exact weight of 3,427 pounds.

By now it was 1:30 a.m. and we had to put this fish to bed, but the crowd was still swarming around it. Everybody wanted to touch the shark, especially its teeth, as the fish lay on its back in the cargo net, with its mouth wide open. Teddy, John, and I had to physically stand guard over the fish's head. When somebody pushed their hand through the crowd, attempting to feel (and steal) its teeth, one of us had to literally slap the person's wrist.

Carl Jr. walked this monster of a shark down the dock with the travel lift, foot by foot through the crowd, to reach the shed where it would be locked up for the night.

Next day, we brought the fish out of the shed for the press to photograph and for the shark scientist to examine. *Good Morning America* had a TV unit on the dock, and four or five helicopters arrived with more newspaper reporters. This fish made newspaper headlines across the United States and the news traveled as far as Saudi Arabia, because we got a newspaper clipping back from Prince Khalid bin Sultan, and a letter from him, congratulating us on the catch. I had fished with the prince in Saudi Arabia the previous winter.

Me with the 3,427-pound fish the day after. We had put the fish on ice all night to preserve it for the Press and ABC's Good Morning America program.

I had asked National Marine Fisheries shark scientists Wes Pratt and Jack Casey to fillet the fish and give me its backbone. I did this purposely so that I had positive proof for everybody that there was no foul play involved in the shark's capture. After Jack and Wes had finished cutting up the fish for scientific study, the only thing left on the dock was saltwater. There were plenty of witnesses who verified that no harpoons or bullets were found in the cut-up carcass and that there had been no signs of foul play. I hoped this public autopsy would put an end to all the crazy rumors that had spread around the Montauk docks like wildfire, but it didn't. The last crazy rumor floating around Montauk was that we had doped the shark.

During this time, the merchants in town sold a lot of gas and Popsicles, and Montauk Marine Basin (the shark's last resting place) was constantly packed with people. I knew long ago that despite what the Montauk Chamber of Commerce said, my big fish would *bring in* the tourists, *not* chase them away.

Four days later, these tourists were coming from all over, still looking for the fish. Montauk Marine Basin eventually put up a five-foot cardboard sign that read:

"THE BIG SHARK HAS GONE"

Donnie and I wanted to officially submit this shark as an International Game Fish Association (IGFA) world record. To claim this record, the angler has to send in a piece of the line that the fish was caught on. I knew that the IGFA was not going to give us this record because I think they wanted to hang on to Alf Dean's 2,664-pound record white shark, caught on April 21, 1959, off Ceduna, South Australia, using seals for bait. After the Marine Mammal Act was passed in 1972, the IGFA banned the use of mammal meat for chum or bait. And despite the fact that we used fish bait, Donnie got word from the IGFA that our fish was disqualified because "the whale was doing the chumming," but as far as I'm concerned, the 3,427-pound white shark still is the largest game fish ever caught on rod and reel.

Congratulations Are In Order

Right from the start, when I first got to Montauk in 1951 and started catching sharks, I was considered an outsider and stayed that way right to the end of 1991, when I moved permanently to Hawaii. I had spent forty years in the social wilderness and decided it was time to move to a warmer climate.

First, the Montauk Chamber of Commerce had wanted to tar-and-feather me and send me out of town. And then it was almost all of the local fishermen, who thought I was crazy, fishing for sharks. As time passed and I started to catch larger sharks on lighter tackle, their disgust grew.

Because I was doing my own brand of fishing—drifting and chumming—I was always treated like an outsider. I hate like hell to think that jealousy had anything to do with it, but it must have played a part. When the *Cricket II* came back to the dock with a swordfish while fishing for sharks, this was marked down in their books as a mistake. In 1960 the boat that "fished for garbage," "low-life" shark, received the Jack Reiber Sportsmanship award for catching three swordfish averaging over three hundred pounds each that season while fishing for sharks. To get even with my detractors, I told them it was not my fault that "the nasty swordfish came along and stole our good shark bait."

When any of them caught a tuna, marlin, or swordfish that was half the size of some of our sharks, and on heavier tackle, I would hear boat after boat radio in to congratulate the crew on their fish. Even if the *Cricket II* brought back a big tuna, around six hundred to seven hundred pounds on forty-five-pound test, nobody ever said "Congratulations on that fish."

I would just flop the fish onto the dock. I didn't have to say anything, and I didn't expect anything from them. Just like on that one special day when Harry Hoffman and I caught a 528-pound tuna on fifty-pound test from an oar-powered rowboat.

I could name a lot of times that my crew and I should have been congratulated; for instance, when we caught a double record, the 1,080-pound mako, which was at that time the largest mako ever caught and also a world record in the fifty-pound test class. This fish hung on the dock all day and only one boat captain, out of about fifty, came over and shook my hand to congratulate me on the fish. I told him that the congratulations should go to my good crew, Dickie Bracht and Tom Hoffman, because without them I could not have done it. As the years went by, I told every one of my mates, "Don't figure on any compliments from the other boatmen; expect nothing but abuse."

The Biggest Catch Of All

The publicity the *Cricket II* got for catching the 3,427-pound white shark in August 1986 hit many overseas newspapers.

Over the next two years, I received a lot of letters from people all over the world and I always answered each letter that I received, but never encouraged anyone to write back. Then one day in April 1988, I received a letter from Jenny, a girl in England. It was only a one-page letter, but I could see from the way the letter was written that this person was very interested and knowledgeable about sharks. In her letter, Jenny wanted to know if the International Game Fishing Association (IGFA) had accepted the 3,427-pound white shark as a world-record fish. In answering her letter, I told Jenny that if she wanted to know anything more about sharks, "Don't be afraid to write back." She did, and wrote me a two-page letter this time, asking more questions about sharks. I answered her two-page letter with my two-page letter. Next time, she wrote a three-page letter. I answered again.

This went on, up to a five-page letter, then I got on the phone and called her, asking if she had a tape recorder. She said yes, so I started off by sending her a sixty-minute tape, which she answered. From the sixty-minute tape, we went to the ninety-minute tape. From one ninety-minute tape, we went up to three ninety-minute tapes. Six months later, I invited her to come over on a vacation because I was finished fishing for the season. We got along together so well that I asked her to stay. I was by myself and enjoyed her company because we had a lot in common besides sharks.

I had been a bachelor for twelve years and my three daughters were all grown up. Bobbie had gotten her x-ray technician's degree, married, and had three sons: Stephen, Brian, and John. (While this book was being written, Stephen, Brian, and John each made me a great-grandfather). Pat went through Fort Schuyler, got her Marine Science degree, and became an officer in the merchant marine. She wound up working for Exxon as a navigator on the super tankers. She has since retired and now takes out private charters on her sailboat, the *Surprise*. And my youngest daughter, Tammy, married and settled down and is raising two sons, Justin and Dylan.

So on November 13, 1988, Jenny and I were married in the living room of my house on Flamingo Avenue. Judge Frood and his wife, Theresa, personal friends of mine from East Hampton, presided over the ceremony. I wanted this to be a private affair because you have telegraph, telephone, and tell-a-friend in Montauk, and tell-a-friend is generally the fastest way of communicating, so what the rest of the people didn't know wouldn't bother them. I figured I was old enough to know what I was doing, so I didn't need to ask permission from anybody to do this.

Because Jenny was over here on a tourist visa, she now had to apply for permanent-resident status. This was the beginning of opening a large can of worms, as far as the Immigration and Naturalization Service (INS) was concerned, so our first job was to find an immigration lawyer who could explain the application process to us. I asked all around Montauk if anybody could help us. Perry Duryea, a local politician, recommended Tom, a Manhattan attorney. As we walked into Tom's office, the first thing I saw was a photo of him shaking hands with Richard Nixon.

Tom agreed to represent us and we began filing out form after form after form, making weekly trips from Montauk to the INS offices in New York, where Jenny was fingerprinted and photographed. They must have thought I was an immigrant smuggler, because the INS took mug shots of me too! We made trip after trip into the city to try and get this situation resolved and both of us began to despair. Jenny and I imagined all kinds of bad things happening and were even told, quite a few times, that our situation was hopeless and Jenny would have to leave the country. For a while there, I had the horrible thought that I might have to move to England. I could just imagine the headlines in British newspapers:

"Frank Mundus in London,
God Save the Queen!"

At one point, we had to fly back from Hawaii to attend a fifteen-minute hearing at the INS building in New York City. Tom advised me to wear a jacket and tie for this occasion, so Jenny and I went tie shopping. As it turned out, I was mistaken for a lawyer in amongst the wall-to-wall immigrants and their lawyers, some of whom wore tattered jeans with holes in them.

For three hours, we sat, watched, and listened in amazement as immigrants milled around, speaking all kinds of languages; some even rushed around frantically searching for interpreters, others sat patiently and waited.

Then it was our turn. Tom, Jenny, and I were taken to a cubicle where an INS officer put us through the third degree.

We had traveled from Hawaii to New York, and waited here three hours, only to spend fifteen minutes at a hearing, and at the end of it all, still had no definite answer as to Jenny's status. Then we spent a couple of weeks back in Montauk, waiting for the INS to make a decision. I was relieved when a temporary green card arrived in the mail for Jenny. Two years down the line, we would have to file more papers for a permanent green card.

Halfway through the battle, poor Tom had a stroke and retired from practice. Now we had to start all over again, searching for a new lawyer. We found one in Queens, Long Island: Barbara Reede. During our first visit to Barbara, Jenny was shocked by some of our biting New York humor when, after looking her up and down, Barbara jokingly remarked, "You're no Farrah Fawcett, but there's something about you!"

On one of our visits to Barbara's office, Harry Hoffman drove us in. While Jenny and I were pushing paper around Barbara's desk, Harry quickly become the office mascot. Everyone thought he was cute and cuddly, like Barney Rubble, and they wanted us to leave him there!

On another visit in, Barbara called us a cab so we could go back to Penn Station to ride the train home. It was to be our brush with an immigrant taxi driver from the twilight zone.

As we climbed into his cab, the driver announced, "Hello, *dis* be my first day on *da yob*." Then he began opening up a huge street map that covered his entire windshield. Now, he mumbled something incoherently. I think he was asking me for directions. It was hard to communicate with him because the man hardly spoke English, but I tried anyway.

After a ten-minute drive, the taxi pulled over, "Here you are," the driver smiled. The brownstone building sure didn't look like Penn Station to me. Meanwhile, his boss was calling him on the radio, wanting to know where he was heading. He couldn't answer because he didn't know, so out came that huge map again. As we watched the meter frantically ticking away, I decided to make a run for it.

At the next red light, I grabbed Jenny by the arm and we jumped out of the cab. Looking over my shoulder, I could see him unfolding his map once more. After this experience, I knew my idiot magnet was still working! We quickly jumped into another cab, hoping we would make Penn Station this time.

By the fall of 1991, we were still tangled up with immigration while I was in the process of selling the *Cricket II* and moving to Hawaii. After a lot of red tape, Jenny's case was transferred to the INS office in Hilo, on the Big Island of Hawaii. Finally, in October 1992, Jenny was sworn in as a citizen of the United States. As we walked down the steps of the court house, amidst a crowd of newly-naturalized Americans, a little man, speaking broken English, tugged on the sleeve of Jenny's jacket and asked, "Is that it or do we pay them more money?" The man was delighted when we told him his ordeal was over now that he was a citizen.

Pistol-Whipped by the Law

Back in the late fifties, Montauk had resembled Mayberry, the fictional town in television's *The Andy Griffith Show*, and "Chiefy," East Hampton's chief of Police, was a close second for lawman Barney Fife. Chiefy had caught me going through a stop sign three times one winter. The first time, he pulled me over and patiently told me that the sign read: "S-T-O-P" and that I should stop. Chiefy threatened to give me a ticket the next time he caught me going through a stop sign.

The second time it happened was at the same stop sign and the same dear old Chiefy came around the corner. He pulled me over and lectured: "That sign is not only for the tourists, but it's for you people who live here all year round! The next time I catch you going through a stop sign, I'm going to give you a ticket." The third time it happened, I can't put into print what Chiefy told me, but the last part of the conversation was the same.

I told this to one of the old-timers and he told me why Chiefy wouldn't give me a ticket. The old-timer said that Chiefy had once given a Montauk local a ticket for going through a stop sign down town by the bank. This person had made him stand there for fifteen minutes, giving tickets to everyone who went through the same stop sign—and some of them had been Chiefy's relatives! That's why he hadn't given anyone a stop-sign-violation ticket since.

I had never had any real trouble with the regular Montauk police until they started moving in officers from New York City. In the spring of 1989, I was down at the boatyard, working on the *Cricket II* and getting her ready for our up-and-coming season, which would begin around the first of June. I had lost my help the season before and needed a new crew. So I spread the word around that I had to have a mate and a licensed captain aboard: this was the year that I had forgotten to renew my captain's license and it had expired.

The first hired hand that showed up looking for a job was a young drifter named Davie. He had driven up from Florida with his brother and their dog, and was looking for work. I mention the dog, because the pooch was the one that started all the trouble. Davie's brother soon found a job as a mate, bottom-fishing for cod on one of the Viking Line boats. After Davie had worked with me for a few days, I mentioned that I needed somebody with a captain's license. He said he knew of somebody nicknamed "The Pope." Now we had a full crew working on the boat in dry dock and everything was going hunky-dory, until . . .

One day Davie showed up for work and asked me if I wanted a brand new nine-millimeter pistol for two hundred and fifty bucks. He had just bought it from somebody down South and brought it up with him. Because he needed money, Davie had to sell it. I did not want a pistol because I never liked hand guns. My plan was to buy it from him and make a swap with one of my customers, during the course of the season, for a rifle or shotgun. And so I bought the gun and put it in the house because I didn't want it or need it on the boat.

Here's where the pooch poked his paw into the picture: Davie's brother had trouble with his wife in Florida and they were in the process of a divorce when he left. She told him that he could have the car, but DON'T take her dog. When she found out that he was headed for Montauk and had taken the car and the DOG, her next move was to get even. She called the Montauk police and told them that her car had been stolen and was full of guns! The car was still registered in her name and she knew that Davie and his brother had a pistol with them. It didn't take the police long, roaming around the docks, to find that car.

On the day we had just put the boat back in the water and got settled in at the slip on the Viking dock, two plain-clothed detectives walked up the dock and grabbed Davie. Then they marched him off to their unmarked car in the parking lot.

I started up the dock toward the car and asked them what was going on. The only thing they told me was that Davie was under arrest. I couldn't get any other information out of them. Davie was handcuffed in the backseat and the window was rolled up tight. I tried hollering through the window to ask Davie what was going on. He motioned with his cuffed hands that he didn't know. The detectives said they were taking him to East Hampton police station, so I tied the boat up, changed my clothes, and drove to East Hampton, only to find that the police had released Davie and he was on his way back to Montauk.

They had mistaken Davie for his brother. While the police had been asking Davie questions, they had also been searching the car for evidence and had found one bullet. Because they found the bullet, the police made Davie tell the whole story. They promised him that if he brought the gun in, everything would be OK and there would be no charges.

When I got back to Montauk, Davie came to my house to tell me what happened while he had been in custody.

He had told them everything.

I told him he was crazy for telling them that I had the gun. The police would hang us up by our thumbs. There had to be a way out of this mess. All of a sudden, I got this idea.

"Do you know how to take this gun apart?" I asked Davie.

"Sure," he said.

When Davie told me he knew how to take the gun apart, I told him to take it apart as much as he could, making as many pieces as possible. I gave him newspaper and tape, telling him to wrap each piece, put it in a bag, and tape it up.

"Now," I told Davie, "*this* is the way you told me that you brought it up from Florida, across all those state lines. This is also the way you gave it to me," I said, taking it from him, "and this is the way I gave it back to you," I said, handing the bag of pieces back to Davie.

So Davie and I went down to the police station, feeling pretty stupid about this gun wrap [*sic*]. We handed the bag of gun pieces to the smiling sergeant on desk duty. He gave us a receipt and we left. We didn't realize that the sergeant was smiling probably because he could put the gun back together after we had left, with no witnesses to prove it had been given to him in pieces, making it legal. Then it would be a gun again and *very* illegal.

Next day, I was arrested without having my Miranda Rights read to me. The one question I had for the detective was, "Why are you arresting me?" He told me it was because I had a handgun in my possession without a permit. I told him that it was not a handgun, only a package of wrapped-up metal.

He said, "No way. The gun was in one piece." That's when I figured out why the desk sergeant had been smiling.

He who smiles last, smiles best, because we got untangled from this mess, thanks to a very intelligent, kindhearted lawyer friend of mine. Although Davie and I had gotten off a jail sentence, Davie's brother's dog wound up in and out of the pound three times that fishing season. We don't know what happened to Davie's new gun after the police confiscated it, but I guess it wound up in good hands.

Three-time Loser, Four-time Winner

I had always said that if we caught the biggest white shark and the biggest mako, I would throw my hat in the ring. In 1979, we caught a 1,080-pound world-record mako on fifty-pound test line. Then the 3,427-pound white shark came along on August 6, 1986—although an unofficial IGFA record, this shark still is the largest fish ever caught on rod and reel.

Now that I had fulfilled my fishing dreams, I hoped that my cocaptain, Ted Feurer, would take over the *Cricket II;* Ted was a natural and well-qualified for the job. He was good with people, could catch fish and fix anything. These are three important qualifications for a charter-boat owner. But in October 1987, Ted told me that he would not be with me next season. He got married, became a cabinet maker, and moved to Upstate New York. So I decided to sell the boat as soon as possible.

While I was still in shock about this mess, a friend of mine, Flip, and his wife, stopped by the house like they always did. He said that someday they would find a business here in Montauk and would move out of the big city. I told him he could buy my boat and I would show him how to run it. Right then and there, they both thought this was a chance of a lifetime and started to talk business. Flip was no spring chicken and he proudly told me he was Polish, but I didn't hold either of those things against him!

I told him right from the start that this business was tough on your body and mind, especially the overnight trips, where you're on the go almost twenty-four hours a day, but he was determined to give it a try. I also told Flip that in this business, you either have to have youth on your side or enough experience to know how to pace yourself.

We sat down and went through the money part, and I told him he could work for me as a mate for the first season to become familiarized with the daily routine. I also told him that between trips, his job was to put fuel in the tanks and check the oil level. My words to Flip were, "This General Motor's diesel will take at least *one quart* of oil on *every* trip." Meanwhile, our new second mate, Rob Osinski, was told that his job was to clean the fish when we got back to the dock and take care of the ice, bait, and chum.

So the season started that June and we sailed five trips. Everything was going along well (all fouled up), with a new crew, what do you expect? On our sixth trip, we were heading out to sea. We left the dock, as usual, around 7:30 p.m. I sat up on the bridge, running the *Cricket II* out to the fishing grounds, while the two mates bullshitted with the customers. I always had a good habit of watching all the gauges on the dashboard—the water temperature, the oil temperature, and the oil pressure gauge—and what did I see? The oil pressure gauge was dropping as I watched it. It was on its way down: forty pounds, thirty-five, thirty . . . twenty-five pounds. My hand went to the throttle and pulled it back to a stop position. I jumped off the bridge and into the cockpit.

"What's going on?" asked the boys.

"I don't want to break up your bullshit session, but I've got to check the motor. I think we've just developed an oil leak," I said.

We took all the food, beer, and fishing tackle off the top of the motor box in order to lift it and see the motor. I expected to see oil squirting all over the place, but there was no oil leak, no oil on the surface, and none down in the bilge. As I inserted the dipstick, my anxious customers were standing close behind me, breathing down my neck. The stick came up dry. It was so low that there was no oil to be seen. I turned around and asked Flip, "How much oil did you put in the motor on this trip?"

He said, "None."

"How much oil did you put in the motor on our last trip?"

"None."

I was afraid to ask him the next question, but I had to, "You mean to tell me that you never put *any* oil in this motor in six trips?"

"No. You told me that the motor would *take* at least a quart a trip, but you didn't tell me to put it in!" he replied defensively.

For three seconds, I was speechless, but then I looked at him and said, in a very loud voice, "YOU ARE POLISH AND YOU REPRESENT EVERY STUPID POLISH JOKE I HAVE EVER HEARD!" This incident got the first laugh of the day from our customers, once we had put more oil in and found that there was no lasting damage done to the motor.

Flip's second mistake was almost permanently hazardous to our health. On July 14, he fell asleep at the wheel for an hour and a half while the automatic pilot steered the boat. Every night on our overnight trips, by the time we rounded Montauk Point Lighthouse, the crew had all their work done and one of them would come up on the bridge so that I could go down and have my last cup of coffee before running the boat the rest of the way to the fishing grounds. On this one evening, Flip came up on the bridge to relieve me. I went down to the cabin, had my coffee, told a few fish stories, and after fifteen minutes, climbed back up on the bridge. I unzipped the canvas curtain that we used to keep out bad weather from our electronics, stuck my head in, and in a loud voice, I said, "OK, Flip, I'll take over."

As I looked at Flip, I saw there was no response. He was just sitting there in the chair, behind the wheel, with his head loosely rocking from side to side.

Flip was sound asleep.

I was so pissed off that I didn't know what to do, so I sat down on the other side of the flying bridge and collected my thoughts. Years earlier, I had another mate do this. I had reacted by grabbing him by the scruff of the neck and throwing him to the other side of the flying bridge, where he landed in a ball and woke up. But I couldn't do this to Flip because he had a lot more years on him and would wind up with broken bones.

After I had sat there for a while, I figured out what to do. I would look at the loran and radar and mark down exactly where he started to sleep. Eventually, I got tired of watching his head nod back and forth, so I went down into the cockpit. The customers knew that there was something wrong because I was back down in the cockpit and kept looking ahead. The weather was on our side. The ocean was calm and the moon gave us plenty of visibility.

Finally, one of the customers asked me what was going on. I told him to look up at Flip and tell me what he saw. After a couple of minutes' observation, the customer said in surprise,

"He looks like he's asleep!"

"He *is* asleep," I said. "And I'm going to see how long he sleeps!"

Up ahead of us, a few miles in the distance, I saw one of the large Connecticut blue-fish boats anchored, with almost one hundred people aboard, fishing. And according to my automatic pilot, the *Cricket II* was on a collision course with her! My customers were not exactly calm. The ones who were not in their bunks, sleeping, stood outside, biting their fingernails. They looked at me, wide-eyed, glanced at the boat ahead, then looked at me. I told them not to worry. "We won't hit that anchored boat. The tide and wind will push us off course enough to avoid a collision."

As we slid past the anchored boat, I jumped up on the bridge and took a radar reading. We had missed the other boat by half a mile. I climbed back down into the cockpit and waited. It was an hour and a half before I saw Flip light up a cigarette. Then I jumped up on the bridge and screamed at him, "DO YOU KNOW THAT YOU WERE

SOUND ASLEEP AT THE WHEEL FOR AN HOUR AND A HALF AND ALMOST HIT A BOAT THAT WAS ANCHORED?"

As he left the flying bridge, Flip tapped at his wrist, mockingly, and muttered, "So, hit me with a wet noodle!"

I sat down behind the steering wheel and was so mad I couldn't say a thing. Neither of us mentioned the incident anymore on that trip; but back at the dock, when the customers had left, Flip tried to downplay his actions, and said to me, "You mean to tell me that you *never* fell asleep at the wheel?"

"Yes, I did fall asleep at the wheel. Everybody falls asleep at the wheel, but only for three seconds. One second you fall asleep. The next second, your head hits the steering wheel, and the third second, you are back up again, but nobody sleeps for an hour and a half," I screamed at him.

Flip started to defend himself again, when I cut him short, "If you don't like what's going on around here, get your shit off the boat." And so on July 15, Flip took his gear off the boat and quit. I returned his $10,000 deposit and now I had to find a new buyer.

A month or so later, Rob, the second mate, wanted to buy the boat and he told me his father would back him financially. After we exchanged all the paperwork, my lawyer advised me not to let the deal go through because Rob's father wanted me to hold a mortgage on his house. So now I began looking for the third buyer. (Rob has since gone on to become a successful chef entrepreneur, starting up a new business he calls "High Seas Offshore Catering," and is currently writing a shark cookbook, tentatively titled *North East Sharks: Hook 'em, and Cook 'em*. Rob is going to include my deep-fried blue-shark recipe[5] in his book).

In the meantime, I forgot to renew my captain's license. In order to update my license for another five years, I just had to mail it in, but forgot. When I realized it was overdue, I contacted the U.S. Coast Guard office, and they told me that because my license and the renewal's grace period had lapsed, I had to take the written test over again. Nowadays, you have to be a college graduate to pass this test and I couldn't, because I only got half a year of high school. Meanwhile, the press picked up the story and contacted the coast guard's head honcho. His hands were tied and he had to go by the book. Meanwhile, the story was starting to make the rounds via local TV and newspapers. It didn't take long to go from here to California. And of course, the story got exaggerated as it made its way across the country.

The press began saying something to this effect:

"Mundus will never pass the test because he only had half a year of high school."

Then they said:

MUNDUS CAN HARDLY READ OR WRITE

And finally:

MUNDUS CAN'T READ OR WRITE

During this Mundus media madness, a friend of mine arranged for me to go in to New York Coast Guard headquarters at Battery Park and take an oral test.

The coast guard examiner started testing me at 8:00 a.m. and didn't even stop for lunch. He hit me with lots of test questions, and things were going well until 3:00 p.m. when he began testing me on navigation. He asked me to plot a course on the chart from Block Island to Connecticut. I told him this was impossible to do because he hadn't told me the strength and direction of the tide. This is when I lost it, so to speak.

"You expect me to show you what I *can do*, that I *have already done* for almost fifty years!" I snapped. The examiner folded up his papers and I went home. That was when I lost my license for the last time.

To get around the problem, I hired a temporary mate who had his captain's papers. Now that I had a licensed captain with me on the boat, this made things legal again.

Later that year, two more prospective buyers stepped up to the plate, Paul, a mechanic, and Jim, a used-car dealer. I had just finished having the motor completely overhauled, a good selling point to them. They wanted to buy the boat if I could give it to them on terms. They agreed to come up with a down payment and so much each year. In addition, I had to show them the ropes for a couple of seasons.

After I sold the boat to Jim and Paul and fished with them for two years, there was no sense in me staying in Montauk. In November 1991, I filled up two large wooden crates (built by my carpenter neighbor, Bill Masin) with all the good junk that I wanted or needed, and then I auctioned off the rest: my truck, the shark mounts, and jaws (which don't hold up in Hawaii's humidity), and donated the money I made from the auction to the Montauk Ladies' Village Improvement Society. When I left Montauk, I was tempted to put up posters of myself, showing me with my arm outstretched and my middle finger pointing toward the sky, but never got around to it! There were no teardrops and wet handkerchiefs from any of the local boatmen on my departure.

Four years went by. Jim and Paul's payments had dried up after the first couple of years. I was forced to repossess the boat and start all over again. One day in 1995, I happened to call a friend of mine, Charlie DiBella, who lived in Florida. Charlie had been a boss carpenter, who I had worked for in the winter time, many years ago, and he had become a good friend. Eventually, the conversation got around to his son, Joe, who was in South Carolina, hoping to have a new boat built. Suddenly, a light bulb flashed in my head; "Maybe Joe might want to buy the *Cricket II*," I suggested to Charlie.

The next day, my telephone rang; it was Joe DiBella, and he *was* interested in buying the boat. Joe still remembers the first time he fished for striped bass on the *Cricket II* as a seven-year-old in 1958, along with his brother and their father.

All went well with the boat purchase, and in 1995, Joe took the *Cricket II* south to North Carolina. Since then, he has remodeled her and made a lot of fancy improvements to the old girl. Now he successfully fishes the *Cricket II* as a charter boat off Radio Island, North Carolina, catching all kinds of fish, including sharks.

After all these years, the old girl is still going strong. Joe and the *Cricket II* rode out the last three hurricanes: Bertha, Fran, and Bonnie. During one of these hurricanes, the boat was hit broadside by fifteen- to twenty-foot swells and Joe says, "She was taking them like a duck." A hundred and eighty-eight boats were put out of commission by that storm. Next day, the *Cricket II* was the only boat running and the only damage she sustained was a broken antenna mount. Once more, the old *Cricket II* was running true to form. In her fifty years, she has come through a bunch of hurricanes, and suffered only minimal damage. If you want to fish with captain Joe DiBella, you can reach him online at *www.cricket2.com* or by emailing him at *ldibella@cox.net*.

Getting to the Heart of Things

After more than four decades of tangling with large sharks, would you believe that my biggest threat came from a heart condition that was five years in the making?

In 1993, during an annual visit to the doctor, I complained about a pain I would get in the high part of my chest, on the left side. Dr. Z told me that it was "vog" from the volcano: sulphur fumes that drifted over the mountain from an active volcano, ninety-two miles away, on the other side of the island. He gave me some pills to take, and because the pain seemed mild, I stopped paying as much attention to it.

A few years later, Dr. Z retired and Dr. Denzer took over my aches and pains. I mentioned the pains I had been having for the past five years because I noticed that these pains increased while I was working hard in the yard: I have to admit that the kind of yard work I did in my one-acre property was a little unusual. I used a machete all one winter to cut down weeds and vines and moved many large rocks around. Then I brought in truckloads of dirt and moved it all by hand with my wheelbarrow.

Dr. Denzer put me through some rigorous tests, including testing for a lung defect, but I passed them all with flying colors.

Then, in June 1998, I was invited back to dear old Montauk for a month to give a lecture for *The Fisherman* magazine, and also to fish with Captain John Arceri on his boat, the *Reel Nice*. John put me up at his new house. It was still under construction, but was only a half-mile's walk to the docks, where his boat was tied up at the fancy Montauk Yacht Club.

On many mornings, I would make the twenty-minute walk from the house to the boat, often stopping by Bob Rando's place to say hello. Bob owns the Sportsman's Dock and he's a good friend of mine from years back. When he saw that I was living in an unfinished place, Bob invited me to stay over at his house for the rest of that month.

During my morning walks, I noticed that the "volcano chest pain" would hit me once in a while. One day, while walking with Bill Masin (one of the good guys in Montauk), I had to slow my walk down. When I asked Bill if there were any active volcanoes on Long Island, he looked at me like I had just lost it and said, "Why do you ask?"

I told him what I was being treated for, and realized this was the proof I needed to rule out "vog" as the cause of my chest pains. When I returned home to Kona, I told Dr. Denzer about my recent chest pains and he covered me in electrodes and put me on a treadmill till my tongue fell out. Dr. Cogan, the heart specialist from Honolulu, was also there. He, too, put me on a treadmill and didn't find anything unusual either. On my next visit to the doctor, on July 21, Dr. Denzer attached a portable heart monitor to me at 8:30 a.m., then Jenny and I went down into town to do our weekly "shoplifting."

My first stop was to see my eyeglass man about picking up a new pair of glasses. I had to walk up a flight of stairs to his office and that did it—a dull steady pain started in my chest, but this time it didn't go away. I didn't tell anyone about it, not even Jenny.

After that, we went to the supermarket to pick up a few items. At this point I still hadn't told her about my chest pain. I said I wanted to sit and wait in the car instead of waiting for her to read all the labels on everything that was on the shelf. I was hoping that the pain would go away, but it didn't; and when Jenny came out of the store, I finally told her about it and said, "Let's head straight back to Dr. Denzer!"

There was no doubt about it; the chest pain had been there for over an hour: I was having a heart attack. Dr. Denzer confirmed this when he removed the heart monitor and read the data; he immediately sent us to the emergency room at Kona Hospital.

I was kept in the hospital overnight for tests, and the next day, I was flown by air ambulance to Queen's Medical Center in Honolulu. The air ambulance is a small two-engine plane specially equipped to fly people (who are in critical condition) from all the islands straight to the Queen's Hospital. To get into the small plane, I had to step up onto the wing. As I clambered over the wing and into the cabin, I fought to keep my scanty hospital smock from blowing upward in the strong, gusty breeze. To my embarrassment, I lost the fight, and a nurse who was standing nearby got an eyeful.

So there I was in late July, tucked between two white sheets at Honolulu's main hospital, hooked up to all these big, fancy machines. After a couple of days of tests, the big boys, cardiologist Dr. Cogan and heart surgeon Dr. Dang, said I was going upstairs to the OR for an angioplasty. It's standard practice for the patient to be semiawake during this procedure, and I vaguely remember seeing them trying to push a balloon-type device up through the arteries in my leg and then in my arm to clear the blockage. No good, they couldn't get all the way up. The only alternative was a quadruple-bypass operation, where the surgeons would use three vein grafts from my left leg and one from my chest to reroute the blood flow.

The worst part of the operation was the first night, when I was in intensive care, recovering from the anaesthesia. I remember lying in bed, struggling for every breath. "I . . . can't . . . breathe . . . Please . . . get . . . the doctor," I gasped to the two nurses on duty. They kept telling me, over and over, "The doctor's coming." I didn't think I was going to make it through that night, but I did.

A few minor things went wrong after they sent me home: some fluid built up in my lungs and I was rehospitalized for one night in Kona; then I had some other aches and pains, but because we could get hold of Dr. Denzer in the middle of the night, he was able to tell me which combination of pills to take to correct the problem.

As if the eight-inch zipper scar in my chest wasn't long enough, I decided to add on to it with an incision that extended from my chest to below the belly button. During a routine check up in January 2000, Dr. Dang, my heart specialist, detected an enlarged abdominal aortic aneurysm, and so I made a return trip to the Queen's Medical Center in Honolulu (because I liked it there so much!) for some major abdominal surgery.

Later that May, my urologist discovered I had the beginnings of prostate cancer and he sent me for radiation therapy in Hilo, located on the other side of the Big Island, 110 miles away from home. I had eight weeks' worth of radiation therapy—one minute a day, five days per week—and stayed in a Hilo hotel in between zaps, coming home on weekends, when Jenny picked me up and returned me to the oncology center each Monday for the next cycle of treatments. During the week, I checked into Uncle Billy's, a local Hilo hotel. Meanwhile, Jenny stayed over on the other side of the island, taking care of our house and the pets: Arnold the wild boar and Joe the dog.

Later on, I met local historian and artist Herb Kane. Our radiation treatment sessions coincided and so Herb and I circumnavigated the island together each Monday and Friday. Along the way, Herb pointed out all the little-known sites and facts about Hawaii and its customs. He even introduced me to the island's famous rock cookies (as hard as a rock unless they were dunked). Herb finished his radiation treatment and then I had to find other transport to Hilo. Shortly after, I met up with Bob Barry, another prostate patient and he took over where Herb left off.

I converted a golf cart into a utility cart for working around the yard.

Me, looking through a coffee plant in my yard.

At Uncle Billy's hotel in the evenings, I was serenaded to sleep by thousands of tree frogs, chirping noisily. I got used to them after a while. Tree frogs are considered a pest in Hawaii. During my days spent as a hotel guest, I took frequent walks to kill time during my radiation treatments. On one of these walks, I visited a local Prudential real estate office and asked to see some properties that had a large acreage. We had lived on a one-acre lot in Kealia for eleven years and the neighborhood was starting to get crowded. I needed more elbow room.

I called up David Taylor, a Prudential real estate agent, and he showed me a twenty-acre place in Naalehu, about thirty-two miles south of Kealia. The front ten acres was pasture land and the back ten was an ohia tree forest. Most of it was badly overgrown with weeds and brush. I considered it another challenge, and so we sold the house in Kealia and bought this piece of property.

We moved south to Naalehu on July 5, 2002. Our packing process took more time than we had anticipated. Like most people, I didn't realize how much junk we had accumulated over the years. One of the funniest things that happened during the move was when we transported Arnold, the orphaned wild boar we had adopted, to our new home. Because he weighed in at over five hundred pounds, I didn't want to have him sitting on my lap during the forty-five-minute ride.

This meant that Jenny and I had to load him into his six-by-three-foot steel cage and haul it on our small two-wheel flatbed trailer. Everything was going OK, until I was doing my usual thirty-five miles an hour along the twisty-turny mountain road that had no guard rail! We got about halfway to our destination, when I noticed through my rear view mirror that Arnold was standing upright. I hoped that I could get the trailer stopped before he leaned against his cage, toppling it over onto the highway and down the side of the mountain! Meanwhile, our large, fat, black hairy

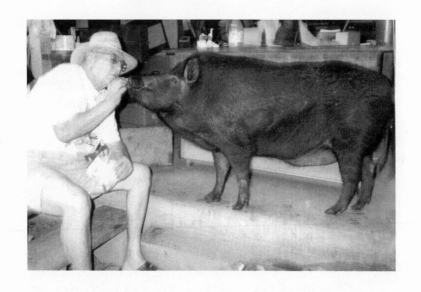

Me, feeding potato chips to Arnold, our pet wild boar.

pet porker was attracting plenty of attention and horn blasts from curious motorists. Thankfully, we did stop in time and retied the cage, reinforcing it with more ropes.

Our twenty acres did not have a house on it, so we bought a sixty-foot-by-twelve-foot trailer that had once been a government freezer. I converted it to a house trailer and hired carpenters to panel and partition the inside into living quarters: a kitchen/living room area, a bedroom, and an office. We spent about eighteen months living in this building.

Because termites are such a problem in Hawaii, I decided to outwit them by putting up a forty-foot-by-sixty-foot steel building. Then a bunch of carpenters cut windows and doors in it and framed the interior with wood. Bill Peebles, a friend of mine from Naalehu, oversaw our house-building project, including ordering all my material for me. Bill hired, fired, and supervised a team of laborers and carpenters to do the woodwork.

Because the front ten acres of our property had been cleared off at one time but had a lot of heavy grass on it, we decided to add some livestock to trim down the weeds. We tried different types of animals for this purpose. First, came Jack the cow and two horses belonging to a friend, but Jack and the horses gave me trouble with the fences. Next, we bought three sheep from a neighbor, and in less than two years the sheep population had exploded to over twenty. One of our biggest challenges was the monthly sheep-worming routine. Thank god we didn't have to shear them as they were the hairless type, the St. Croix hair sheep. We also added two goats, five chickens, and four geese to the farm. I found out that it's hard to make a farmer out of a fisherman because sheep are a lot tougher to catch than any one-thousand-pound shark I ever came across. It took the two of us to subdue some of the large rams. One time, Jenny and I sat on one to restrain it during the worming process, and he still managed to toss us both up in the air.

Even the female sheep, which are smaller, gave us one hell of a hard time hanging on to them. We named one Psycho Fuzzball, because restraining her was like holding on to a powerful, psychotic forty-pound fuzz ball or a giant white tick. We eventually got used to our monthly thrashing and settled in to life on the farm.

The Last Hunt

In November 1999, Harry Hoffman and his son, Tommy, came to Hawaii for a couple of weeks to visit with me and Jenny; and as usual, Harry and I got into trouble together—for the last time in his life. After a couple of days' sightseeing around the island, Harry grew restless for the saltwater. "Let's go fishing," he suggested.

"Harry, there ain't nothing out there now," I told him. But you know Harry; we had to go. One of our neighbors, Tony, owned a small private boat that had nothing on it for fishing except a few rods and reels. "Just cover the expenses and I'll take you guys out," Tony offered.

"Thanks, Tony. Pick a day and we'll go," I told him.

The next Sunday found us loading all the unnecessary junk on the boat, under Harry's supervision of course. I considered fishing poles unnecessary because I was convinced there wasn't any fish out there. After hours of dragging fishing lures around, I decided to take a nap. I had hardly gotten settled in a good spot when it happened: "Fish on!" Tommy yelled. I raced out from my little cubby hole and saw Tommy hanging on to a bent pole—a small blue marlin was jumping in the distance, about forty yards from the boat. We were trolling three rods. "Wind in that other line," I hollered to Harry, "and I'll wind this one in." As I was winding in the line, it came to a stop. "I think this line is fouled up with yours," I told Tommy.

"No, it isn't," he said. "My fish is way out there." And then it happened—I had a fish on and it jumped. Now we had *two* blue marlin hooked *at the same time*: this was very unusual, even at the right time of year when there were plenty of fish to be caught. Now the fancy footwork began; in order to prevent the two jumping, zigzagging fish from tangling our lines, Tommy and I had to perform a silent, well-choreographed fishermen's ballet, passing under and over one another's bent fishing poles, back and forth, while

walking from one side of the boat to the other. While all
this was happening, Harry knew he had better stay out of
the way or get run over. All three of us were veterans at
this game. I glanced over my shoulder: Tony was wedged,
wide-eyed in a corner, up against the steering wheel, about
as far forward as he could go in this small cockpit. Tony
had never seen a double-header, never mind one handled
so easily.

After fifteen minutes, we lost one fish right at the boat
because the hook pulled out, but landed the other blue
marlin, which was in the hundred-and-fifty-pound class.

"So there's no fish out there," Harry laughed, "*Hah,
hah, hah.*" What could I say? I had egg on my face: Harry
had gotten me again.

Right down to Harry's last fishing trip, he had to get
into some kind of trouble! That was the last time I went
fishing. It also turned out to be Harry's last hunt.

My South-African Shark Safari

It took years before I finally got recognition for being the fisherman who had inspired author Peter Benchley's character "Quint." Finally, in the spring of 2004, photographer Joe DiMaggio made the connection for me with the Discovery Channel and they allowed Joe to direct a one-hour biographical Frank Mundus documentary for their 2005 *Shark Week*.

Producer Jeff Kurr of Shark Entertainment brought his film crew, sound man Mike Gatt, and photographer Tony Sacco over from California and they began shooting the program. It would be a three-part shoot.

First, they filmed me here in Hawaii. My neighbor, Bill Peebles, generously allowed the film crew to convert his garage into a makeshift "boathouse" for interviews. Next, Joe, Jeff, Tony and Mike flew to Montauk in early May, filming more interviews and shooting reenactment footage of my early days. Rob Osinski, my ex-mate and now head chef at "The Dock" restaurant in Montauk, was a big help during the New York filming, and so was my old neighbor Bill Masin, who made his home and garage available as a location shoot for interviews.

Finally, I joined Jeff, his wife Cat, and the crew in California, and by May 17 we were on our way to South Africa for a two-week shoot. We hoped to get "up close and personal" with the awesome "air jaws" flying white sharks, off Cape Town.

It had been a long ride from Hawaii to South Africa—a four-plane trip, spread over two days. They sent me first class all the way. I particularly enjoyed the British Virgin Atlantic Airlines leg from California to London and on to Johannesburg. First-class passengers who fly these long trips with Virgin get a free pair of pajamas and socks to walk around and relax in and a free in-flight massage. During my six-hour layover at London's Heathrow Airport, the crew and I visited Virgin's VIP Lounge, where they had everything you could possibly want or need, from a shoeshine to a haircut, shower, or shave. Before boarding my connecting flight to Johannesburg, I picked up a bunch of British newspapers that I brought home for Jenny. It felt funny to be on a plane surrounded by flight attendants who all had the same British accent as my wife.

When I arrived in Africa, the cold temperature in the evenings surprised me until someone there told me that Cape Town is less than five thousand miles from Antarctica. We spent the first week off Simonstown, with shark researcher and conservationist Chris Fallows. Chris has been studying the habits of these magnificent creatures for quite a while now and has shot some tremendous photos of white sharks jumping in pursuit of seals. These white sharks hang around the outer islands, in deep water, waiting for a lone seal to waddle off the rocks. When one detects a seal in the water, the white shark shoots to the surface, blasting all the way out of the water like a surface-to-air missile! If it hits a seal on the way up, the shark stays on the surface, devouring the animal.

Next, we spent a week in Gansbaai with dive master and skipper Andre Hartman. By boat he took us six miles off Gansbaai to an area known as "Shark Alley," a channel between Dyer Island and seal hangout, Geyser rock. After we anchored in the channel, Andre demonstrated how he "snout touches" the white sharks, a technique he personally developed. To snout touch a shark, Andre teased it up close to the boat with a bait on a rope, then he took hold of the shark's nose, and using the fish's forward momentum, raised its head about a foot and a half straight out of the water. Once the shark stops moving forward, the jaws and mouth open at their widest. Then Andre lets go and the shark settles back down below the surface. There were plenty of sharks milling around Shark Alley. We always had a couple of them under the boat all the time. On one day, there were five boats anchored all in a row and each had a couple of white sharks nearby that they were playing with.

Andre is a hardened, fearless scuba diver, and the Discovery crew showed me a video of him and Jeff's wife Cat free swimming with white sharks, without the protection of a cage! I wondered what Peter Gimbel, the first man I put in the water with blue sharks, would have thought of this. Things have changed so much since I started shark fishing more than fifty years ago. Now the white sharks are protected, you can't catch them anymore. You can't even swim with them. Would you believe that environmentalists call that "harassing" the sharks!

After fifty years of being a hooker, it was time to move on. The job I have now is to convince fishermen to use hooks that will catch their sharks in the jaw, and not the stomach, when they tag them. This way, the shark will live to be caught again, and the tagging data retrieved will help us better understand their growth and migratory habits.

This is not the end of my true stories, but all that Jenny and I could squeeze between the covers of this book. We might be back . . .

WHAT IF?

What if that little nine-year-old boy hadn't broken his arm? Think about what would have happened: He would have gotten a good education and wouldn't have started fishing. Then he might have gone into some kind of business instead of the monkey business he got into. If he hadn't caught fish and catch sharks, then author Peter Benchley would never have heard about him, collected newspaper clipping about his big catches, chartered his boat, or written the book *Jaws*. Steven Spielberg wouldn't have gotten his great start. The three principal stars of *Jaws*—Roy Scheider (*Brody*), Richard Dreyfuss (*Hooper*), and Robert Shaw (*Quint*)—wouldn't have gotten theirs either. But best of all the wouldn'ts, if he hadn't caught that big white shark at the end of his career, the fish that hit all the newspapers, including England, his wife wouldn't have written to him asking about sharks and she wouldn't have been here to write this book. Then you wouldn't be reading it right now.

A Proposition from an Ex-hooker

For sport fishermen, I propose a shark-fishing contest that is conservation-minded in the top-ten class. In *Fifty Years a Hooker*, I have told you how many sharks are killed every day by fishermen who use cheap throwaway hooks. In this tournament, the circle hook or Gamakatsu hook would be mandatory. Only one fish would be killed and brought back to the dock, a shark with a golden tag. This fish could not be shot or harpooned. If the winning fish is brought to the weigh-in with a regular hook in it, that fish would be disqualified. A day before the tournament, one shark would be caught, tagged, and released. The angler who catches this golden-tagged shark is the winner. Tournament headquarters could be any place, for instance, Montauk Point, Long Island. The shark tagged off Montauk might head to Connecticut or New York. Boats can fish out of their home port. Duration: Any boat could fish all day and night, seven days a week, for as long as the tournament lasts, let's say two weeks.

All sharks would be hooked in the jaw because the circle hook is designed to slide up and out of the shark's stomach and then lodge in the jaw. All released sharks will live because the hooks in their jaws will rust and fall out in time. This idea of mine would be the first shark-fishing tournament of its kind. Let's hope that all of the up-and-coming tournaments will use this no-kill method of sport fishing for sharks. I have learned a lot in fifty years of hooking and have made plenty of mistakes—but I hope that all of my readers will benefit from what I have learned.

ENDNOTES

Chapter 1: An Unusual Childhood

1. Sister Fingerwhacker. Not her real name. At least I don't think it is!

Chapter 3: The Move to Montauk

2. Ralph Ryder. Not his real name.
3. Frankie Macarena. Not his real name.

Chapter 6: Life's Problems

4. *Joe Munchkin.* Not his real name.

Chapter 7: The St. Maarten Sting

5. *Bobby Hogan.* Not his real name.

Chapter 8: Three-time Loser, Four-time Winner

6. My Blue Shark Recipe.

    I have cooked blue shark in my house for a lot of guests and served them deep-fried blue-shark fingers. They raved about them, but never knew what they were eating! I just called them "fish sticks."

    First, cut the blue shark into hunks. Freeze the hunks—freezing breaks down the fibers and removes all the water after thawing at room temperature. After thawing at room temperature, cut the hunks into fingers or any way you want them. Next, wrap the pieces in a clean towel and place in the refrigerator for another four to five hours to make sure you have removed all the water. Now you have firm white meat to work with. Dip the shark fingers in egg and coat in a mix of breadcrumbs and Potato Buds, or a combination of Aunt Jemima Pancake Mix and Potato Buds. Deep fry for two to three minutes.

AUTHOR'S BIOGRAPHY

FRANK MUNDUS has been publishing nonfiction since 1971. His first book also happened to be the first shark-fishing manual ever published, *Sportfishing for Sharks* (coauthored with Bill Wisner) by Macmillan, 1971.

Mundus's second book, *Monster Man* (coauthored with Robert F. Boggs in 1976), was a humorous, biographical account of his career as a shark fisherman.

Frank Mundus was the inspiration for Peter Benchley's shark hunter "Quint" in the movie *Jaws*. Frank has just completed his autobiography, *Fifty Years a Hooker*, cowritten with his wife, Jeanette. This work traces Mundus's rise from poverty-stricken boyhood in Brooklyn, New York, through five decades of triumphs and setbacks as the maverick charter-boat captain of Montauk, on the eastern tip of Long Island. Mr. Mundus writes about his encounters with large great white sharks and relates highlights from his five decades as a fish guide and psychotherapist to eccentric customers.

In 1975, Peter Benchley and ABC's *American Sportsman* show filmed a TV special onboard Mundus's boat to promote the nationwide release of the movie *Jaws*. As a result of his work, Mundus has been featured on many national radio and television shows, including *Late Night with David Letterman* (three appearances) and *Larry King Live*. He also starred in a 1980 Schaefer Beer Commercial. Mundus has also traveled extensively across the United States as a paid lecturer at various sportsmen's shows.

In 2001 Frank Mundus coproduced a television documentary on his life and recently traveled to South Africa with the Discovery Channel to film a one-hour biographical special for their 2005 *Shark Week*.

JEANETTE MUNDUS is Frank Mundus's wife and coauthor. She was born in England and immigrated to the United States after her marriage to Frank. Jeanette was educated at the University of Hawaii and has a BA degree in English. *Fifty Years a Hooker* is her first book.

BOOK DESCRIPTION

The stories in *Fifty Years a Hooker* range from dramatic, nerve-pounding accounts of shark hunts to tales of comic misadventures, involving a host of eccentric characters who could not resist the pull of Frank Mundus's legendary "idiot magnet." Mundus's extensive compilation accurately reflects the book's title. He was, indeed, a hooker. For fifty years he sold his services, took good care of his customers, and saw to it that they had a good time, hoping that they went away satisfied and would come back again.

Among the stories you'll find in *Fifty Years a Hooker* are:

- *White Shark, White Pineapple.* The agony of waiting for the right writer.
- *How I Got Started Shark Fishing.* How a broken arm and two train wrecks kept me on the right track for a fishing career.
- *The Pelican Disaster.* My involvement in one of the worst maritime disasters off Long Island.
- *More Tales of Hoffman.* The zany fishing misadventures of my friend, Harry Hoffman, and me.
- *The 4,500-pound. White Shark.* My mate, my customers, and I fight one of the largest whites ever taken commercially by harpoon
- *Peter Gimbel.* The first man who swam with sharks while I rode shotgun.
- *Close Calls.* The time an ice-cream cone saved my life, plus other close calls.

- *Tap-Tap.* The time I hollered at Jackie Onassis for jaywalking on the island of St. Maarten.
- *The St. Maarten Sting, or How I Sold the Cricket III.* Borrowing a storyline from the movie, *The Sting,* I sell my other boat and outsmart a couple of Caribbean pirates.
- *Portrait of the Artist as an Idiot.* A mysterious artist (who lost the Mayor of Shelter Island's bust) claims me as his muse for a watercolor of a white shark.
- *Mundus of Arabia.* A Saudi Prince hires me to pioneer shark fishing in the Red Sea. I just miss a public beheading and narrowly escape one year in jail.
- *The 3,427-pound White Shark.* In 1986, I achieve my lifetime ambition of catching the largest fish of any kind on rod and reel with the help of some seasoned mates and an experienced angler.
- *Pistol-Whipped by the Law.* A mate's dog and his ex-wife set off a chain reaction which culminates in my arrest for possession of a firearm.
- *Three-time Loser, Four-time Winner.* The two happiest times in a man's life are when he buys a boat and sells it . . . and sells it and sells it, and hopefully sells it again, like I did.
- *Getting to the Heart of Things.* I remarry, burn my snow shoes, and retire to Hawaii, where I plant pineapples and fruit trees, adopt an orphaned 350-pound wild boar, and survive open-heart surgery, aneurysm repair, and prostate cancer.
- *African Shark Safari.* In which I travel to South Africa with the *Discovery Channel* and hook up with white sharks once more—this time through the lens of a camera.